Vera und Ansgar Nünning

Translated from the German by Jane Dewhurst

An Introduction to the Study of English and American Literature

Klett Lerntraining

Bibliografische Information der Deutschen Nationalbibliothek
Die Deutsche Nationalbibliothek verzeichnet diese Publikation in der Deutschen
Nationalbibliografie; detaillierte bibliografische Daten sind im Internet
über http://dnb.d-nb.de abrufbar.

Auflage 12 11 | 2014 2013
Die letzten Zahlen bezeichnen jeweils die Auflage und das Jahr des Druckes.

© Klett Lerntraining GmbH, Stuttgart 2009. Alle Rechte vorbehalten.
www.klett.de/uniwissen
Redaktion: Manfred Ott
Umschlaggestaltung: Sabine Kaufmann
Umschlagbild: Avenue Images/ Corbis RF
Satz: media office gmbh, Kornwestheim
Druck: AZ Druck und Datentechnik GmbH, Kempten

Printed in Germany
ISBN 978-3-12-939619-3

Contents

Preface

The main objective of the present volume, which is a translation of an updated and slightly revised version of our book *Grundkurs anglistisch-amerikanistische Literaturwissenschaft* (Stuttgart: Klett 2001, ⁴2004), is to provide a concise introduction to the subject-matter, major issues and research fields in English and American literary studies, and to detail the most important foundations, methods and models relating to the analysis and interpretation of literary texts. It is aimed primarily, but not exclusively, at students of English and American literary studies. As a familiarity with the analytical categories and methods used to approach narrative, dramatic and lyric texts is essential, especially at the beginning of the course of study, particular attention is paid to the use of clear conceptual language. We have also focused on fundamental and general aspects (such as central technical terms, generic categories and transferable methods of textual analysis from various genres and media), as such elements enable the student to situate the material covered within broader contexts and therefore provide helpful guidance for those new to the discipline.

When the German version of this book was published, some reviewers and any number of colleagues and students indicated that an English version of this introduction would be much appreciated. However, rendering a text of this type in English has naturally not been without its difficulties. Despite the common subject-matter, the discipline of literary studies takes different forms in English- and German-speaking countries, and methods, models and terminology do not always overlap. Where a standard equivalent to a German term was available, this has been employed; where an equivalent term was not available, efforts have been made to define or paraphrase the German term. When German authorities are cited, the standard or approved translation has been employed where one exists; otherwise the translator has supplied her own translation. Throughout the volume, every effort has been made to bridge the differences between the disciplinary traditions and create a text that is accessible to students of English and American literature from all backgrounds.

As general and comparative literary studies, like English and American literary studies, encompass a wide variety of objects, areas of enquiry and methods, which cannot be covered comprehensively within an introductory volume, we have taken a mixture of pluralism and pragmatism as our guide in writing this book. We have consciously adopted an approach which uses illustrative examples to afford insights into the practice and 'nature of real, existing English and American studies' (SCHWANITZ 1985: 9), and thus serves the needs of students beginning their course of study, but which simultaneously offers a general overview of the discipline in all its factual and methodological diversity.

This short, introductory volume is obviously not the place for a comprehensive introduction to the history of literatures in English. More important for the student who is anxious to derive the greatest possible benefit from the diverse selection of courses on offer is a general understanding of the basics of literary studies, and of the spectrum of literary-historical themes. The present volume aims to provide such a preliminary understanding, along with a basic introduction to the terminology and content necessary for orientation in English/American literary studies. Instead of supplying 'ready-made' interpretations, we therefore aim to provide the reader with the terminological and methodological tools that will enable him or her to interpret unfamiliar texts independently.

However, the volume is not only aimed at new students who wish to cultivate the skill of interpreting literary texts in a systematic and methodologically informed manner, and of employing a terminologically precise idiom. It should also prove helpful to more advanced students who are preparing for seminars or exams and desire a brief overview of the fundamental terms and methods of literary studies, as well as more precise information about the interpretation of lyric, dramatic and narrative texts.

This introduction is not only written *for* students; it is also the result of many years of fruitful cooperation *with* students. We would therefore like to thank the numerous students in Brunswick, Gießen and Cologne, who have contributed more to this book, with their active and constructive cooperation in introductory and other courses in literary studies, than they are probably aware. Special thanks are due to our assistants, who made diverse contributions to the preparation of the present volume. Wibke Bindemann, Hanna Bingel, Stefanie Bock, Katharina Engelhardt, Meike Hölscher, Nora Redhardt and Katja Zinn read the manuscript with meticulous attention and carefully checked all quotes and bibliographical references. Gaby Allrath, Dorothee Birke, Stella Butter, Klaudia Seibel, Annegret Stegmann and Carola Surkamp completed the lay-out and commented constructively on earlier versions of individual chapters, as well as contributing invaluably to the composition of the various figures and the glossary.

Our greatest and most heartfelt thanks, however, go to three colleagues to whom we owe a special debt: to Jane Dewhurst, the eminently competent, skillful and patient translator of the present volume, as well as to research assistant Dorothee Birke and Richard Humphrey. First and foremost, we should like to express our sincere gratitude to Jane Dewhurst, who did an excellent job in turning heavy-duty teutonic scholarly prose into readable English, finding any number of elegant solutions for complex problems. Dorothee Birke not only meticulously checked and proof-read the translation, she also made a number of very useful suggestions for improvement, which we have gratefully incorporated. This book has benefited enormously from Jane's linguistic resourcefulness and expertise, both as a translator and literary scholar, and from Dorothee's unparalleled conscientiousness, exemplary competence, and fine eye for terminological and stylistic details. Both of them not only did a marvellous job, they have also been, and are, a great pleasure to work with. Last, but not least, we are also very grateful to Richard Humphrey, who provided invaluable help and extremely good advice in the final stages of the revision, resourcefully helping us across a number of terminological hurdles. Any remaining mistakes or failings are, of course, entirely our responsibility, not theirs. If the present volume is successful in its aim of enabling students to pursue a course in literary studies independently and successfully, then this is to a large extent thanks to their efforts.

We would also be grateful if readers of the present volume would send their comments, critical or otherwise, to us at ansgar.nuenning@anglistik.uni-giessen.de or v.nuenning@urz.uni-heidelberg.de.

Vera and Ansgar Nünning
September 2004

1 Literary Studies: Subject-Matter, Major Issues and Research Domains

The two greatest (complementary, but unfortunately entirely compatible) mistakes that can be made in a literary studies course are therefore, first, to deprive the participants of their spontaneous enjoyment of literature and, then, to abandon them, wordless and open-mouthed, before this literature.

HARALD FRICKE/RÜDIGER ZYMNER

1 Structure and Approach of the Present Volume

At the majority of universities, a degree course in English/American studies begins with introductory courses in literary studies and linguistics. The title of the present volume alludes to this practice, but also sums up the content and overall approach of what is to follow: the volume offers an introduction, not to the history of literature written in English, but rather to literary studies, to the academic study of literature.

Introducing literary studies

What exactly, then, is studied in English and American literary studies? At first glance, the answer seems to be self-evident: literary texts written in the English language. However, on closer examination, this statement merely begs further questions: What are literary texts? Which works should be classified as 'English' literature? What is meant by 'the analysis of literary texts'? What, in addition to literary texts, is the subject-matter of literary studies?

Subject-matter of study

This introductory chapter aims first and foremost to answer these questions and to provide students with an introduction to the subject-matter, the central issues and the research domains of English and American literary studies. English and American studies as well as their research domains are all based on a logic with which the student should familiarise him- or herself at the earliest possible stage, to ensure direction and enjoyment in the chosen course of study.

Objectives of this chapter

In order to avoid the *"two greatest mistakes that can be made in a literary studies course"* mentioned in the introductory quotation, we will attempt to set our course to the practical aspects of the study of English and American literature, and to offer an initial overview of the major issues and methods of this discipline. The primary aim of the present volume is to supply students in the early stages of their studies with some theoretical, terminological and historical categories so as not to *"leave them standing, wordless*

Practice as a guide

and open-mouthed" before the huge diversity of literature in the English language, but also to avoid depriving them of *"their spontaneous enjoyment of literature"* (FRICKE/ZYMNER 1991: 17).

Two pre-conditions for studying successfully	Pursuing this 'middle way', with practice as a guide, involves performing a difficult but necessary balancing act. Anyone who does not enjoy reading and does not take an interest in literature in English will have considerable difficulty fulfilling the reading requirements; without some terminological foundation, however, this enjoyment cannot be communicated. Anyone who wishes to talk in a competent, academic manner about the literary texts read in the course of their studies must of necessity familiarise him- or herself with some of the foundations and terminology of literary theory, textual analysis and literary history. Once this first hurdle has been cleared, the student will notice that not only reading, but also communicating about literary texts and mastering the methods and terminology of literary studies can be a fascinating enterprise.
Transferable skills and knowledge	Of central importance in the analysis and interpretation of literary texts is the acquisition of a basic knowledge of the terminology and the methodological skills. This includes an awareness of the fact that the analytical categories are all grouped together within individual fields (for example, metre, techniques of characterisation or the presentation of consciousness) and within theoretical contexts (for example, structuralism). A thorough familiarity with the theoretical foundations is essential, because the resulting knowledge and skills are transferable. To put it simplistically: a student who attends an introductory course on a certain novelist, dramatist or poet will, at the end of the course, know a good deal about the life and works of this author, but may still be helpless when confronted with other authors and texts. A student who attends a primarily methodologically oriented course dealing with the analysis of lyric, dramatic or narrative texts, on the other hand, acquires the knowledge and skills which enable him or her to tackle new subjects and texts independently. In the first case, only general knowledge is increased; in the second, transferable skills are acquired which increase the student's ability to study independently.
Fundamental terms and methods of textual analysis	For this reason, the following chapters are structured with the intention of shedding light on the characteristics of each genre, on the methods of textual analysis and on the various interpretative approaches. The following examinations of the various forms of lyric, dramatic and narrative texts, as well as diverse media genres, are intended firstly as a detailed introduction to the fundamental terms and techniques of textual analysis. However, this volume also aims to equip students to access independently a

broad spectrum of texts from a variety of cultures and periods within the literatures of the English language. The glossary at the end of the book is intended not only to provide precise definitions of the most important terms used here, but also as a reference aid for the reader.

2 The Subject-Matter of Literary Studies

Like any other academic discipline, the area of literary studies must first give the most precise definition possible of the subject-matter or phenomena with which it is concerned. The variety of attempts that have been made to define the subject-matter, aims and interests of literary studies testify to the fact that this task is considerably more difficult than it may seem at first sight. Naturally, the study of literature is concerned with texts that are classed as 'literary'; however, this merely transfers the problem to the definition of the term 'literature'. We will see in chapter 1.3. why it is so difficult to reach a satisfactory definition of this term.

Preliminary definition

Beginning with the assumption that writing is always a form of communication, the first task must be to gain a preliminary insight into some of the fundamental factors and contexts of literary communication. The most important factors in written communication are generally the author of a work, the text produced by the author, and the addressee or reader, to whom the text is addressed.

Literature as communication

This conception of literature as communication can be developed further with the help of a model from communication theory: that of the transmission of messages. The variant of this conception which is probably most widespread sees communication as a phenomenon that begins with the speaker addressing a message to others. This message, which refers to some form of context (for example, certain aspects of the extralinguistic reality), travels along some form of channel or material medium to reach the addressee. One precondition for successful communication is that the speaker (also called addresser) and the addressee share at least to some degree a common code (a system of rules that enables the interpretation of linguistic signs). The relationship between these various factors in the communication process is represented in the diagram below (figure 1.1.).

Model of communication

The six functions of language postulated by ROMAN JAKOBSON, which are of relevance to many issues in literary studies (and are also helpful when differentiating between literary and non-literary texts), are derived from the relationship between an act of linguistic communication and the various factors in the commu-

Functions of language

nication process. The addresser is associated with the emotive or expressive function of conveying his attitude towards the object. The conative function, which is directed towards the addressee, aims to influence the opinions and behaviour of the recipient, whereas the referential function denotes the relationship of a message to the facts, objects or models of reality to which it alludes. The phatic function, on the other hand, is related to the channel of communication, that is to say, the establishment and maintenance of communicative contact between the addresser and the addressee. The metalingual function refers to the way in which the linguistic code is thematised or highlighted. The poetic function, finally, is based on a reflexive reference made within a message to its own form or structure.

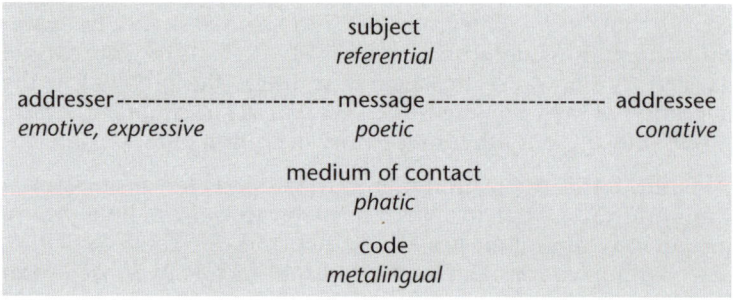

Figure 1.1.: Communication model and functions of language

Peculiarities of written communication

Literary modes of writing or of textual communication are therefore special cases within general linguistic communication and characterised by a number of peculiarities. In contrast to face-to-face oral communication, written communication is usually characterised by a time lag between production and reception. The text becomes the medium through which the message from the addresser reaches the addressee. The addressee, therefore, has no opportunity to influence the addresser directly (for example, by means of body language or facial expressions) or to ask questions concerning the latter's intention. The text forms the only link between the addresser and addressee. All attempts at precise definition and further differentiation within the general communication model depend on the medium used in each case. Furthermore, as we will see in subsequent chapters, each form and genre of literary communication is characterised by a number of distinguishing features.

Literary system

This communication model effectively broadens the scope of literary studies beyond the examination of literary texts alone to include the entire social sphere in which literary texts are written,

Literary Studies: Subject-Matter, Major Issues and Research Domains published, read, discussed and reviewed. This sphere is described as the 'literary institution' or the 'literary system'. The literary system can be described schematically as a network of relations consisting not only of literary texts, but also of the people that produce, mediate, read and process these texts, including authors, publishers, readers and critics.

Roles within the literary system

The sphere of society described as a 'literary system' is in fact a particular communication system which comprises four possible roles: production, mediation, reception and processing or criticism. When defining the subject-matter of literary studies we should therefore take care to consider the author (as the producer of literature) and the reader (as the recipient) as well as the literary works themselves. In addition, publishing houses, the book trade, the media and other institutions involved in the mediation of literature and in literary reviews should be taken into account. Censorship and changes demanded by publishers are only the most obvious instances which illustrate the influence of the literary system on literary texts. A glance at the shelves in any bookshop or at the literary section of a newspaper, in which the books are arranged according to (at the very least) the categories of 'fiction' and 'non-fiction', should suffice to illustrate the extent to which these institutions determine which texts can legitimately be classified as literature.

Model of literary communication

The following model of literary communication, which is based on JAKOBSON's communication model, offers an illustration of the subject-matter of literary studies:

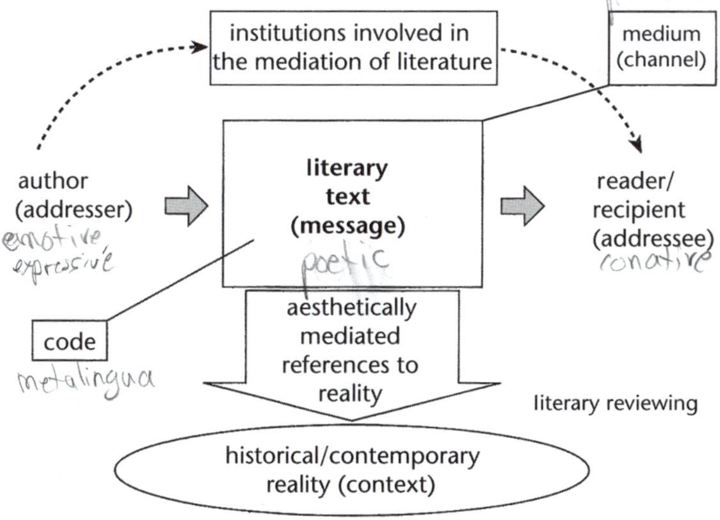

Figure 1.2.: Model of literary communication (see NÜNNING/JUCKER 1999: 49)

Constituents of the communication model	This model of literary communication offers a simplified representation of the most important elements and agents involved in the communication process. An author (addresser) produces a literary text (message) which is simultaneously the material basis or medium (channel) via which the message reaches the recipient or reader (addressee). If the addressee is to understand the text, he or she must share a common language and similar generic conventions (code) with the addresser. Literary texts generally incorporate references to the historical or contemporary reality (context), but these references are subject to techniques of aesthetic mediation.
Literature as symbolic and social system	This model of literary communication facilitates the task of showing the difference between literature as a textual or symbolic system and literature as a social system. Literature can be regarded as an ensemble of texts which are classified as 'literary' thanks to their fulfilment of certain criteria (see below). Considered from such a perspective, literature is understood as a symbolic system, which is characterised by certain aesthetic features and differs significantly from texts in other social systems (for example, economic, legal, academic, and so on). The approaches and methods of textual analysis introduced in the following chapters are concerned with the investigation of literature as a symbolic system. However, the extended social sphere of the literary institutions can also be the subject of investigation, as a social system which is composed not merely of literary texts, but also of a variety of agents, roles and institutions.
Field of study	The study of Anglo-American literature thus encompasses an extraordinarily broad field, including not only the interpretation of literary texts, but also all other aspects of literature as a symbolic and as a social system. It is concerned on the one hand with the development of theories, models and methods of textual analysis and with the histories of British, Irish, American and Canadian literature, as well as other literatures written in the English language. On the other hand, it is also concerned with the biographies of authors, the development of the book trade, the media and censorship as well as with the reception and criticism of literature. However, a university course will often focus on literary texts which are written in English, and particularly on the analysis and interpretation of literary texts. To reach a more precise definition of the field of literary studies, then, we must first elaborate a working definition of 'literature', and clarify what kind of texts can be classified as literary.

3 Criteria for a Definition of Literature

Generations of literary theorists have attempted to answer the question *"What is literature?"*, which was asked by JEAN-PAUL SARTRE along with countless others; however, it remains to this day hotly disputed. And yet the word 'literature' is known to everyone, and occurs in all manner of educational and everyday contexts. Academics pore over secondary literature, bookshops are well-stocked with travel and children's literature, and so on. However, although we may all have an intuitive understanding of what is meant by the term 'literature', such subjective notions are obviously of limited use when attempting to delimit the scope of an entire discipline. In order to reach an adequate definition of the subject-matter of literary studies, we need reliable criteria which enable us to differentiate between literary and non-literary texts. We need not, however, concern ourselves here with defining the 'essence' of literature, nor with reaching definitive conclusions about what literature 'is'. What we need is a viable working definition of the term.

What is literature?

An examination of definitions in encyclopaedia and implied definitions in literary histories demonstrates that a fundamental distinction can be made between broad and narrow definitions of the term (see GRABES 1981b). 'Literature' in the broadest sense encompasses all written communications, i.e., the entire corpus of written and printed works. However, even a definition of this breadth (on which, despite the obvious practical problems relating to its application, most English literary histories are based) excludes oral literatures. A huge number of narrower definitions also exist, although they show a remarkable lack of consensus concerning the precise nature of 'literature'. They generally only agree insofar as many of them limit 'literature in the narrow sense' to poetic and imaginative texts.

Broad vs. narrow definitions of literature

Yet the problem remains that, in order reach a satisfactory definition of 'literature', concrete characteristics and criteria that can form the basis of a categorisation as 'literary' or 'non-literary' must be identified. A good deal of ink has been spilt in the attempt to define the 'literariness' of literary texts; however, again, there is little consensus about the precise qualities described by this term.

Literariness

The question of what constitutes the 'literariness' of a literary work becomes all the more difficult when one considers that the term 'literature' has always been subject to historical change and that it can vary considerably from one cultural context to the next. As a result, there *can* be no perennially valid answer to the question

'Literature' and history

of what literature is, 'in essence'. The historical and cultural variability of the term 'literature' becomes particularly evident when we consider the historical transition from the orally mediated literature, which is still common in many areas of the former British Empire, to the written word, and to other, more modern media (for example, cinematic adaptations of novels). As a result of these changes in medium we are constantly being confronted with new 'texts', such as radio plays and screenplays, which introduce yet more nuances to the term 'literature'. To attempt to discuss all historical varieties of 'literature' in the course of a short introduction would, of course, be impossible. However, it is important to familiarise oneself with at least the most important criteria which have been applied in previous attempts to distinguish 'literature' from other forms of texts.

Normative vs. descriptive definitions

Scholars of literature generally agree that definitions based on particular normative or qualitative criteria (which differentiate, for example, between 'high-brow' and 'low-brow' literature) are problematic, not least because such criteria do not stand up to objective scrutiny. Normative aesthetic or value-based definitions of 'literature' are therefore usually avoided nowadays. There is also a general consensus that any differentiation between literary and non-literary texts should follow descriptive (as opposed to prescriptive) criteria, and base itself on certain textual and contextual factors.

Literature and reality

Two central criteria for differentiating between literary (in the narrow sense) and non-literary texts have traditionally been the specific way in which literature positions itself in relation to reality, and, in particular, the view that literature makes no claim to convey or represent 'facts'. In contrast to 'referential' texts, then, literary texts make no pretence of referring directly and explicitly to reality, nor of making 'factual' statements about this reality. Whereas we, quite reasonably, expect a travel guide to give us reliable information about a country or town, we do not have the same expectations of a play or a novel. Literary texts may well incorporate many general or even quite specific references to a contextual 'reality' (for example, to general knowledge or to certain existing places, people and events), but they generally exhibit a more relaxed relationship to factual reality.

Mimesis vs. poesis

Literary theory has long been concerned with the central question of the relationship between the imaginative world evoked by a literary text, and reality. The term 'mimesis' (Greek for 'imitation'), which has been a concept central to aesthetics since Antiquity, considers literature's relationship to reality to be grounded in its imitation of the real world. The modern view, however, is that literary texts do not merely imitate extra-literary contexts; instead, reality and literary texts are in dynamic interplay. The term 'poesis' (Greek for 'the making'), on the other hand, emphasizes that literature creates independent models of reality with specifically literary tools. The question of the relationship between literature and reality is thus superseded by the question of *how* literary texts transform the knowledge, the experiences, as well as the values and norms of the period in which they have their genesis.

Fictionality

The different claims made by literary and non-literary texts in terms of the 'truthfulness' of their content or their proximity to 'reality' lead on to a further important criterion for the differentiation between the two: the 'fictionality' of literary texts. This term, derived from Latin (from *fingere*, meaning 'to form, invent, feign') refers to the fabricated or imaginative nature of the worlds presented in literary texts. The places and characters that feature in such texts are therefore described as 'fictional' and/or 'fictive'.

The aesthetic convention

Fictionality is nowadays no longer considered to be a feature of the text itself, but rather a set of social conventions or consensually recognised rules concerning how certain texts should be approached. Agents in the literary system, therefore, conform to this so-called 'aesthetic convention', which holds that literary texts should be judged not in terms of 'true' versus 'false' or 'useful' versus 'useless', but rather according to specific aesthetic criteria. When acting in accordance with this aesthetic convention, individuals are prepared to abandon, or rather to 'suspend', the expectations of factual accuracy with which they generally approach non-fictional texts. The English Romantic poet SAMUEL TAYLOR COLERIDGE described this attitude of mind, whereby the reader allows him- or herself to be transported to an invented world in the full knowledge that the literary text will supply no 'true' information about reality, as a *'willing suspension of disbelief'*.

Signals for fictionality

Whether a reader classifies a text as fictional or non-fictional is dependent to a large degree on the signals given by the text itself. Rather than being inherently fictional, a literary text presents itself as such by giving certain signals. By 'signals' or 'indicators' of fictionality, we mean all those signs which indicate to the reader that the world presented within the text is fabricated, and that it is to be read according to the rules of the aesthetic convention. Non-fictional texts, conversely, incorporate contrasting indicators, which can be described as 'reality signals'. Signals for fictionality, which can occur with varying degrees of frequency and concentration and frequently allow diverse interpretations, are subject to historical change and to a variety of conventions.

There are certain textual features which play an important role in signalling fictionality and in constituting the different modes

Textual signals for fictionality	of referring to reality in fictional and non-fictional texts. These include particular introductory or concluding formulae; for example, 'Once upon a time' signals a fairy-tale. The use of certain deictic elements, particularly those whose spatial, temporal or personal reference cannot definitively be related to extra-textual reality, a high degree of ambiguity, and the inclusion of allusions to other literary texts can all serve as signals for fictionality. Further pointers towards the fictionality of a literary work can be found within the repertoire of representational techniques which are considered specifically 'literary', for example, representation of consciousness, monological speech, and other devices which have no parallel in non-fictional texts.
Contextual and paratextual signals for fictionality	A clear distinction should be made between the textual signals listed above, and contextual, as well as paratextual signals for fictionality. Among the contextual signals are communication situations (for example, theatre visits, poetry readings) as well as signals relating to the publishing process (certain publishing houses, for example, are primarily known for specialising in 'fiction', whereas others publish mainly 'non-fiction' books) and the external presentation of a book. Paratextual signals for fictionality, on the other hand, include the title and subtitle, subdivisions of the text, generic terms such as 'novel' or 'comedy' and legal disclaimers ('any similarity to any person, living or dead, is purely coincidental').
Ambiguity and the polyvalence convention	A further characteristic feature of literature is its ambiguity, also described as 'polyvalence'. In contrast to the ideal of the greatest possible explicitness and clarity, which is applied to non-fictional texts, literary texts (and often even short excerpts from such texts) typically allow for various interpretations, thanks to their internal ambiguities. When polyvalence occurs in literary texts, then, it is considered a seal of quality rather than a flaw. In contrast to readers of timetables, of legal texts or newspapers, who expect straightforward information, within the literary system readers approach literary texts in accordance with the 'polyvalence convention'; instead of rejecting polyvalence, they expect literary texts to be open to a variety of interpretations. As a result of the aesthetic and polyvalence conventions, therefore, literary texts are expected to accord the recipient a certain amount of freedom to construct meaning. Instead of one particular meaning, they offer a greater or lesser number of potential meanings, which the reader has to negotiate. This also impinges upon the possible interpretations of a text, which are usually manifold and always determined by the analytical categories applied and their underlying theoretical bases.

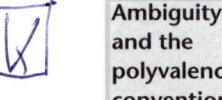

There have been any number of other attempts to distinguish between literary and non-literary texts (see EAGLETON 1983; chapter 1). A fundamental division can be made between 'text-intrinsic' definitions, which attempt to define literariness on the basis of certain linguistic or formal characteristics of literary texts, and 'context-oriented' conceptions of literature, which draw on extrinsic factors. The second approach includes theories which focus on the production or reception aesthetics of literature, i.e. on the genesis of a work or the specific response it elicits from the reader. There now follows a résumé of some of the most important criteria for differentiating between fictional and non-fictional texts, and the approaches in which these are grounded.

Further definitions and demarcations

According to text-intrinsic approaches, which form the basis of stylistic and formalistic conceptions of literature, literary texts are distinguished by particular linguistic and stylistic features. Literary language, then, is characterised by a high degree of deviation from everyday language, a feature which is also referred to as 'deautomatisation' or 'defamiliarisation'. According to these approaches, the main task of literary studies is to identify the typical literary techniques in which this defamiliarisation finds concrete expression.

Literature as a particular use of language

According to a widespread view which is based on JAKOBSON's communication model (see above), the literariness of linguistic expression is determined by the dominance of a particular function of language, the aforementioned poetic function. This view holds that, in literary texts, language is focused on itself, i.e. on certain formal characteristics of the linguistic building blocks of a text. This dominance of the poetic function is particularly evident in poems (see chapter 3). It cannot be regarded as a watertight criterion for the classification of literary texts, however, as similar techniques can be found in other types of language use, for example, in advertising.

Poetic functions of language

Rather than focusing on style or language, other approaches take the specific properties of literary communication as their starting point. As a result, literature is often defined as a non-pragmatic discourse, because a poem or a tragedy, unlike, for example, a user manual, does not serve a specific purpose and gives no directions for action. This definition does not, however, apply to all literary texts, because some genres or individual works (for instance, political novels or plays by GEORGE BERNARD SHAW) are intended to serve a certain purpose.

Literature as non-pragmatic discourse

In contrast to approaches which attempt to tie literariness to certain textual features, other attempts to define the term assume that literariness is based primarily on the attitude of the individual

Literariness as based on an attitude towards texts	reader towards a text. As became apparent in the discussions of the aesthetic and polyvalence conventions, there are certain socially recognised rules concerning how literary texts are generally approached. There is, of course, nothing that prevents us from reading a novel or a play as if they were non-fiction, and to draw specific information from them. If we did that, however, we would not be acting in conformity with the aesthetic and polyvalence conventions, which govern communication within our society on the subject of literature.
Literature and the aesthetics of production and reception	Whilst text-intrinsic approaches proceed from the assumption that literary texts can be 'objectively' shown to have certain aesthetic qualities, definitions of literature which are based on production aesthetics focus on the creation or genesis of the text. They take the basic view that a work is classed as 'literature' because it is the product of a specifically poetic imagination or poetic inspiration. Definitions based on the aesthetics of reception, on the other hand, hold that literary texts differ from others in the specifically 'aesthetic' effect that they have.
Literary studies in general vs. English/ American literary studies	Everything that has been said up to now about criteria for a definition of literature, and a good deal of the material in the forthcoming chapters, is not only applicable to the study of English/American literature. Other areas of literary studies, including comparative literary studies, are also concerned with these basic questions. However, although English/American literary studies share many general concerns and methods with literary studies in general, they focus primarily on literature written in the English language and published in certain geographical regions.
English literature vs. literature(s) in English	What do we mean when we say 'English literature'? Contrary to the commonly held view that the expression refers to a particular 'national literature', that is to say, the literature of England, Great Britain or the British Isles, we should be careful to make a primary distinction between 'English' literature, and the huge variety of literatures written in the English language. English and American studies are concerned not only with English and American literature, but also with all other literatures written in the English language, for example, Canadian, South African and Australian literature.

4 Interpretation and Criteria for Literary Analysis

Questions of interpretation	Explaining the working practices and criteria of literary studies is no less important than demarcating their subject-matter. Precisely because 'interpretation' often appears to be a rather vague and nebulous term (as many of those who studied German or English

at school can testify), it is important to clarify which terminological and methodological criteria should be fulfilled by an analysis of a literary text. This raises certain questions: What do we mean by a literary analysis or interpretation? What are the aims (and limitations) of such an interpretation? What criteria should a literary interpretation fulfil if it is to have any academic merit?

It is important, firstly, to clarify the difference between the subject-matter of literary studies, and the academic discourse surrounding this subject-matter. The subject-matter encompasses all those factors such as the literary texts, authors, readers and so on, which were previously identified as concerns of literary studies. The academic discourse includes the theories, methods and terms by means of which literary studies analyse and classify this subject. On the level of the subject-matter, then, we find literary texts which are characterised – as explained above – by their polyvalence. The scholars and students who analyse and interpret these texts, however, take heed of the conventions which govern communication within the academic system.

Literature vs. academic discourse

A corresponding distinction is made between literary language, or the language of the subject-matter of literary studies, and academic or scholarly metalanguage. The language of the subject-matter is the artistically crafted language of the literary text. The term 'metalanguage', on the other hand, refers to every utterance that focuses on the code, i. e. the language itself. In contrast to the ambivalent language of literature, the metalanguage of literary studies is a specialist language, which must satisfy the criteria of academic discourse (for example, clarity, use of well-defined terminology, comprehensibility). Those who recommend that literature specialists should write in as 'literary' manner as possible are confusing the language of the literary text with academic discourse and metalanguage. It would be as logical to recommend that an ornithologist give up studying birds and learn to fly himself.

Literary language vs. metalanguage

As interpretation frequently has the reputation of being an artistic discipline which at school only the teacher succeeds in mastering, or which involves purely subjective judgements and tastes, it may be helpful to draw a distinction between the type of literary analysis frequently found in the arts section of newspapers, and the scholarly analysis and interpretation of texts carried out by those studying literature at university. A review in a national daily newspaper or in the *Times Literary Supplement* informs us about new publications and assesses their quality, without making any claims of verifiability or denying the subjectivity of its judgements. In contrast to the metalanguage of literary studies, such reviews often approach the style of literary language. It would, therefore,

Literary reviews vs. literary interpretation

be erroneous to confuse newspaper or televised reviews of literature with literary interpretation, and to expect the same standards of entertainment from one's lecturers that one expects from literary critics active in the popular press. Instead, we should be aware that such popular forms of criticism and academic literary interpretation are different social institutions, pursuing entirely different objectives.

Analysis – Interpretation – Reading

Various terms, the most common being 'analysis', 'interpretation' and 'reading', are employed to describe the process of examining literary texts. The expression 'textual analysis' refers to the systematic examination of a text in terms of its individual components. Analysis has less to do with relaying the meaning of a text than with describing its formal and thematic characteristics in the most precise way possible, that is to say, with describing the modes of representation which are used to generate meaning. Textual interpretation, on the other hand, focuses primarily on exploring the potential meanings of a text and formulating hypotheses concerning how it should be understood. The precise analysis of a text is a prerequisite for its successful interpretation. Modern critical approaches frequently attack the notion of 'interpretation' and replace this term with 'readings', by which they stress that there is no single meaning and correct interpretation of a literary text, but rather a variety of possible ways of deriving a meaning from or attributing a meaning to a text.

Factors that influence the understanding and interpretation of a text

The complexity of this process of textual interpretation becomes clear when we examine the numerous factors that influence our understanding and interpretation of a text (see GRABES 1981a: 21ff.). Most important for a simple understanding are the text itself, the language skills and general world view of the reader, the linguistic meaning of the text and the concrete meaning that is attributed to it, and, finally, the context. In the case of an interpretation, however, various other factors can be influential, most importantly, the text written by the interpreter, without which the primary text would not be accessible to others, and the language of the individual interpreter.

Hermeneutics

Literary studies has reacted to the complexity of the process of understanding and interpreting texts by developing particular methods of interpreting literary texts. The term 'hermeneutics' is generally used to refer to the process of interpreting and explaining texts. An interpretative understanding is reached, on the one hand, by means of a grammatical and rhetorical examination, which can uncover the linguistic meaning of a text; on the other hand, it involves identifying any figurative significance beneath the literal level of meaning. The interpretative methods of hermeneutics and other approaches (see chapter 2) are, in a manner of speaking, rules that must be observed by anyone who wishes their interpretation to have scholarly merit.

Given the numerous factors that influence our understanding of a text, it should come as no surprise that our comprehension of single parts of the text and that of the text as a whole are mutually dependent. The view that we reach an understanding of a text by moving within the so-called hermeneutic circle is one of the most important insights of hermeneutics. Put simply, this means that we must approach the whole via its parts and the parts via the whole (HANS-GEORG GADAMER). The hermeneutic circle, however, applies not only to the relationship of interdependence between the single elements and the whole of the text; it also refers to the interdependence of linguistic understanding and factual knowledge (see VOGT 2001: 60) as well as of the information conveyed by the text and the interpreter's previous knowledge: *"We constitute our first assumptions about the whole from our own world view; we then analyse the parts, draw conclusions from the parts for a more concise understanding of the whole, and on the basis of this understanding, begin again to constitute the parts."* (PETER RUSTERHOLZ, in: ARNOLD/ DETERING 1996: 124)

Hermeneutic circle

In addition to the aforementioned factors that influence our understanding and interpretation of a text, there are additional factors that can influence the interpretation of literary texts (see GRABES 1981a: 24ff.). These include the author, as well as his language and world view; those who are involved in mediating the text and its meanings; the political, socio-economic and cultural context; references to other texts and genres; the contemporary and later reception of the text and its interpretative tradition. Admittedly, these factors can only influence an interpretation insofar as the individual interpreter is aware of them and can thus bring them to bear on the process of interpreting the text. Literary interpretations are therefore subject to numerous historical variables, to an even greater extent than other forms of textual understanding.

Additional factors that influence the interpretation of texts

The model of literary communication which appears above presents the three factors author → text → reader in accordance with the logic of the genesis of the text and of literary production. However, we should note that the processes of reading and interpreting a text are based on a different chronology. Instead of the author, who can play a part in the process of interpretation only insofar as the interpreter knows anything about him and applies this knowledge in the course of his interpretation, it is the text that represents the point of departure. Drawing on his linguistic and factual knowledge, the interpreter assigns a particular meaning to the text which is then recorded in his written interpretation. This sequence can be represented as follows:

Sequence of factors influencing textual interpretation

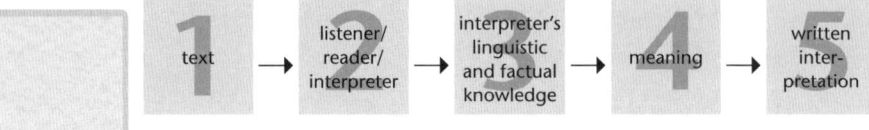

Figure 1.3.: Factors influencing textual interpretation
(see GRABES 1981a: 31)

Importance of other disciplines

The sheer variety of factors that can influence the understanding and interpretation of literary texts is indicative of the difficulty of making reliable statements concerning the meaning of a literary text. These factors also make us more aware of literary studies' perennial reliance on other disciplines: linguistics (particularly historical linguistics and sociolinguistics) is central to determining the meaning of a text; conclusions concerning the context, world view and reception of a work can generally only be reached with prior knowledge of cultural and intellectual history, philosophy and sociology; references to other texts, genres and media are only intelligible to those well-versed in textual analysis as well as genre, literary and art history.

Criteria for the interpretation of literary texts

This begs the question of which criteria an interpretation has to fulfil in order to be classed as 'scholarly'. Firstly, any interpretation of a literary text *"is required to reflect on the factors that have influenced the interpretation, and to inform us about these factors"* (GRABES 1981a: 25). Those who compose scholarly interpretations should therefore not only make explicit their premises, objectives and methodological presuppositions, but also be able to give an accurate account of the factors which have contributed to the composition of their interpretation. Like all other areas of literary studies, textual interpretations should be measured against the yardsticks that are applied to pieces of academic scholarship in general. Among the most important criteria for assessing the academic merit of an interpretation, which are also applied to the work produced by students in the course of their literary studies, are the following (see GRABES 1981a: 30ff.; LUDWIG 1994: 247ff.):

- precision, comprehensibility and communicability
- terminological clarity
- logical coherence and systematic application of analytical categories
- methodological clarity
- coherence of argument and conclusions
- consistency and plausibility
- reference to and critical consideration of previous research
- documentation of all the sources and secondary literature consulted
- relevance, contribution to scholarship

- concision and revenue on efforts invested
- intersubjectivity, or intelligibility and verifiability

The use of well-defined scholarly terms and methods is a fundamental requirement, if interpretations are to meet these criteria.
Just like every other branch of scholarship, literary studies has its
own standardised terminology, which enables us to discuss literary subject-matter in a precise, sophisticated and economical way.
The categories and methods of literary studies represent a clear
and systematic means of attaining plausible, coherent and intersubjective results. If the interpretation of a text, or indeed any
other kind of scholarly composition based on literature (including,
for example, a biography of an author, a reconstruction of the
original reception of a work or an investigation of changes in the
aesthetic criteria used by literary reviews) is to have scholarly
merit, then it must fulfil the criteria listed above.

**Termino-
logical
language**

5 Types of Textual Interpretation

The primary concern of anyone analysing or interpreting literary
texts, then, is to employ well-defined categories and methods in
order to produce a precise and comprehensible account of the
content, as well as of the linguistic, formal, and structural characteristics of literary texts, and to interpret these characteristics
and their possible effects. It follows from this that the goal of
interpretation is not to investigate 'the' meaning of a text, and
certainly not to determine the intention of the author. Instead,
interpretation can be described as a rational discourse on thematic and structural textual characteristics, as well as on the relationship between these characteristics and their potential
meaning(s). In practice, the goal should be a synthesis between
the methodical analysis of textual processes and interpretative
understanding.

**Interpreta-
tion as a
rational dis-
course
about tex-
tual charac-
teristics**

It is also important to note that there is no such thing as 'the'
interpretation of a text, but rather various different types of interpretation (see STRUBE 1993: 91), focusing on various aspects of the
text. Among such aspects are the style, the theme and the structure
of a literary work. An initial distinction can be made between
thematic and formal (that is, structural) interpretations of texts,
the first of which focus primarily on the content, or the 'what' of
a literary work (for example material and motifs), whereas the
latter focus on formal techniques, or the 'how' of its composition.

**Textual
interpreta-
tion: theme
vs. form**

Function	However, the task of interpreting a literary work is not confined to a description of its thematic and formal characteristics; it is also concerned with the function of these characteristics. The term 'function' is one of the most frequently used terms in literary studies, and can refer to a wide range of phenomena, depending on the individual approach and context. 'Function' generally means 'the task, role, capacity or effect of a part or an element within a larger whole'. It is used more specifically when applied to the six functions of language which were explained earlier (see chapter 1.2., figure 1.1.). Moreover, it is helpful to distinguish between an 'internal function' (the function of elements or modes of representation within a text) and an 'external function' (the relationship between texts and outside factors). Contrary to the common erroneous use of the term, it can be equated neither with the intention of a real historical author, nor with the actual effect of a text on its readers.
Semantici-sation of literary forms	Since form-oriented interpretive approaches also take into account the function(s) of textual characteristics, they serve to investigate the so-called 'semanticisation of literary forms': they proceed from the premise that literary modes of representation and literary structures function as independent carriers of meaning, which can play a central part in the allocation of meaning by the recipient. The concept of the semanticisation of literary forms, which goes back to Russian Formalism and the Prague School, investigates the semantic function of artistic techniques. It is concerned less with the external composition of literary works than with the way in which poetic techniques of representation can contribute to the process of constructing meaning. The analysis of formal processes of representation can yield useful insights into the potential meaning(s) of a literary work.
Types of textual interpreta-tion	The broad spectrum of types of textual interpretation extends far beyond a basic differentiation between thematic and formal approaches, however. In the final analysis, there are as many different types of textual interpretation as there are theories and methods in literary studies (see chapter 2). Each of these various approaches takes different factors into account during the interpretative process (for example, the author, the world view and ideals dominant at the time of a work's genesis, the cultural context, and so on). In addition, the various types of textual interpretation differ in their angles of enquiry and their goals, as well as the kind of argumentation and the theories of literature they imply. Some of the most widespread types of textual interpretation and their most important characteristics are represented schematically in the diagram below (see STRUBE 1993).

Semanticize =
give mea-
ning to sth

	structural interpretation	stylistic interpretation	psychological interpretation
goal	identification of the structuring principle	identification of the stylistic principle	explanation of (one aspect of) the text according to the specific mental condition of the author
argumentation	'proof' of the structuring principle	'proof' of the stylistic principle	'interpretation' or psychological explanation of the genesis of the text
implicit theory of literature	literary work = closed, structured whole, autonomous	literary work = unitary whole (organism); autonomous; characterised by stylistic harmony	literary work = creation of an author and therefore not autonomous

Table 1.1.: Types of textual interpretation
(see AXEL SPREE, in: EICHER/WIEMANN 1997: 180)

It is not the text itself that determines the type or goal of an interpretation, but rather the individual interpreter and his or her specific angle of enquiry. The types of interpretation listed above represent different ways of interacting with literature, and serve diverse interests: *"Structural, stylistic, psychological interpretations, to name but a few, are ways of interacting with literature, or behavioural modes, which were created on the basis of specific interests and were not, so to speak, drawn from or dictated by the text. No text forces the scholar of literature to adopt a structural or psychological interpretative approach; the text cannot determine the interest or the goals of the scholar of literature."* (STRUBE 1993: 94) It follows, therefore, that anyone embarking on an interpretation of a text must first choose a fruitful angle of enquiry and clarify their goal, methods, and the theoretical assumptions implicit in all of these.

Objectives of the interpreter

6 Fields and Research Domains in Literary Studies

As was made clear in the course of the discussion concerning the subject-matter of literary studies, the fields in English and American literary studies are not by any means only concerned with the interpretation of the major works written in the English language. The analysis and interpretation of literary texts do, in practice, comprise a large part of literary studies; however, the discipline is also concerned with other subject areas, fields of enquiry and methods. Among the related fields of study is the investigation of

Fields of study

all the other aspects of the literary system (for example, the production, mediation, reception and processing of literature) which are included in the model of literary communication presented above (see chapter 1.2., figure 1.2.). In addition, literary studies are concerned with a number of fundamental questions, which go far beyond the analysis of individual texts. A further important area of enquiry is that of historical change within the literary system and in literary forms of expression.

Systematic vs. historical areas of enquiry

A preliminary distinction can therefore be made between systematic and historical areas of enquiry. The former of these focuses on fundamental and timeless aspects, whereas the latter is concerned with the historical development of the objects under investigation, whether they be literary texts or phenomena within the literary system. However, in the context of literary studies, these two areas are very closely related, as the majority of systematic questions can only be answered adequately if due consideration is given to historical factors.

Central concerns of literary studies

Literary studies can be schematically divided into three research domains, each of which focuses on a different area of enquiry and uses different methods; they are literary theory, textual analysis or interpretation, and literary history. These areas do not by any means account for the discipline in its entirety; instead, they comprise the central areas for a student of literature. Far from being homogeneous, these research domains can themselves be divided into further sub-categories.

Literary theory

In general, literary theory focuses on the systematic areas of literary studies. These include certain fundamental questions (for example, the definition of literature and theories of interpretation) as well as categories which enable us to order the objects of enquiry in a methodical and structured manner (for example genre theory). Literary theory also includes literary aesthetics (the branch of philosophy dealing with beauty and taste), poetics (the description of literary art) and genre theory. It comprises a broad spectrum of competing approaches, models and methods, which will be systematised in the second chapter.

Textual analysis and interpretation

A second central area comprises the analysis and interpretation of literary texts, which were discussed to some extent above. Thanks to the wide variety of literary genres and media, this area includes a large number of analytical categories and methods specific to these genres and media, the most important of which will be discussed in chapters 3 to 6.

Literary history

The third research domain of literary studies is literary history, which focuses on historical areas of enquiry into the development of literatures written in English. Like the disciplines of English and

American studies, the broad field of literary history can be divided into (at least) two major areas: English and American literature. These two central areas have been joined over the past decades by the histories of a number of New English Literatures (see chapter 7).

In addition to these central areas, literary studies also includes a number of other important fields, such as textual criticism and scholarly editing. These research domains focus on assessing the reliability of textual editions; this is an extremely important element of the study of older texts. They are also responsible for supplying us with annotated (or critical) editions of major works, which include detailed critical commentaries on the text (for example, information on the genesis and transmission of the text, a selection of textual variants, documentation of the reception history and interpretative explanations).

Further fields of study: textual criticism and scholarly editing

Literary theory, textual analysis and interpretation, and literary history are not discrete and separate areas of enquiry; they are in fact very closely related. Literary theory occupies a central position in this relationship, as every textual interpretation and literary history is based on particular theoretical preferences, even if they are not acknowledged. None of these three research domains should be omitted, however, as the student who concentrates on literary theory, models and methods may lose sight of the text itself and of literary history, thus neglecting the core of the discipline; while a student who only focuses on the texts without giving due consideration to theory, models and methods, risks foundering *"wordless and open-mouthed"* before the literature and interpreting it in a purely subjective and impressionistic manner.

Relationship between the research domains

Every effort should be made to develop a mind-map of each of these three research domains as soon as possible, as this 'map' will enable the student to navigate his or her way far more effectively through the maze of subject areas, approaches, angles of enquiry and literary histories. Such an overview is necessary in order to be able to make an informed choice from the wide range of courses on offer and to fit these courses into some kind of overarching framework. It can also aid students in overcoming their initial (and, unfortunately, often justified) impression of having very little firm ground beneath their feet. The models presented in the following chapters are meant to serve as such 'maps' in that they are to help students orientate themselves in this initial phase, to enable them to fit the subject areas and topics covered in their literature classes into a larger disciplinary framework, and to assist them in deciding how to broaden their knowledge and skill base in a systematic manner.

Mind-maps of subject areas

7 Classifications in Literary Studies: Genres and Periods

Classifications
One of the goals of literary studies, as of other academic disciplines, is to describe, classify and interpret the objects of enquiry as precisely as possible. Therefore, a variety of literary terms have been coined, which serve to order and structure the discipline. These enable us to classify the multitude of texts, and thus to impose some order onto the, at first sight, chaotic and diverse proliferation of literary works. As a glance in any literary history will confirm, there is large variety of criteria for the differentiation and categorisation of texts; some of the most common and most important of these criteria are listed in the table below.

language	literature in the German, English, Romance, etc. languages
nation	German, English, Scottish, American, Irish, French national literatures
categories of aesthetic evaluation	high-brow and low-brow literature, popular literature, pulp fiction
sociological categories	children's, women's, working class literature
historical categories	classical, medieval, contemporary literature
media-related categories	oral, written, audiovisual literature
relation to reality	realistic and mimetic (from 'mimesis' meaning 'imitation') versus fantasy (anti-mimetic) literature
conventionality of mode of representation	traditional versus innovative or experimental literature

Table 1.2.: Criteria for the classification of texts

Genres and text types
One of the most important, and the most helpful, categories in literary studies is that of the literary genre, or the 'text type', in the case of non-fictional texts. However, although in theory there is a system of distinct genres and types, the different kinds of texts actually form a continuum, with permeable boundaries between the various categories. The following tree diagram suggests a typology of the most important literary genres.

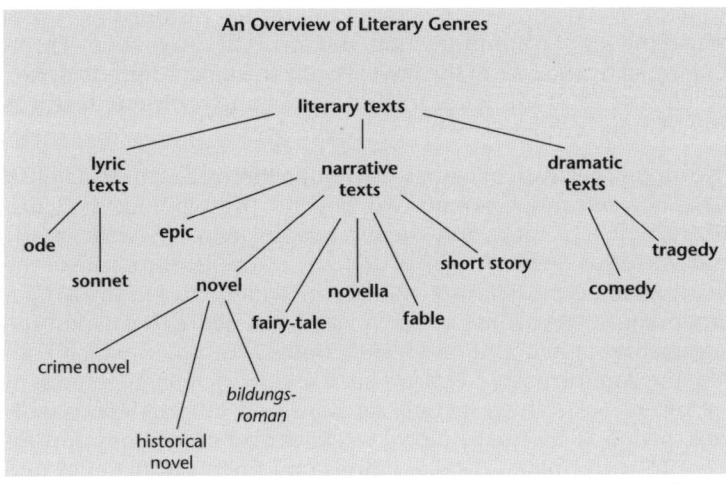

Figure 1.4.: *Typology of literary genres* (see NÜNNING/JUCKER 1999: 66)

The term 'genre' is derived from the biological term *genus*, and refers to a group of literary works that share significant characteristics in terms of content, form and/or function. Such 'generic features' or 'generic conventions' do not only serve as a classificatory system for literary works, they are also important signposts for authors and recipients. Genres are *"constructs based on sociocultural, literary and social consensus"* (VOSSKAMP 1992: 256), which manifest themselves in the form of groups of texts.

Generic features

Various criteria are employed in order to classify and differentiate between genres, including external form (for example, length; verse or prose composition) and medium (book; stage, radio or film production; see chapter 6). Another widespread, but more problematic form of generic classification is based on thematic criteria. Content-based genre typologies are useful insofar as they can give a preliminary thematic and contextual view of a group of texts. However, such content-based classifications are also problematic in that they risk devoting so much attention to sifting through a potentially limitless variety of themes that they neglect the representation techniques and the specific literary qualities of the texts under consideration. Those typologies that are based on stylistic and textual aspects, by contrast, focus primarily on the formal characteristics, and therefore the specific literary qualities, of a text.

Criteria for generic classification

Models of the genre system such as the typology of literary genres sketched above should not blind us to the fact that single genres, and, indeed, the entire genre system, are subject to historical change. Genres are not atemporal 'natural forms of literature'

Genre system and genre change

(JOHANN WOLFGANG VON GOETHE), but rather historically conditioned modes of communication and forms of convention. This is illustrated by the case of the novel, today the most common genre, which rose to prominence in the 18th century, although it was preceded by various forms of narrative prose.

Genres and text types beyond the three 'main genres'

The broad spectrum of genres within the literatures of the English language naturally extends far beyond the typology sketched above, which includes only the three main genres (lyric, dramatic and narrative texts). We could add, for example, the genre of the essay, which is particularly valued and widespread in the Anglo-American sphere. There is also a variety of genres located at the intersection of fictional and non-fictional writing, in which English and American studies have been taking increasing interest in the recent past. These include sermons and other religious writings, pedagogical tracts, moral weeklies and magazines, historiography, travelogues, letters, diaries and memoirs, fictional and non-fictional biographies and autobiographies, street ballads, pamphlets and various forms of popular literature and popular culture (for example, reality TV, docu-drama, cyberpunk).

Modes of writing

In addition to the genre system, text types can also be classified by reference to the mode in which they are written. 'Modes of writing' is a broad and often imprecisely used term, which has at least two main meanings: it can be used in a more precise sense to refer to *"ahistorical constants such as the narrative, dramatic and satirical"* (HEMPFER 1973: 27), and also more loosely as an umbrella term to designate various different textual structures such as metaphor, rhetorical figures, narrative form and so on (see chapters 3 to 5), as a virtual synonym for 'modes of literary representation'. The former narrow use of the term allows us to make a clear distinction between 'mode of writing' and terms such as 'genre' or 'subgenre', the *"concrete historical realisation of these general modes, such as satirical verse, novel, epic and so on"* (HEMPFER 1973: 27). KLAUS W. HEMPFER also makes a distinction between 'primary modes of writing', which *"can be used only in particular speech situations (for example, narrative in a report, dramatic in a performative context), whereas secondary modes of writing (the comical, the satirical, and so on) can occur in various types of speech situations"* (ibid.: 225).

Periods

A further important organisational category in literary studies, in addition to that of the genre, is the concept of the 'period'. Periodization enables us to subdivide the history of literature into a chronology of 'ages' or phases. The term 'period' refers to a space of time or phase of variable length, in which literary works sharing particular ideological, thematic, formal or stylistic features (also known as the 'period style') originate.

The organisational categories listed above also influence the structure of the present volume, which is concerned primarily with the most important genres. The second chapter offers an introductory overview of the nature and application of the most important theories, models and methods of literary studies in the form of a typology. The four subsequent chapters are introductions to the analysis of the three main genres (poetry, drama and narrative) as well as to the analysis of media genres. The final chapter comprises an explanation of the most important terms, problems and forms in literary historiography, and an overview of the major periods of English and American literary history.

Structure of the present volume

2 Literary Studies: Theories, Models and Methods

Hostility to theory usually means an opposition to other people's theories and an oblivion of one's own. One purpose of this book is to lift that repression and allow us to remember.

TERRY EAGLETON

1 The Use and Necessity of Literary Theory

The theory boom

A preliminary acquaintance with the most important approaches and issues in literary theory is an important precondition for gaining an insight into the various fields and research domains of English and American studies. Such an acquaintance is not easily obtained, however, and the following typology of literary theories, models and methods is intended as a guide. The progressive trend towards theorisation in literary studies, which has been in evidence since the 1960s, has resulted in a multitude of competing approaches and methods, which also affects English and American studies. Whether this increase in approaches and models is a positive or a negative development is a contentious question, and opinions range from insistence in the undeniable usefulness and indispensability of theory, through a sober evaluation of the advantages and disadvantages, to an open, and even militant, hostility to theory.

Attitudes towards theory

However inclined we may be towards the final position, it is not a particularly helpful stance. To dismiss theories and methods is to hide one's head in the sand, like the proverbial ostrich. The well-known disadvantage of this course of action is that the threat does not disappear merely because one hides from it. Understandable though phobia and scepticism with regard to theory may be, there are a number of reasons why such attitudes are likely to prove counterproductive to the success of one's studies.

Omni-presence of theory

It is now generally accepted that every form of analysis and observation has its basis in theory of some kind. For those of us concerned with literature, this implies that literary studies, literary historiography, textual interpretation of every kind, and even those approaches which claim to be 'theory free', are all based on a number of theoretical assumptions. If an analysis and interpretation of a literary text is to fulfil the criteria listed in the first chapter (for example, intersubjectivity, plausibility and coherence), then it must acknowledge its theoretical foundations. TERRY EAGLETON (1983: viii), one of the most prominent English literary theorists, succinctly summarised the agendas that frequently lie behind hostility to theory in the quote that heads this chapter: rejection of theory is indeed often merely hostility towards the theories of other people, and frequently means that one has forgotten, or is at least insufficiently aware of, one's own theoretical presuppositions.

The opposition between a theory-oriented and a 'direct' or 'undistorted' approach to literary texts, much touted by the 'anti-theorists', therefore reveals itself to be a false one. What is at issue is not whether or not scholars of literature *use* particular theories, models and methods, but rather, how conscious they are of their theoretical and methodological premises, and how explicitly they present the categories they use: *"The question must be put whether the model is merely a set of the scholar's assumptions, that is, relatively unconscious. Or does it consist of a set of consciously chosen categories, collected in a scheme which allows reflection, criticism, and thus development?"* (BONHEIM 1990: 37)

Conscious and explicit use of theory

In addition, today's students of literary and cultural studies must, for various reasons, familiarise themselves with theoretical approaches and terminology as a matter of necessity. A glance at a lecture list of a German, British or American university should suffice to convince anyone that this area is of ever greater importance in English and American studies syllabi. Moreover, a steadily increasing proportion of secondary literature is only accessible to those with a basic knowledge of recent literary and cultural theory. A familiarity with theory and awareness of methodology are therefore necessary for independent academic study, particularly in view of the fact that most scholarly books and essays can only be evaluated with the help of these tools. In addition, students can exploit the merits of their preferred theories and analytical categories in their written coursework, by testing the various approaches and selecting those models and methods that are most suited to their topic, to the texts they are discussing, and to their argument.

Necessity of theory

The question as to why it is useful and important to familiarise oneself with certain fundamental theories, models and methods in the early stages of one's university career is not hard to answer. The main argument is that these concepts are indispensable analytical tools, which enable the student to formulate the premises and arguments of their literary analyses, to describe textual phenomena in an appropriately differentiated manner, and to render their analytical approaches transparent and their interpretative conclusions comprehensible. A familiarity with theoretical bases and methods is important, then, because their transferability en-

Usefulness of theory

ables the student to access literary texts without help from the lecturer. A course of study which is oriented towards theory and method is therefore neither an end in itself, nor a means of scaring away the young literature enthusiast. It is rather an important prerequisite for acquiring transferable skills and progressing independently to more advanced approaches.

2 Theories, Models and Methods: Terminology

Theories

Although the terms 'theories', 'models' and 'methods' are frequently used synonymously in literary studies, they can actually be clearly differentiated. The term 'theory' refers to explicit, detailed, organised and consistent systems of categories, which are used to investigate, describe and explain the subject-matter of the respective field. Theories are expected to give a full account of their terminology and structure, and to be unified, systematic and intersubjective. Within the discipline of literary studies, many theories have been developed that deal with particular aspects of literature (for example, the production and reception of literary works, the relationship between literature and its context, the system of literary genres); however, literary studies have also adopted theories from many other disciplines in the humanities.

Models

Models are formal or graphic representations of a theory or a component part of a theory. Despite the loose way in which the term is frequently used, models can be identified by a number of specific characteristics. Models are always representations of something; they are concerned only with the limited number of characteristics that are regarded as relevant for the area of enquiry. The structure of the model is therefore determined by the aspects that are selected. In literary studies as in other disciplines, models represent a means of reducing complexity, as they attempt to provide an overall, schematic representation of complex subject-matter. Among the models that have been influential in literary studies are the communication model presented in chapter 1 (see Figure 1.2.), diagrammatic representations of literary genres (see Figure 1.4.), and FRANZ K. STANZEL's typological circle of narrative situations (2001 [1979]), which will be introduced in chapter 5.

Methods

The term 'method', which in Greek means approximately 'the way towards something', refers to well-defined, planned and therefore also verifiable procedures for dealing with something. It refers to the means by which one reaches a particular goal. Methods are composed of a systematic sequence of rules, principles and analytical stages, which follow a particular angle of enquiry or point of departure in pursuit of a particular predetermined goal. Different methods can yield different results. Jochen Vogt (2001: 209) gives a concise account of the way in which they differ from each other: *"From a systematic point of view, one 'method' of interpretation differs from another in that it designates certain aspects of the text as important and integrates them into an argument, and simultaneously ignores or disregards other aspects (which are perhaps privileged by another, competing method)."*

A number of other terms are also used to refer to the theoretical and methodological foundations of an analysis. For example, the terms 'approaches', 'directions' or 'frames of reference/analysis' are often employed instead of 'theories', while methods are frequently being referred to as 'procedures', 'interpretative/analytical processes' or (again) 'approaches'. The term 'approach' is also often used to designate the basic theoretical assumptions and methods preferred by scholars who 'approach' literature in a way that is distinct from those adopted by other groups of scholars. However, the immediate priority for the student is generally to attain some kind of overview of the plethora of approaches, angles of enquiry and methods of literary studies, regardless of the terms in which they are couched. The following section aims to provide just such an overview.

'Approaches', 'procedures' and similar terms

inconsistent system of categories!

3 Approaches and Methodologies of Literary Studies: A Typological Introduction

As we saw in the explanation of the various types of textual interpretation in the first chapter, literary studies comprise a large number of different theories and methods. This 'methodological pluralism' may at first seem daunting, but it has its advantages, too, for many of the approaches summarised below can also be applied to other media genres (see chapter 6). In order to do justice to these diverse angles of enquiry and objectives, a large arsenal of different theories and methods must be applied. The methodological pluralism that currently exists in literary studies is, then, to a large extent a consequence of the plurality of objects and goals of study.

Methodological pluralism

In what follows we will present a typology (i. e. an overview subdivided into different types) of the main theoretical approaches in order to assist students in finding their way through this bewildering methodological plurality (the word 'approach' is here used in the sense of 'basic theoretical assumption', see above). This typology aims to provide guidance in classifying the various theoretical currents. Also, it highlights the diversity of ways in which one can approach a literary text, and the various aspects of texts that are

Use of a typological introduction

privileged by specific approaches. In the following short introduction of the most important types of approaches and methods we aim, firstly, to examine which aspects of the broad field of literary studies provide the focus of each approach, and, secondly, to identify and explain some of the most important characteristics of the various approaches and methods.

Communication model as a frame of reference

The various theoretical approaches in literary studies can be roughly divided into groups (according to the respective objects of enquiry). A frame of reference for such a systematization of the plethora of approaches can be found in chapter 1 in the form of the model of literary communication (see chapter 1.2.). The various groups of different approaches each concentrate on one element of this model, or they consider the various elements to be related to one another in particular ways.

Text-oriented vs. context-oriented approaches

A preliminary distinction between text- and context-oriented approaches can be made on the basis of whether an approach focuses on the literary work itself or on its relationship to the various contexts in which it is situated. Following on from this distinction, various types of context-related approaches can be identified according to the different kinds of contextual relationship (author – text, text – historical reality, text – other texts or text – reader). Moreover, both author- and reader-oriented approaches can be primarily psychological, primarily sociological or primarily historical in orientation. The following diagram illustrates which aspects of the chain author – text – reader – historical reality are of prime concern to the various approaches and methods.

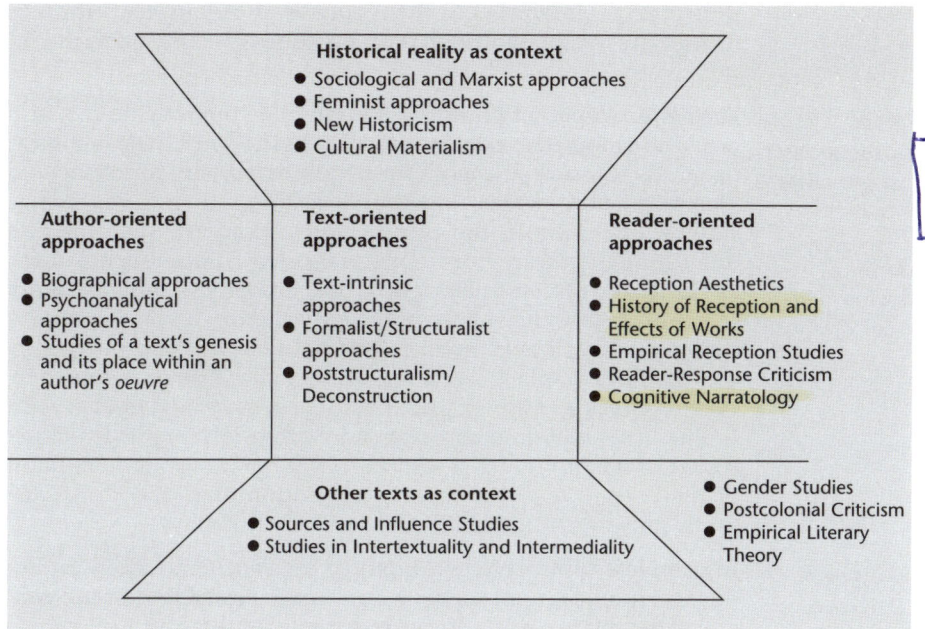

Figure 2.1.: Theoretical approaches and methods in literary studies
(see NÜNNING/JUCKER 1999: 60)

Text-oriented approaches

Text-oriented approaches are concerned primarily with matters related to the analysis of thematic, formal or linguistic characteristics of literary texts. Due to their focus on the text itself, some of these methods are also described as 'text-intrinsic' or 'intrinsic' approaches (the German term *'werkimmanente Interpretation'* having become well established in German studies). For a long time, New Criticism was the most influential text-oriented approach in the Anglo-American sphere; however, text-oriented approaches also include textual criticism, stylistic interpretations and all approaches concerned with the content of a work. Among the latter are, for example, certain currents in feminist literary theory such as images-of-women criticism, which subjects literary representations of women to critical examination.

Structuralist approaches

Formalist and structuralist approaches, which can be counted among the 'structural interpretations' presented in chapter 1.5., should also be classified as predominantly text-oriented. Such approaches deliberately disregard contextual aspects and concentrate on providing an exact description of the structural features of literary texts, for example, the plot structure of dramatic and narrative texts (see chapters 4 and 5). Structuralist approaches are therefore less interested in the meaning of literary texts than in techniques of representation or in processes of constituting meaning.

Poststructuralist approaches

Further examples of primarily text-oriented approaches can also be found among the more recent currents in French literary theory, generally subsumed beneath the headings 'poststructuralism' and 'deconstruction', which have had a lasting influence on literary studies, especially in the United States. However, such theories differ fundamentally from other text-oriented approaches. Text-intrinsic and structuralist approaches emphasise the ambiguity of literature, but they also assume each literary text to be unitary and to form a closed structure. Deconstructionist approaches, by contrast, which take the concept of *différance/différence*, coined by JACQUES DERRIDA, as their watchword, are concerned neither with finding 'the' meaning of a text, nor with analysing its structure. Instead, such approaches aim to formulate an exact description of the text's internal differences, discontinuities and contradictions, thus negating the idea of a unitary meaning.

Author-oriented or production-oriented approaches

In complete contrast to text-oriented approaches, author- or production-oriented approaches focus on the production or the genesis of the literary work. Typical examples of this attitude towards literature, which is nowadays regarded as rather passé, can be found in biographical approaches, which investigate the possible influence that the biography of the author could have had on a particular work, or treat literary texts as biographical sources. Psychoanalytical approaches attempt to ascertain the role that certain childhood experiences and the psyche of the author play in a particular work, or to draw conclusions from a literary text about the unconscious of the author. Rhetorical studies (the study of oration) and studies which focus on the genesis, production and revision of a text, or which analyse the text within the context of an author's *œuvre*, are also author- or production-oriented.

Reader-oriented or reception-oriented approaches

Unlike some of the now rather antiquated author-oriented approaches, methods of studying the relationship between text and reader have only been in existence since the 1970s. Reception-oriented approaches shift the focus away from pure textual analysis towards the reception or processing of a literary work by the reader, and can be separated into two sub-categories. The first is concerned with the text and its potential meanings or effects, and with the ways in which these could hypothetically be realised by the reader. This sub-category includes reception aesthetics and reader-response criticism, both of which are concerned with the potential of meaning inherent in the literary work. The second sub-category is concerned with the actual recipient and reception process and includes empirical reception studies, which are concerned with the actual impact of texts on real-life, contemporary readers. Situated between the two sub-categories are reception history and the history of aesthetic effects, which investigate the horizon of expectations of the original (reading) public and the historical reception of a literary work.

Like reception studies, approaches which focus on the relationship between a specific literary work and other texts and media have been booming for some years now. These approaches, which are known as 'studies in intertextuality and intermediality', had several precursors, including source and influence studies, as well as studies of the history of specific themes, motifs or materials, which look in particular at the sources and literary models for a text, and the text's adaptation of these sources. However, in contrast to these older approaches, theories of intertextuality are not merely concerned with thematic and formal similarities between individual literary texts. Instead, they aim to carry out a systematic investigation of the relationships between literary texts and genres. Theories of intermediality (see chapter 6.3.), on the other hand, examine the interaction between different forms of art, for example, film adaptations of novels, or references in literary works to other art-forms or media. Given the enormous growth in importance of audiovisual mass media and the increasing tendency towards combining various genres and media, this represents an interesting new area of research that offers students a variety of prospects in terms of both success in their studies and in their professional career.

Studies in intertextuality and intermediality

In contrast to the methods discussed previously, context-oriented approaches focus on relationships between literary texts and their historical context. Now that the dominance of structuralist and other text-based or intrinsic approaches has receded somewhat, it is again deemed acceptable to investigate the relation of literary texts to extratextual reality. As a glance in many of the older histories of English and American literature will demonstrate, traditional historical approaches generally took the historical and political context of a literary work into consideration. A typical example is the recourse to the so-called 'Elizabethan world picture', which is still influential in many analyses of WILLIAM SHAKESPEARE's works. Marxist and sociological approaches to literature, which proceed from the assumption that literature mirrors social reality, focus on the axis 'text – historical reality'. Some feminist approaches which examine the relationship between literature and the historical situation of women also attach a great deal of importance to issues of context.

Context-oriented approaches

New Histori-cism and Cultural Materialism	Since the beginning of the 1980s, the influence of historicising tendencies has been growing, particularly in Anglo-American literary studies. In North America, the so-called New Historicism has played an important part in broadening literary studies into a theory-conscious discipline that also pays due attention to cultural history. New Historicism is based on considerations relating to the historicity of texts and the textuality of history, and argues that information concerning 'contexts' can only be accessed via texts themselves. It is primarily interested in the interaction between literary texts and the standard of knowledge or cultural discourses (i. e. the socially accepted discursive conventions) which prevailed at the time of their genesis. The approach known as Cultural Materialism, which originated in Great Britain, also differs from text-intrinsic interpretations by taking the literary text's relation to reality into consideration; however, it places a greater focus than New Historicism on the political and ideological dimension and on the analysis of power relations.
Comprehensive theories	This necessarily simplified typology does not, however, cover the entire spectrum of currents in contemporary literature. There are also a number of approaches which cannot be assigned to any one area within the diagram. They include a variety of innovative and comprehensive theoretical currents which examine the entire domain of the literary system. Among these approaches are, for example, gender studies, postcolonial criticism and Empirical Theory of Literature, the latter of which purports to replace all other hermeneutic approaches to literature with a new empirical paradigm. Whilst these approaches differ in many respects, they also have a number of similarities: They all favour a broad definition of literature (see chapter 1.3.) and open up new areas of investigation. Moreover, they all aim to extend 'traditional' literary studies to include interdisciplinary approaches, and, in particular, to integrate approaches from cultural and media studies within the discipline of English studies.
Theoretical imports from other disciplines	In addition to the theoretical currents discussed above, which take literature as their direct subject-matter, there are also several influential theoretical approaches that were developed in other disciplines and have (often eclectically) been imported into literary studies. Among the most significant comprehensive theoretical imports are JACQUES LACAN's psychoanalysis, MICHEL FOUCAULT's historical discourse analysis, PIERRE BOURDIEU's theory of social milieus, JACQUES DERRIDA's deconstruction and philosophy of language and NIKLAS LUHMANN's systems theory. As these names indicate, contemporary literary theory is not only increasingly interdisciplinary and intermedial in approach; the spectrum of approaches has also absorbed many international influences.

The various approaches do not only differ in respect of their individual focus. They also employ different methods and analytical procedures. In the case of text-oriented interpretations, New Criticism and deconstruction, for example, 'close reading' of the individual literary text is the favoured method. This involves an extremely detailed, thorough and intensive reading and text-centred interpretation, which assumes the autonomy of the work of art, disregards the context and concentrates on the linguistic peculiarities, formal characteristics and nuances of meaning within the work under consideration. This is still the dominant method of analysis in Great Britain. New Historicism and approaches which favour intertextual methods of analysis, on the other hand, are very popular in the United States and focus on comparisons between several texts, New Historicism preferring to investigate the dialogue between literary and non-literary texts with the aid of discourse analysis. Other areas such as literary sociology, empirical reception studies and empirical literary studies, the latter of which investigates literature as a social system, employ methods borrowed from empirical social research.

Methodo-logical differences

4 Functions of Theories, Models and Methods

Although the preceding typology cannot serve to provide a comprehensive understanding of the particularities of the various approaches, it should suffice as a preliminary guide to the bewildering array of literary theories, models and methods. Such a guide should prevent students from losing heart immediately when confronted with a multitude of methods and technical terms in an introductory course, and will hopefully demonstrate that literary theory is accessible, even to the beginner.

Typology as a guide

Instead of being intimidated by the plurality of approaches, students should therefore obtain a preliminary overview of these approaches as quickly as possible. The numerous encyclopaedia of literary and cultural theory are a good source of information on the specific approaches, theoreticians and basic terminology dealt with in university courses. With the help of this basic knowledge, you will be in a far better position to follow the methodological procedures discussed in secondary literature and seminars, and to understand what questions are being asked and how they can best be answered.

Basic knowledge

There is, of course, no magic formula for dealing with the confusing multitude of approaches, models and methods in literary theory. However, it is advisable to find a reasonable compromise between uncritical identification with particular approaches and

Attitude towards methodological pluralism	an excessive, needless fear of all theory. The student who uncritically adopts a particular theory for the simple reason that it has been used by the lecturer runs the risk of becoming an uncritical disciple, who, at worst, can merely parrot terminology. The student who rejects theories and models from the outset, however, forgoes the opportunity of learning about diverse new ways of thinking and interpretative procedures and, additionally, restricts him- or herself to reading literature perpetually through the distorting lens of everyday assumptions and personal prejudices.
Open-minded and critical attitude	Instead of inclining to one of the extremes described above, it is advisable to adopt a simultaneously open-minded and critical attitude, to compare the diverse approaches and to make independent judgements concerning their advantages and disadvantages. This is an important precondition if students are to be able to select the most appropriate approach for each individual subject and angle of enquiry. As the usefulness of a theoretical system, a model or a methodological approach can only be determined by application, every individual student must decide which theoretical approach and procedure to apply in each individual situation. The yardstick for assessing the value of an approach is whether or not it yields new insights and contributes significantly to the study of literature.
The uses and functions of theories, models and methods 	The uses and advantages of theories, models and methods is best illustrated by means of a brief summary of their diverse functions. Models serve primarily to provide a visual illustration of complex material, and can therefore be useful guides when teaching literature; it is for this reason that so many have been included in this introduction to literary studies. Theoretical approaches, methods and clearly defined analytical categories also perform

- explanatory or cognitive functions: they can be used to formulate the premises of literary investigations, define basic terminology and explain the objectives of the investigation;
- heuristic functions: they enable us to develop precise areas of enquiry within textual analysis, and to formulate clear hypotheses concerning the potential of meaning of a literary work;
- descriptive functions: they enable us to identify and describe textual phenomena in a precise way;
- communicative functions: they are an important prerequisite for the coherence and comprehensibility of textual interpretations;
- typological functions: they enable a systematic classification of texts and their respective characteristics;
- literary-historical functions: they enable us to position texts within broader historical contexts;

- comparative functions: they supply yardsticks for comparative studies;
- didactic functions: they facilitate learning and teaching procedures and enable the transferral of analytical procedures;
- mnemotechnic functions: they facilitate the process of memorising complex material;
- application-oriented functions: they function as analytical aids in textual interpretations.

This brief outline of literary approaches and their functions leads on to the question of how students of English should approach literary works in practice. The numerous modes of analysing and interpreting literary texts are as diverse as the theoretical approaches, models and methods in literary studies outlined above. Each one of these approaches can in theory be applied to every poem, drama and novel in the English language. However, the selection of one particular approach generally involves focusing on specific aspects of the text, and neglecting or entirely disregarding other aspects.

Textual analysis: from theory to practice

The choice of approach and analytical or interpretative procedure will generally depend on the area of enquiry, the objective and the topic or subject-matter of the individual investigation. To offer an example: a student who is writing an essay entitled 'Forms and functions of plot structure in the spy novel' would probably not be well advised to adopt an approach from psychoanalysis or reception aesthetics, as his or her topic calls for a text-centred approach. For a student who is investigating a thematic topic at the intersection of literary and cultural history (for example 'The social position of women in Victorian literature'), however, a theoretical framework or approach that considers the relationship between the text and historical reality or the text and other texts, as well as the arguments of feminist literary theory, would be more appropriate.

Criteria for choosing an approach

The genre and period to which the text belongs are also an important consideration when choosing an approach. The following four chapters will provide an introduction to the various genre-specific approaches and analytical categories. Rather than offering 'ready-made' interpretations, these chapters aim to supply students with terminological and methodological aids, which will enable them to undertake independent analyses of unfamiliar texts. We will therefore be providing explanatory introductions to various central terms and methods and illustrating their uses by means of some examples from the analysis of lyric, dramatic and narrative texts.

Genre-specific approaches and analytical categories

Further reading

An exhaustive survey of the multitude of theoretical currents would far exceed the scope of this introduction. We therefore advise those who wish to learn more about individual approaches, methods and concepts to consult the introductions listed in the appendix of this work, as well as the *Metzler Lexikon Literatur- und Kulturtheorie: Ansätze – Personen – Grundbegriffe* (1998/2004). This encyclopaedia, interdisciplinary in approach, offers a compact survey of the diverse approaches in literary and cultural studies, in addition to explaining important terminology and introducing those authors who have contributed significantly to the theoretical debate. For those who prefer to consult English reference works, we should like to recommend the *Encyclopedia of Contemporary Literary Theory* (1993), edited by IRENA MAKARYK, and the *Dictionary of Cultural and Critical Theory* (1996), edited by MICHAEL PAYNE. As all the entries in the *Metzler Lexikon Literatur- und Kulturtheorie* give suggestions for further reading material which provides information on specific approaches and the work of individual theoreticians, we have restricted the reading lists in the appendix of the present volume to general introductions to literary theory. The works by JONATHAN CULLER, TERRY EAGLETON, RAMAN SELDEN, PETER WIDDOWSON and HUBERT ZAPF in particular offer strong footholds for those new to the discipline.

3 An Introduction to the Analysis

CHAPTER **of Poetry** $1 = witzeln$

The Hippopotamus
Behold the hippopotamus!
We laugh at how he looks to us,
And yet in moments dank and grim
I wonder how we look to him.
Peace, peace, thou hippopotamus!
We really look all right to us
As you no doubt delight the eye
Of other hippopotami.
                    (OGDEN NASH)

1 The Poem as an Ultra-Complex Textual Structure: Fundamental Features of Lyric Composition

"*Everyone knows what a [...] poem is; no-one knows what a [...] poem is*", quips OTTO KNÖRRICH (1992: xii) in the introduction to an encyclopaedia of lyric forms. This striking, paradoxical observation succinctly summarises the fact that, on the one hand, everyone has an intuitive understanding of what a poem is, but, on the other hand, no-one is confident about giving an exact definition of a poem. Most people would instantly classify the poem by the unconventional American poet OGDEN NASH (1902–1971) cited above as a (short, humorous) poem, despite its very unpoetic theme. It exemplifies some of the basic characteristics of the genre: relative brevity, tendency towards a very selective and limited treatment of the chosen theme (think of all the other things he could have said about a hippopotamus!), the subjective perspective of the speaker (also sometimes called the 'lyric persona'), as well as the rhyme scheme (rhyming couplets), an (almost) regular metre, the division into stanzas, the lack of any plot, the repeated use of exclamations and other deviations from everyday language – although this poem (like NASH's poems in general) is, for the most part, written in a register close to everyday speech. All these elements imbue poems with an enhanced level of artistry, something that is also said to be characteristic of poetry in general.

> How to recognize a poem when you see one ...

The objective of this chapter is to give an introductory overview of some of the fundamentals of the theory of poetry, or lyric texts and to present some of the most important categories for the analysis of poems. Firstly, the most important generic features of poetry will be summarised. Following this introduction to the fun-

> Aims and content of this chapter

damental features of lyric composition and the presentation of a communication model for lyric texts, the most important areas and problems in the analysis of poetry will be presented systematically and explained by reference to select examples.

The 'essence' of poetry

The question of what constitutes the 'essence' of poetry has not as yet been answered satisfactorily, and it probably never will be. There are many reasons for this. Firstly, poetry – like many other literary genres – is characterised by a high degree of diversity. Secondly, both poems themselves and our conception of poetry and its characteristics are subject to historical change. Thirdly, in addition to the individual genres, the entire system of genres and media is continually changing and being transformed.

Normative theories of poetry

There have been many attempts, however, to determine and identify the 'essence' of poetry or lyric texts once and for all. Many of these attempts simply define poetry according to one single characteristic, thereby universalising a single 'type' or manifestation. The resulting, frequently rather grandiloquent, definitions find their way, not only into school syllabi, but also into encyclopaedia of literary terminology, as is demonstrated by the following entry under 'Lyrik' from the widely used *Sachwörterbuch der Literatur*: *"Lyric (Greek lyra = lyre), the most subjective of the three basic forms (→ genres) of literature, an unmediated expression of processes within the poet's innermost soul, which are created by emotional interaction with the outside world (→ experience), and, in the process of being put into words, are elevated from the individual to the universal and symbolic, and are accessible to the recipient by means of an empathic response."* (WILPERT 1955: 328)

Descriptive criteria

Rather than formulating such normative definitions of poetry, we will take the more constructive approach of listing some criteria that can be used to differentiate between poetry and other literary genres. In what follows, then, a list of the most important characteristics will be composed, which, although not applicable to every poem, should allow us to develop a more concrete notion of the characteristics of poetry. The following brief overview owes a good deal to EVA MÜLLER-ZETTELMANN's (2000) sophisticated and balanced 'multi-component model', which assembles a number of criteria for definition and systematises them in the form of a comprehensive analytical arsenal.

Brevity, density and reduction of the topic

A typical characteristic of the majority of poems (the 'epic poem' is the exception that proves the rule) is the tendency toward relative brevity. This is generally accompanied by a reduction and compression of the subject-matter represented in the poem. Spatial and temporal relations are also typically compressed in lyric texts, which frequently place the subjectivity of the speaker in the foreground.

Subjectivity

Most definitions of poetry agree on the importance of the category of subjectivity for a generic classification. Subjectivity is expressed, not only in the attitude and perspective of the lyric persona, but also in the individual mode of linguistic expression and the theme of the poem, which is often centred on individual experience. A typical instance exemplifying a high degree of subjectivity is the poem "London" (1794) by the early Romantic poet WILLIAM BLAKE (1757–1827). The frequent repetition of the personal pronoun 'I', which punctuates the entire text, is established in the first stanza, and the constant intrusion of the perspective of the speaker into the portrayal of the city epitomises the pronounced subjectivism that is so characteristic of Romantic poetry:

I wander through each chartered street
Near where the chartered Thames does flow,
And mark in every face I meet
Marks of weakness, marks of woe. [...]

Musicality and lyricism

The etymology (the study of the origins and original meaning of words) of the word 'lyric' gives some indication of certain additional characteristics of lyric texts. The Greek word 'lyric' refers to a lyre, a stringed instrument; and the term 'lyric' was originally used to refer to those songs that were sung to the accompaniment of the lyre. Thanks to this connection between poetry and music, musicality remains one of the main characteristics of poetry, and is the origin of a variety of other features that are specific to the genre: *"Metre, rhythm, frequent recurrence of structures, compactness, succinctness of formulation, (relative) brevity."* (LINK 1992: 86)

Structuralist theory of poetry

We have structuralist approaches to the theory of poetry to thank for the insight that poems are not the unmediated expression of feelings and moods; they consist in the first instance of words and are distinguished by a particular form of language use. Structuralist approaches also propagated the view that various categories from linguistics (for example, from phonology, semantics and pragmatics) can be usefully employed when analysing poems.

Paradigmatic and syntagmatic relations

The distinction between the paradigmatic (Greek *parádeigma*: example, exemplar, model) and syntagmatic (Greek *syntagma*: that which has been put together) axes, which forms the basis of the structuralist theory of language, is particularly important for the theory and analysis of poetry (and other literary texts). According to ROMAN JAKOBSON, the term 'paradigmatic' refers to the relationship between linguistic elements that can be substituted one for another in one specific slot within a sentence, thanks to their

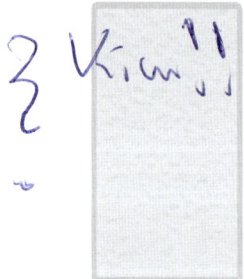

similarity. The selection of linguistic elements on the basis of paradigmatic relations is therefore concerned primarily with the similarity or equivalence between the respective elements. Syntagmatic rules, by contrast, govern relations of contiguity and possible combinations of elements within a sentence or a text. Paradigmatic and syntagmatic relations do not only exist on the level of individual words; they can be applied to diverse aspects of poetry from phonological and rhythmical repetitions through metrical and grammatical structures to lines of verse and metaphorical content.

Poetic function

As was discussed in the first chapter, literary texts can be distinguished from other types of text by the predominance of the 'poetic function of language', a term which refers to the fact that the recipient's attention is drawn towards the linguistic composition of the text (see chapter 1.3.). Taking the distinction between the paradigmatic and syntagmatic axes explained above as a basis, JAKOBSON (1960: 358) was able to give a concise definition of the poetic function: *"The poetic function projects the principle of equivalence from the axis of selection into [sic] the axis of combination."* According to JAKOBSON, poetic structures result from the imposition of the principle of equivalence, which actually governs paradigmatic relations, onto the combination of elements on the syntagmatic axis; the resulting repetitions or recurrences on various linguistic levels create relations between textual elements. In a non-aesthetic text, for example, the principle of equivalence governs the selection of words like 'freeze', 'make cold' or 'chill', all of which are roughly similar on the paradigmatic axis and could be taken at random in a sentence like 'she is chilled by the wind', or 'she is made cold by the wind'. EDGAR ALLAN POE, however, projects the principle of equivalence onto the axis of combination in his poem "Annabel Lee": *"the wind came out.../Chilling and killing my Annabel Lee"*. Here, the principle of phonological equivalence determines the selection of 'chilling'. As a consequence, the linguistic structure of the text is foregrounded, and the recipient is prompted to search for connections between the contiguous elements. The relationship between the paradigmatic axis of selection and the syntagmatic axis of combination, and the projection of the principle of equivalence onto the syntagmatic axis, are represented in the following model (see LUDWIG 1981/1994: 19).

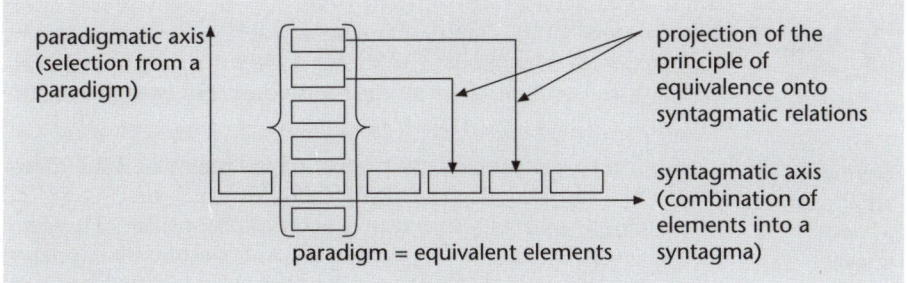

Figure 3.1.: Relation between the paradigmatic and the syntagmatic axes

A consequence of the employment of parallelism and equivalence as constitutive processes governing the combination of elements on the syntagmatic axis is the tendency towards increased artificiality and self-referentiality or self-reflexivity often found in poetry. The referential function of language, which points towards the extratextual context or reality, is reduced to a minimum or even suspended. Simultaneously, the recurrence of linguistically equivalent elements in lyric texts has the effect of foregrounding the text itself and its language.

Increased aesthetic self-referen-tiality

According to structuralist theories of poetry, poems are 'texts with an ultra-complex structure' (see LINK 1981; 1992), distinguished from other literary and non-literary genres by their high degree of linguistic equivalence and parallelism. The central features of poetry can therefore be described as aspects of this high degree of structural complexity, which manifests itself on a variety of linguistic levels:

Levels of structural complexity

- on the level of sound, metre and rhythm, as well as on that of relations between sounds (phonological level), for example by means of rhyme and other sound patterns,
- on the level of individual words and their formation (morphological level) in the form of the repetition of words,
- on the level of sentences (syntactic level) in the form of the parallel arrangement of sentences or sentence components,
- on the level of meaning (semantic level) in the form of figurative language.

Other aspects of the structural complexity specific to poetry are related to its external form. Lines as well as metric and stanzaic structure, for example, are fundamental forms of lyric composition. Theoretical approaches to poetry which focus on formal criteria consider lines to be a feature peculiar to poems: *"In fact, the only watertight distinction between poetry and most non-poetic discourses is that poetry is set out on the page in lines, whereas prose runs*

Lines, metric and stanzaic structure

right to the far edge." (Furniss/Bath 1996: 12) The term 'metre' refers to the scheme of stressed and unstressed syllables that forms the basic structure of a poem. The metre does not merely emphasise certain parts of a line, the resulting equivalences also enhance the structural complexity of the text.

Rhyme scheme and phonological structures

In addition to the subjectivity typical of the genre and the afore-mentioned formal criteria, rhyme scheme and specific sound structures represent further features of lyric composition. These are naturally also aspects of the great structural complexity of poetry: the rhyme scheme establishes connections between lines and between individual words, and other sound structures create further phonological equivalences.

Deviation from everyday language and increased artificiality

All of the aforementioned generic characteristics contribute to the impression of increased artificiality or of deviation from everyday language which is characteristic of poetry. In the case of the majority of poems, this impression of a deviation from the norm is enhanced by a tendency towards structural, phonological, morphological and syntactic complexity. In the remaining sections of this chapter, we will examine examples of the various figures or modes of expression that can be employed on each of these levels. *= apply*

Generic features of poetry

To recapitulate, then, the most important generic features of poetry are (see Müller-Zettelmann 2000: 64–156):

- a tendency towards relative brevity,
- a tendency towards compression, condensation and reduction of the represented subject-matter,
- a tendency towards increased subjectivity,
- a tendency towards musicality and proximity to songs,
- a tendency towards structural and phonological complexity,
- a tendency towards morphological and syntactic complexity,
- a tendency towards deviation from everyday language and increased artificiality,
- a tendency towards increased aesthetic self-referentiality.

2 A Communication Model for Poetry: Speech Situation, Perspective and the Lyric Persona

Speech situation

An analysis of the communication or speech situation of a poem is often a good starting point for interpretation. The speech situation is one of the fundamental structuring principles of literary texts; its constituent elements are the addresser and addressee of a poem and their respective spatial and temporal situations. In the case of a poem, the central issues are, firstly, who the textual

speaker is, secondly, to whom his or her remarks are addressed, and, thirdly, where and when both speaker and addressee are situated. An analysis of the personal and possessive pronouns and their referential function can be fruitful in answering these questions.

When analysing the speech situation in a poem, a distinction must be made between the real author and the speaker or voice. The poet does not generally express him- or herself directly in a poem; instead he or she delegates statements and feelings to the fictive speaker in the text. The term generally applied to this mouthpiece is 'lyric persona' (it could also be described as the 'lyric I'). This persona can be presented to a greater or lesser degree as a subjective personality, but cannot be equated with the historical author.

Author vs. 'lyric persona'

An analogous distinction must be made on the side of the addressee between the real reading public and the fictive addressee named or implied in the poem. Even if the reader is at first inclined to identify him- or herself with the 'lyric thou', it soon becomes apparent that this would be as erroneous as an equation of the author with the lyric persona. In both cases, a distinction must be made between the historical individuals reading and writing literary texts, and the fictive characters that speak and are addressed in these texts, for the lyric persona and its complement on the side of the addressee are merely literary devices or textual strategies.

Reader vs. 'lyric thou'

A systematic arrangement of all these aspects can serve as a basis for a communication model applicable to poems. The communication relations that characterise this genre can be represented graphically as follows:

A communication model for poetry

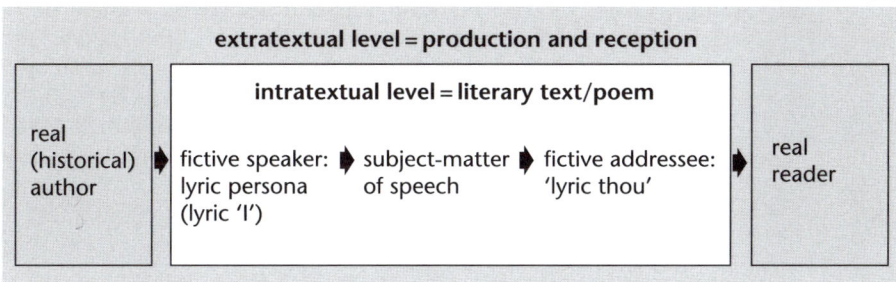

Figure 3.2.: A communication model for poetry

Pragmatic figures	Rhetorical figures that refer to the context and the communication or speech situation are classed as 'pragmatic figures'. They include, for example, the apostrophe (not the punctuation mark, but a rhetorical figure whereby the audience, a person or a thing are directly addressed as if present), and the rhetorical question (a question that does not require an answer, or whose answer is obvious).
Explicit vs. implicit subjectivity	The generic feature of subjectivity, when examined more closely, can help us to describe the speech situation in specific poems more precisely. In different poems, there can be considerable variation in the extent to which the 'lyric persona' materialises as the speaker. A fundamental distinction is made between implicit and explicit subjectivity (see MÜLLER 1995/1998), based on identifiable textual characteristics, and on *"a scale measuring the presence of an 'I' [...], which can range from a subjective colouring of the utterances through to the construction of a concrete character, whose social environment and inner life are clearly defined"* (MÜLLER-ZETTELMANN 2000: 110). The two poles on this scale are, on the one hand, the 'hidden' or covert speaker who barely appears in the poem, and, on the other hand, the manifest, overt, clearly perceptible and more or less individualised lyric persona.
Explicit subjectivity	The term 'explicit subjectivity' describes this clearly perceptible and present lyric persona, who refers to him- or herself in the first person singular, appears as a communicating individual and gives expression to his or her innermost thoughts, feelings and impressions. Such poems are remarkable for their high degree of self-expression; among the numerous examples are WILLIAM SHAKESPEARE's sonnets, many poems by the metaphysical poets, and a good deal of Romantic poetry such as the poem by BLAKE ("London") discussed previously. A sub-genre of poetry which is characterised by a particularly high degree of explicit subjectivity is the dramatic monologue, in which a speaker, who is generally highly individualised, describes an occurrence from his or her own subjective perspective. A typical example is ROBERT BROWNING's dramatic monologue "My Last Duchess" (1842), in which a historically specified character addresses a particular audience in a clearly defined situation:

That's my last Duchess painted on the wall,
Looking as if she were alive. I call
That piece a wonder, now: [...].

Examples of explicit subjectivity	The following opening lines of three poems demonstrate the variety of possible uses of explicit subjectivity to express, for example, private spiritual experiences ("The Collar"), erotic encounters ("The Canonization"), or experiences of nature (as in WILLIAM WORDSWORTH's well-known poem):

An Introduction to the Analysis of Poetry

I struck the board and cried, "No more;
I will abroad!
What? shall I ever sigh and pine? [...]."
(GEORGE HERBERT, "The Collar")

For God's sake hold your tongue, and let me love,
Or chide my palsy, or my gout,
(JOHN DONNE, "The Canonization")

I wandered lonely as a cloud
That floats on high o'er vales and hills,
When all at once I saw a crowd,
A host, of golden daffodils;
(WILLIAM WORDSWORTH, "I wandered lonely as a cloud")

Implicit subjectivity, by contrast, occurs in those poems in which the textual speaker appears not as an individualised lyric persona, but rather can be discerned merely in the choice and subjective coloration of the content, as well as in the form of linguistic expression employed. Implicit subjectivity is in accordance with the ideal of impersonality that characterises the aesthetics, novels and poetry of modernism. An interesting example of implicit subjectivity is EZRA POUND's famous metro poem, which also exemplifies many of the traits of the Anglo-American imagist movement, a school of poetry in the 1910s, which strove for the greatest possible concision and a suggestive use of images. As this poem consists of only two lines, is can be quoted in full:

In a Station of the Metro

The apparition of these faces in the crowd;
Petals on a wet, black bough.

Implicit subjectivity

Even though the title itself indicates that the text refers to an unspecified metro station in Paris, this poem does not offer an 'objective' description of reality, nor does it exhibit complete impersonality. Instead, the linguistic expression of a momentary impression, the infusion of the perceived scene with a subjective perspective, and, finally, the image selected by the poet (what sort of person associates faces in a crowd with petals on a wet, black bough?), all imply *"some kind of consciousness, even if it does not express itself directly in the poem"* (MÜLLER 1995/1998: 98).

Subjectivity in Ezra Pound's metro poem

Like the lyric persona, the addressee or 'lyric thou' can also appear more or less explicitly in a poem. The more frequent the occurrence of forms of address and personal pronouns referring to the second person singular, the more contours the 'lyric thou' acquires as interlocutor. Some poems, which are addressed entirely to a particular individual, naturally place great emphasis on the

Degree of explicitness of the 'lyric thou'

addressee, who therefore appears as an 'explicit lyric thou'. A well-known example is SHAKESPEARE's "Sonnet 18": *"Shall I compare thee to a summer's day? / Thou art more lovely and more temperate."* A further example of an explicit 'lyric thou' occurs in SIEGFRIED SASSOON's (1886–1967) sonnet "Glory of Women", whose subject-matter is typical of much of the poetry of the First World War:

You love us when we're heroes, home on leave,
Or wounded in a mentionable place.
You worship decorations; you believe
That chivalry redeems the war's disgrace.
You make us shells. You listen with delight,
By tales of dirt and danger fondly thrilled.
You crown our distant ardours while we fight,
And mourn our laurelled memories when we're killed.
You can't believe that British troops 'retire'
When hell's last horror breaks them, and they run,
Trampling the terrible corpses – blind with blood.
  O German mother dreaming by the fire,
  While you are knitting socks to send your son
  His face is trodden deeper in the mud.

Speech situation in "Glory of Women"

The first line, and every alternate line in the first ten, begin with the second person singular personal pronoun 'you'. It is not entirely clear at first who exactly is being addressed. However, the poem contains a variety of signals, which give hints as to the identities and attitudes of the speaker and his addressee. The plural in the title and various statements by the speaker indicate that the poem has a collective rather than an individual addressee. We can infer that the addressee of this disillusioned accusation is an unspecified group of women, a hypothesis that is strengthened by the contrast established between the speaker and the addressees, which is accentuated formally by the opposition between 'you' and 'we'. The frequent repetition of the pronoun 'you' (it occurs seven times) also enhances the presence of the addressees. A significant change in the speech situation occurs in line 12, however, when the speaker suddenly addresses a single, more closely identified individual. Whilst it can be inferred from the context in the first eleven lines that the speaker is addressing British women (this is particularly explicit in the line *"You can't believe that British troops 'retire'"*), in the last three lines the speaker addresses a German mother.

Changes of speech situation and perspective

As this example illustrates, the speech situation in a poem is by no means constant, but can change in the course of the text. A typical example of such a shift of speech situation and perspective occurs in STEVIE SMITH's (1902–1971) frequently cited poem "Not Waving but Drowning", whose title now has proverbial weight in English. By means of a series of abrupt changes in perspective, the poem creates a striking image of human isolation and misunderstanding. The drowning person's cries for help are misunderstood by those present as cheerful waving, but the (dead) lyric persona has the last word – which would naturally be impossible in reality:

Nobody heard him, the dead man,
But still he lay moaning:
I was much further out than you thought
And not waving but drowning.

Poor chap, he always loved larking
And now he's dead
It must have been too cold for him his heart gave way
They said.

Oh, no no no, it was too cold always
(Still the dead one lay moaning)
I was much too far out all my life
And not waving but drowning.

Taking the speech situation as our point of departure, we can differentiate when describing the characteristics of poetry *"between the levels of the enounced and enunciation"* (MÜLLER-ZETTELMANN 2000: 139). The level of the enounced, or the level of content, encompasses all entities, such as people, spaces, objects, moods, thoughts, feelings, experiences, and so on, that are represented or contained in a text – in other words, it refers to the 'what' of the poem. The level of enunciation, or textualisation, on the other hand, refers to all elements related to the linguistic and formal composition, and the infusion of the poem with various perspectives, i. e. to the 'how' of the poem.

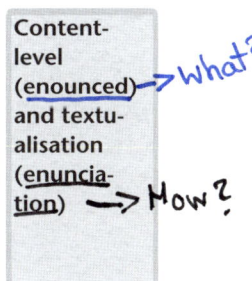

Content-level (enounced) and textualisation (enunciation)

A question that is closely related to the speech situation and this distinction between the levels of the enounced and enunciation is that of the spatio-temporal distance that exists between the thoughts, feelings and experiences of the lyric persona as represented in a poem, and the act of turning this subject-matter into language. The greater the distance, the stronger the impression that the represented subject-matter is being mediated by a speaker: *"An unmediated poem presents experience and the expression of this experience in language as simultaneous occurrences; a mediated poem, on the other hand, can be recognised by the temporal, but also the spatial, emotional and evaluative distance between the speaker and the facts presented in his discourse."* (MÜLLER-ZETTELMANN 2000: 140) This distinction between unmediated and mediated poems should not, however, be seen as a binary 'either/or' opposition; instead they form two poles of a graded scale which allows for numerous intermediate stages.

Distance between represented elements and linguistic realisation

3 The Structure of Poetry: Metre and Rhythm, Feet, Stanzas

Metre and metrical pattern

In addition to the speech situation and subjectivity, the metrical pattern, consisting of stressed and unstressed syllables, represents a further formal principle of organisation that is fundamental to poetry, but not to the other main literary genres (with the exception of a small number of verse narratives and verse dramas).

Feet

When describing the metre of a poem, we use a specific inventory of terminology, some of which dates back to Antiquity. Any description of the metric structure of a poem will generally begin with the smallest unit of verse: the foot. The sequence of an unstressed syllable followed by a stressed one, which is generally represented as follows ᵕ/, is described as an iamb, whereas the opposite sequence of a stressed syllable followed by an unstressed (/ᵕ), is called a trochee. In addition to these two most common types of foot, the following also occur frequently in English poems: the dactyl (/ᵕᵕ), the anapaest (ᵕᵕ/), and, rather less frequently, the spondee (//) and the amphibrach (ᵕ/ᵕ).

Number of feet

As well as identifying the type of foot, an analysis of the metrical pattern of a poem must state the number of stressed syllables (or 'beats') that occur in a line of verse. Again, specific terminology exists; a line with four stressed syllables, for example, is known as a 'four-beat line' or 'tetrameter'. Both the type of foot and the number of stressed syllables must be determined in order to describe or classify the form or genre of a poem; the 14-line traditional sonnet form, for example, generally consists of iambs with five stresses per line, the metre commonly known as the iambic pentameter. Also common in English poetry are the trimeter with three stresses and the hexameter with six. The following lines of verse serve to illustrate these different kinds of metrical forms:

Trimeter	*The kíng	sits in Dúm	ferline tówn* (ballad)
Tetrameter	*Behóld	the híp	popó	tamús!* (OGDEN NASH)
Pentameter	*My mís	tress éyes	are nó	thing líke	the sún* (WILLIAM SHAKESPEARE)
Hexameter	*Ánd, as I	líve, you will	sée my he|xámeters	hópping be|fóre you.* (SAMUEL TAYLOR COLERIDGE, "Hexameters")

Table 3.1.: Examples of the most important metrical forms

Rhythm

The rhythm of a poem is not determined solely by its metre; the length of the syllables, the repetition of phonological and syntactic elements and, not least, the meaning of individual words or sentences can also influence the rhythm. It is therefore important that we also take the word, clause and sentence structures of a poem into consideration, in addition to the metric organisation. The rhythm of a poem is determined by the interplay between its metrical structure and the linguistic realisation of the individual lines.

There is often a degree of tension between the line structure of a poem and its syntax. When sentences, or syntactic units, extend beyond the end of a line, this incongruence between sentence structure and line structure is known as 'enjambment' (or 'run-on line'). If, on the other hand, the end of a line of verse corresponds to a break in the syntax (which usually coincides with the end of a unit of meaning) this is known as an 'end-stopped line'. Enjambment is particularly noticeable if the subsequent line of verse contains sentence components that are necessary in order to complete the meaning of the preceding line. The following excerpts from MARTIN AMIS' poem "Point of View", in which the run-on lines support the view that everything is dependent on the perspective of the observer, are illustrative of the potential of enjambment to surprise and unsettle the reader:

Enjambment

Point of View *POV*
Policemen look suspicious to normal
Murderers. To the mature paedophile
A child's incurious glance is a leer anzüglicher Grinsen
Of intimate salacity; in more
Or less the same way, live people remain
As good as dead to active necrophiles.
[…]
Anyone who has ever walked into
A lamp-post knows that all speeds above nought
Miles per hour are really pretty fast, thanks.
[…]
If you don't feel a little mad sometimes
Then I think you must be out of your mind.
No one knows what to do. Cliches are true.
Everything depends on your point of view.

A break in metre which divides up a line of verse into parts is known in the study of metre as a 'caesura'. The best known example of a metrical pattern that incorporates a caesura is the so-called 'alexandrine', which consists of an iambic hexameter with a caesura after the third stress, or the sixth syllable. The most famous instance of the alexandrine in English poetry is in the final line of verse of the Spenserian stanza, named after EDMUND SPENSER (1552?–1599), in which an alexandrine follows eight lines of verse written in iambic pentameters, with the rhyme scheme ababbcbcc

Caesura and alexandrine

(for more information on rhyme scheme, see chapter 3.4.). Caesuras are often not merely a break in the metric structure of a poem, but also serve to emphasise thematic oppositions and breaks in thought sequences by means of the tension they introduce into the line structure. An illustrative example occurs in the sonnet "Glory of Women" by SASSOON (quoted above). The fifth line of this sonnet is divided by the end of a sentence, which brings the metre to an abrupt halt. This metric division corresponds to the content of the sonnet, which is concerned with juxtaposing the women's alleged romantic glorification of the war with their supposed role in ensuring its continuation, and pitting both against the real horror of the trenches.

You máke | us shélls. || You lí\sten wíth | delíght,
By táles | of dírt and | dánger | fóndly | thrílled.

External structure: stanzaic form

Any analysis of the structure of a poem will generally also include an examination of its external structure and division into component parts. The appearance of the poem on the page often gives some indication of this structure. This is particularly the case if the lines of verse are organised into stanzas according to certain structural principles. Poetry that has no such stanzaic structure, however, and is composed of lines which follow one another in unbroken sequence, is described as 'stichic'.

Heroic couplets

We generally classify forms of stanza on the basis of how many lines of verse they comprise. Paired lines of verse (i. e. rhyming pairs) are known as 'couplets'. The category of 'heroic couplets' refers in English-language poetry to rhyming couples composed in iambic pentameters, a metrical form which is known for its, often epigrammatic, concision. The following excerpt from ALEXANDER POPE's (1688–1744) didactic poem *An Essay on Criticism* (1711/1713) is characteristic of this type of verse. Here the neoclassical writer states that the task of the poet is to give expression to general thoughts and to the universal and immutable laws of nature:

True wít | is ná\ture tó ad\vántage | dréss'd
What óft | was thoúght, | but né'er | so wéll | expréss'd. (line 297f.).

Other forms of stanza

Stanzas consisting of three or four lines of verse are known as 'tercets' and 'quatrains'. Many sonnets are composed of two tercets, which are joined to form a sestet, and two quatrains fused into an octave. An English variation on the sonnet form, invented by HENRY HOWARD, EARL OF SURREY (1517–1547), and known as the 'English' or 'Shakespearean sonnet', consists of iambic pentameters divided into three quatrains (in alternate rhyme) and a concluding heroic couplet, often a pithy, epigrammatic statement of the poem's central message.

The internal structure of a poem can be analysed using formal as well as thematic criteria. A break can be marked by a shift in the communication context or the speech situation; a change of theme or of spatial and temporal reference, as well as formal or stylistic variations (for example, vocabulary and sentence structure) can be indicative of the internal organisation. In addition, the structure of a poem is determined to a degree by its rhyme scheme, which can also mark units of meaning.

> **Internal structure**

❹ Complex Phonological Structures: Rhymes and Other Sound Patterns

The rhyme scheme often serves as starting point for an analysis of the structure of a poem. 'Rhyme' is generally taken to refer to the consonance of words from the last stressed vowel; more exact definitions are based on the position of rhymes in a line of verse, the number of rhyming syllables, the degree of consonance and the way in which the rhyming syllables are divided into words. In the most narrow sense, rhyme refers to a rhyme occurring at the end of the line of verse (end-rhyme), with a consonance between all phonemes following the last stressed vowel (full/perfect/true/exact rhyme), and with all rhyming syllables occurring within the same word. However, by applying certain criteria, we can differentiate between various types of rhyme. These criteria and types are presented systematically in the table below.

> **Rhyme and rhyme scheme**

Classification according to position in line
End-rhyme: rhyme between stressed final vowels in lines of verse *Tyger! Tyger! burning bright* *In the forests of the night,* (WILLIAM BLAKE, "The Tyger")
Internal rhyme: special case; full rhyme between two or more words within the same line of verse *And a clatter and a chatter from within [...].* (T. S. ELIOT, "The Waste Land") *Sister, my sister, O fleet sweet swallow.* (SWINBURNE, "Itylus")
Classification according to number of syllables
Masculine/Monosyllabic rhyme: consonance as from the vowel of the stressed final syllable *As you no doubt delight the eye* *Of other hippopotami.* (OGDEN NASH, "The Hippopotamus")

Feminine/Disyllabic rhyme: consonance as from the vowel of the stressed penulti-mate syllable
[...] *but when I reached / That tenderest strain of all the <u>ditty</u>,*
My faltering voice [...] / Disturbed her soul with <u>pity</u>!
(Samuel Taylor Coleridge, "Love")

Triple rhyme: consonance as from the vowel of the stressed third syllable before the end
Descending rather quickly the <u>declivity</u>, / [...] /
'Midst other indications of <u>festivity</u> (Lord Byron, *Don Juan*)

Classification according to purity of rhyme

Full/Perfect/True/Exact rhyme: exact consonance of phonemes in the rhyming syllables

Congruence between more sounds than in the preceding definitions of rhyme

Rich rhyme/rime riche: consonance between the consonants preceding the final stressed vowels, as well as between the vowels themselves. Usually involves hom-ophonic (= identical in sound, but different in meaning) words
That crazed that bold and lovely <u>Knight</u>, / [...] /
Nor rested day and <u>night</u>, (Samuel Taylor Coleridge, "Love")

Identical rhyme: goes one step beyond rich rhyme: rhyme formed by the repetition of the same word
But I said, "I've a pretty <u>rose-tree</u>", / [...] /
Then I went to my pretty <u>rose-tree</u>, (William Blake, "My Pretty Rose Tree")

Congruence between fewer sounds than in the preceding definitions of rhyme

Near/Imperfect/Slant/Approximate/Off/Half rhyme

(a) **End assonance /Vowel rhyme:** congruence between vowel sounds only
The apparition of these faces in the <u>crowd</u>
Petals on a wet, black <u>bough</u>. (Ezra Pound, "In a Station of the Metro")

(b) **Consonance at the end of two lines:** congruence between consonants only
Futile – the Winds –
To a Heart in po<u>rt</u> –
Done with the Compass –
Done with the Cha<u>rt</u>! (Emily Dickinson, "Wild Nights – Wild Nights!")

(c) **Pararhyme:** special case of consonance; initial and final consonants are repeated, but the vowel is varied
Courage was mine, and I had <u>mystery</u>
Wisdom was mine, and I <u>mastery</u>. (Wilfred Owen, "Strange Meeting")

Eye/Sight rhyme: use of homographs (written in the same way, but different in pro-nunciation) as rhyme words
Many times man lives and <u>dies</u>
Between his two <u>eternities</u>, (W. B. Yeats, "Under Ben Bulben")

CHAPTER 3 An Introduction to the Analysis of Poetry

Historical rhyme: rhyme words that used to be, but are no longer, consonant, owing to changes in pronunciation *We die and rise the same, and <u>prove</u>,* *Mysterious by this <u>love</u>.* (JOHN DONNE, "The Canonization")	
Classification according to division of rhyming syllables	
Mosaic rhyme: division of one of the rhyme words into more than one word *Oh, do not ask, 'What <u>is it</u>?'* *Let us go and make our <u>visit</u>.* (T. S. ELIOT, "The Love Song of J. Alfred Prufrock")	
Broken rhyme/Split rhyme: rhyme created by dividing a word at the line break (see chapter 3.3., 'enjambment') *[…] on an age old anvil wince and <u>sing</u>* *Then lull, then leave off. Fury had shrieked 'No <u>ling-</u>* *<u>ering</u>!* (GERARD MANLEY HOPKINS, "No Worst, There Is None")	

Table 3.2.: Types of rhymes

The schematic representation of the sequence of end-rhymes within a stanza or a poem is described as its 'rhyme scheme'. The rhyme scheme is conventionally represented by a sequence of lower case letters, with identical letters used for rhyming lines of verse. Rhyme schemes are, of course, not restricted to the aforementioned couplet, in which the final words of two consecutive lines of verse rhyme. The most common rhyme schemes, and the terms used to refer to them, are represented in the table below:

Rhyme schemes

Definition	Rhyme scheme
Rhyming couplets	aa bb cc
Alternate rhyme *Kreuzreim*	abab cdcd
Embracing rhyme/envelope rhyme *Umarmender Reim*	abba cddc
Chain rhyme/interlocking rhyme *Kettenreim*	aba bcb cdc
Tail rhyme *Schweifreim*	aab ccb

Table 3.3.: Rhyme schemes

An analysis of the rhyme scheme can yield a variety of insights into poetry. The interpretative value consists firstly in the fact that the rhyme scheme subdivides a poem. While end-rhymes link lines of verse, a new rhyme frequently marks the beginning of a new unit of meaning. Rhymes also create a link between the rhyming words by means of repetition on the phonological level. This sometimes serves to heighten contrasts which reach to the core of a poem, such as the alternate rhymes 'delight/thrilled' (referring to British women) and 'fight/killed' (referring to the soldiers) in

Interpretative value

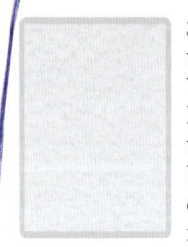

SIEGFRIED SASSOON's "The Glory of Women". By creating such intra-textual parallels, rhymes also highlight the coherence of the text. The representation of the rhyme scheme as a series of lower case letters enables us to give a schematic representation of sound patterns and thus to gain an overview of the structure of a poem. Even poems that are composed entirely of stichic verse can have a structure, which can generally be discerned by examining their rhyme scheme.

Other sound patterns

In addition to the various types of rhyme and rhyme schemes, poems can include other internal sound patterns, which contribute to their phonological complexity. Internal links can be established not only by means of end-rhyme and other types of rhyme, but also by means of repetition and accumulation, of sounds or phonemes and groups of phonemes. The most important phenomena are explained below:

Alliteration: succession of words with the same initial sound or succession of accented syllables with the same consonant or consonantal group
Nothing is so beautiful as spring – / When weeds, in wheels, shoot long and lovely and lush (GERARD MANLEY HOPKINS, "Spring")
And live alone in the bee-loud glade (W. B. YEATS, "The Lake Isle of Innisfree")

Consonance: congruence of consonants short of alliteration; repetition of a sequence of two or more consonants, but with a change in the intervening vowel (see table 3.2., pararhyme)
Gobbets of blubber spill to wind and weather
(ROBERT LOWELL, "The Quaker Graveyard in Nantucket")

Assonance: congruence between vowel sounds only
Blind eyes could blaze like meteors and be gay
(DYLAN THOMAS, "Do Not Go Gentle into That Good Night")

Onomatopoeia: use of words to imitate sounds
Only the stuttering rifles' rapid rattle / Can patter out their hasty orisons.
(WILFRED OWEN, "Anthem for a Doomed Youth")

Table 3.4.: Phonological rhetorical figures

Functions of sound patterns

Rhyme and other sound patterns can have a wide range of diverse functions. Three of the most important are the structuring or organisational function, the function of enhancing the content of the poem by imitating aspects of external reality (for example, sounds, objects) and of internal processes (for example, perceptions and feelings), generally referred to as 'mimetic/evocative function', as well as general aesthetic functions. As in the case of the analysis of the morphological, syntactic and semantic levels, the central question when analysing these aspects is what contribution they make to the poem's potential of meaning.

5 Complex Morphological and Syntactic Structures: Word Repetition and Poetic Syntax

In addition to thematic, structural and metrical characteristics, various rhetorical figures can also contribute to the form and the effects of a poem. Rhetorical figures occur plentifully in poems; however, they are also common in the dramatic and narrative genres as well as in non-fictional texts. As in the study of metrical phenomena, an inventory of terms dating back to Antiquity can be employed when analysing rhetorical figures. These terms can be categorised according to the dimension of language to which they refer. In addition to the 'phonological figures' introduced above, which are employed on the level of sounds, there are also

Rhetorical figures

- 'morphological figures', i. e., rhetorical figures which work on the level of words and word formation,
- 'syntactic figures', or rhetorical figures that are employed on the level of sentence structure (syntax),
- 'semantic figures', or rhetorical figures involving the meanings of words or expressions, and
- 'pragmatic figures', or rhetorical figures involving language use.

Like the speech situation, the metric and stanzaic structure and the sound patterns, all rhetorical figures contribute considerably to the coherence of a poem. As poems generally have little in the way of characters or plot, they rely for their coherence on other features. Coherence is produced by certain elements in the content of the text, for example the circumstances of the speaker and/or the addressee, as well as all the thematic and formal elements that recur throughout the poem and link the various units of meaning together.

Creating coherence

As was mentioned earlier, repetitions and recurrences do not only occur on the phonological level. Analogous complex structures can be found on other linguistic levels of many poems; these include the repetition of morphemes, words, groups of words, sentence components and entire sentences. Such structures are described as 'morphological figures', and are presented in brief in the table below.

Word repetition

Morphological = create coherence (function) (handwritten annotation)

Figures involving repetition
Exact word repetition
Anaphora: repetition of a word or group of words at the beginning of successive clauses or lines of verse *So long as men can breathe or eyes can see,* *So long lives this, and this gives life to thee.* (William Shakespeare, "Sonnet 18")
Epiphora: repetition of a word or group of words at the end of successive clauses or lines of verse *The yellow fog that rubs its back upon the window-panes,* *The yellow smoke that rubs its muzzle on the window-panes,* (T. S. Eliot, "The Love Song of J. Alfred Prufrock")
Epanalepsis: repetition of words in close succession ('immediate repetition') or after other intervening words *Peace, peace, thou hippopotamus!* (Ogden Nash, "The Hippopotamus") *I celebrate myself, and sing myself* (Walt Whitman, "Song of Myself")
Anadiplosis: repetition of end of the preceding clause/line of verse at the beginning of the next *And gentle wishes long subdued,* *Subdued and cherished long!* (Samuel Taylor Coleridge, "Love")
Repetition involving variation of repeated elements
Polyptoton: repetition of a word in different inflected forms *Thus vainly thinking that she thinks me young* (William Shakespeare, "Sonnet 138")
Figura etymologica: repetition of a root in different forms *I had [...] / Lit some lighter light of freer freedom* (Oscar Wilde, "Flower of Love")
Synonymy: repetition by the replacement of one word with another of the same meaning *For thee I watch, whilst thou dost wake elsewhere* (William Shakespeare, "Sonnet 61")

Table 3.5.: Morphological rhetorical figures

Deviation of poetic syntax

Rhetorical figures that are related to sentence structure (syntax), are subsumed under the heading 'syntactic figures'. A typical example is parallelism, i. e. the successive use of parallel clause or sentence structures. Linguistically oriented conceptions of poetry regard such syntactic equivalences and other notable features of poetic syntax as 'deviations' from 'normal syntax'. In addition to parallelism, particular forms of conjunction, deviations from the normal word order and figures involving omission are also com-

  **An Introduction to the Analysis of Poetry**

mon. The following table offers an overview of syntactic rhetorical figures and the terms applied to them (see LUDWIG 1981/1994: 115ff.).

[handwritten: Syntactic = interaction with content level (parallels or contrasts)]

Parallelism between clauses or entire sentences
Parallelism: succession of clauses or sentences of the same structure *Happy my studies, when by these approved!* *Happier their author, when by these beloved!* (ALEXANDER POPE, "An Epistle to Dr. Arbuthnot")
Chiasmus: reversal of structures in successive clauses *With wealth your state, your mind with arts, improve* (JOHN DONNE, "The Canonization")

[handwritten: K ; surplus meaning!]

Connection of sentences and sentence components
Asyndeton: succession of words or phrases without conjoining words *All whom war, dearth, age, agues, tyrannies,* *Despair, law, chance hath slain [...]* (JOHN DONNE, "Holy Sonnet VII")
Polysyndeton: succession of words or phrases linked by conjoining words *After the sunsets and the dooryards and the sprinkled streets,* (T. S. ELIOT, "The Love Song of J. Alfred Prufrock")

Deviation from normal word order
Inversion: reversal of normal word order *Here rests his head upon the lap of earth* (THOMAS GRAY, "Elegy, Written in a Country Churchyard")
Hysteron proteron: reversal of the logical succession of events *I die! I faint! I fail!* (PERCY BYSSHE SHELLEY, "The Indian Serenade")

[handwritten: K]

Figures involving omission
Ellipsis: omission of sentence components *Authors are partial to their wit, 'tis true, / But are not Critics [partial] to their judgment too?* (ALEXANDER POPE, "An Essay on Criticism")
Aposiopesis: abrupt cessation before the end of an utterance *His dying words – but when I reached* *That tenderest strain of all the ditty,* *My faltering voice and pausing harp* *Disturbed her soul with pity!* (SAMUEL TAYLOR COLERIDGE, "Love")
Zeugma: application of one verb to more than one object in different senses *Here thou, great Anna! whom three realms obey,* *Dost sometimes counsel take – and sometimes Tea.* (ALEXANDER POPE, "The Rape of the Lock")

[handwritten: K]

Table 3.6.: Syntactic rhetorical figures

Functions of morphological and syntactic figures	As was the case with the sound patterns, an analysis of the functions performed by repetitions and figures involving words and sentences is more important than their mere systematization and classification. These word repetitions and syntactic structures can acquire a semantic function by means of their interaction with the content of a poem, and can therefore generate a surplus of meaning within the poem. The main function of syntactic figures is *"to establish relations of correspondence and opposition"* (LUDWIG 1981/1994: 135). Like phonological equivalences, such grammatical figures are frequently employed to lend formal emphasis to certain elements of a poem's content. Alternatively, they can be set in conflict with semantic elements, as sources of tension or dissonance.
Form as expression of content	*"Verbal parallelism resembles free verbal repetition in that it is physically sensible – i. e. audible to the listener, and visible to the reader. This means that the parallelism sets up a special relation between expression and content: the outer form of the message not only expresses underlying meaning but imitates its structure. […] [v]erbal parallelism says the same thing twice over: the expression hammers home the content."* (LEECH 1969: 85)

6 Complex Semantic Structures: Imagery

Imagery as a figurative mode of expression	Imagery is also central to the analysis of poetry, and, thanks to the omnipresence of metaphors and other linguistic images (or rhetorical tropes), it is moreover an important analytical tool for various other genres and media such as film. The term 'imagery' subsumes all the rhetorical figures explained below, including metaphor, metonymy, synecdoche and synaesthesia. All are figurative forms of expression and complex semantic structures. In literary texts, these semantic figures are expressed in words, whereas in films they take the form of visual images.
Structure of metaphor	The term 'metaphor' refers to 'word pictures' that are used to convey a figurative meaning. The actual referent is not named directly; instead it is replaced or paraphrased using words from another field of reference. Metaphors are often described as shortened or covert comparisons, because, in contrast to the direct comparison or simile, the comparative particles 'like' or 'as' are not used: *"Simile is an overt, and metaphor a covert comparison."* (LEECH 1969: 156)
Terms used in the analysis of metaphor	Metaphor involves the removal of a word from its original semantic field and projection of this word onto an element from another semantic field. The original semantic field, from which the metaphorical term, or 'vehicle', is taken, is described as the 'source

domain' or 'donor field', whereas the actual referent, or 'tenor', is situated in the 'target domain' or 'recipient field'. Vehicle and tenor must be linked by some similarity of content or structure (a so-called *'tertium comparationis'*), which connects the two ideas to form a metaphor. Metaphors are figures of similarity, because they operate by means of comparison and substitution, replacing one element with another.

The metaphorical process involves some kind of transfer of characteristics, because central semantic characteristics of the vehicle (also known as its 'salient features') are projected onto the tenor. The so-called 'substitution theory' is based on the view that, by means of a metaphor, one element is substituted for another and that in the course of this substitution a connection is established between the semantic characteristics of the vehicle and those of the tenor. Moreover, the tenor is re-presented or restructured by the metaphor.

Transfer of characteristics

Like the term 'picture/image field' ('*Bildfeld*'), coined by HARALD WEINRICH, the expression 'semantic field' can be used to describe the way in which metaphors are organised into overarching structures, and the specific relationship that connects the different elements of an image. By taking these different fields of meaning into account, we can give a more exact account of the semantic structures of the metaphorical process. The theory of semantic fields enables us to demonstrate that a metaphor does not merely link two isolated linguistic phenomena; it also connects the linguistic and conceptual fields in which the vehicle and the tenor have their origins. If a beloved's eyes are called 'diamonds', for instance, the features 'sparkling', 'precious' and 'beautiful' are transferred onto the target domain, whereas the feature 'hard' (which accounts for the fact that diamonds are used for drilling) usually is not. Metaphors therefore operate as a sort of 'double filter' (DIETMAR PEIL), in that they only admit those characteristics from the source and the target domain that are of relevance for the specific context.

Semantic fields and image fields

The 'interaction theory' is based on the assumption that metaphors connect two different fields of meaning, which leads to a reciprocal interchange between the two semantic fields. In contrast to the substitution theory, then, the interaction theory assumes that metaphors create a link between two superordinate semantic fields. The interaction theory also emphasises that the metaphorical process does not merely comprise a transfer of characteristics from a vehicle to a tenor, or from one word to another one from a different semantic field; as the name suggests, the interaction theory argues that an interchange takes place between the two semantic fields that are thus connected. The various com-

Metaphors as interaction between semantic fields

ponents of semantic field of the source domain impose a particular structure onto the target domain of the metaphor.

Example: Empire metaphor

The metaphor of the British Empire as a family, which was widespread in English poetry of the 19th century and in non-fictional text types, provides a good example of the fact that metaphors shed new semantic light on both the tenor and the vehicle. The metaphor of the motherland not only creates a link between colonial power and the matriarch; the two fields of family and colonialism are also associated with each other by means of this image. Within this semantic field, the colonies are conventionally given the role of the children, and a relationship of political hegemony and economical exploitation is presented as a personal relationship. The metaphor of the motherland therefore structures, interprets and evaluates the tenor – i.e., the relationship between a colonial power and its dependent colonies – in a new and ideologically loaded way. This metaphor of the family, which was also common in the political discourse of the American War of Independence, vividly illustrates the fact that such images are not merely decorative, but that they can be used to reinterpret historical and political circumstances in a propagandistic way.

Functions of metaphors

As can be seen from the example discussed above, the analysis of semantic fields and the function of metaphors can extend its remit beyond literature to include socio-cultural considerations. Metaphors and other forms of imagery, then, do not merely perform the function of opening up new possibilities of meaning that cannot be conveyed by fixed expressions. Metaphors also perform a variety of other functions as conceptual models and instruments for creating meaning. The metaphor of a family to represent the British Empire, for example, offers new perspectives because the image of the family restructures and reinterprets the Empire. The main creative achievements of this metaphor, then, are on the one hand structural, because it is able to impose some of its internal logic and denotations onto the relationship between England and its colonies (in this case, the parent/child relationship with its concomitant rights and duties of both parts). Additionally, however, the connotative power of the images supplies particular criteria for the perception and interpretation of historical and political circumstances. Such interpretative schemata do not merely have a cognitive function; they also have normative, emotional and ideological implications, as they represent a relationship of political dominance as an organic, affectionate relationship, which cannot be dissolved and which imposes the duties of gratitude and obedience on the colonial 'children'.

A precise semantic analysis of the denotations and connotations of a metaphor is indispensable in order to arrive at a competent interpretation of its structure and effect. 'Denotation' refers to the literal and basic meanings of a word, whereas 'connotation' describes all the additional and peripheral meanings that can be inferred from the word's associations. These additional meanings are by no means subjective or arbitrary; however, the associations that are awoken by the vehicle and linked implicitly to the tenor cannot always be clearly or completely identified. It is this phenomenon that is primarily responsible for the much-discussed ambiguity of literary texts.

Denotation and conno- tation

Any analysis of a metaphor must begin with an identification of the source and target domains. Following this, those denotations and connotations of the vehicle which are projected onto the tenor by the metaphor must be examined. Only after investigating the usual meaning (the semantic characteristics) of the vehicle are we able to evaluate the potential effects or the functions of the individual metaphor. In doing this, we must also take into account the semantic fields from which the metaphor is taken.

Analysis of metaphors

Many metaphors are highly complex, consisting of several partial images, all of which are organised into superordinate structures. Instead of merely replacing one word with another, such images link together two different semantic fields. An illustrative example of such a complex metaphor is the formulation *"When hell's last horror breaks them"*, used by SIEGFRIED SASSOON in the poem "Glory of Women" to represent British soldiers' desertion in order to escape certain death in battle. The noun 'hell' and all its associated torments are transferred onto the semantic field of war, in order to adequately express the horror to which the soldiers are exposed. This complex metaphor is particularly effective because the associations of the word 'hell' can vary according to historical and cultural context. Each individual will have his or her own image of hell and will therefore develop an individual conception of the experiences of the soldiers. The structure of a metaphor is represented schematically in the model below:

Complex metaphors

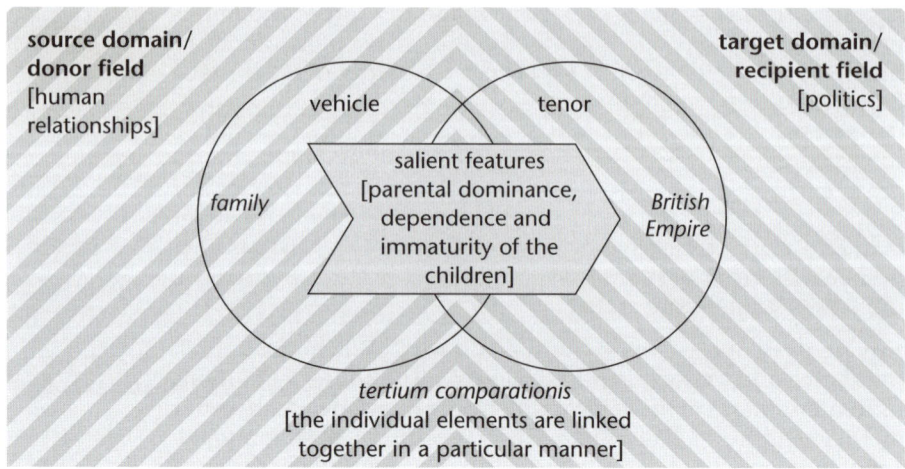

Figure 3.3.: Structure of metaphor

Metonymy und Synecdoche	The term 'metonymy' refers to the replacement of one word with another to which it is ontologically, logically or causally connected. Whereas in the case of metaphor, a connection between formerly disparate elements is forged by means of language, in the case of metonymy, the two phenomena are already associated by physical or thematic contiguity. Synecdoche represents a particular form of metonymy, in which one term is replaced by a narrower one, or a part is used to represent a whole (*pars pro toto*), or vice versa (*totum pro parte*). Whereas metaphor involves the transferral of semantic components from one field into another, in the case of synecdoche the designated entity is replaced by a narrower or broader term from the same semantic field. Metonymy and synecdoche are therefore 'figures of contiguity'.
Synaesthesia	The term 'synaesthesia' refers one or several words that combine perceptions or sensations that are produced by different sensory organs. Synaesthesia is a rhetorical figure that operates on the semantic level. It involves the fusion of several sensory impressions within one linguistic expression, or the association of one sensory impression with another sensory organ. Two complex examples of synaesthesia can be found in WILLIAM BLAKE's poem "London": in the line *"The mind-forged manacles I hear"*, an abstract element is presented as a palpable object which can be heard. A particularly notable example of BLAKE's use of metonymy and synaesthesia in order to criticise society can be found in the lines *"And the hapless soldier's sigh / Runs in blood down palace walls"*. Here an acoustic quality, a sigh, is presented as an actual substance that can be seen to run down palace walls, which themselves serve as

a metonymy designating the monarchy and its power. Since instances of synaesthesia do not make sense if taken literally, they encourage the reader to infer meanings and causal relationships.

When several images are taken from the same semantic field, the resulting interpretative scheme which governs the text is referred to as 'isotopy' (from the Greek *iso-topos*, meaning 'the same place or level'). The isotopy of a text often consists of semantically opposite or of parallel elements. In EDMUND SPENSER's (1552–1599) "Sonnet 15" from the "Amoretti" cycle, whose highly stylized description of the eyes, lips, teeth, forehead, hair and hands of the beloved draws on the inventory of traditional tropes used in the Elizabethan sonnet to describe beauty, various comparisons occur that originate from a common source domain: that of precious gems, jewellery and other valuable objects. The recurrent use of images from this semantic domain or isotopy serves to present the beauty of the lady as the apotheosis of nature's achievements:

Isotopy

Ye tradeful merchants, that with weary toil
Do seek most precious things to make your gain,
And both the Indias of their treasures spoil,
What needeth you to seek so far in vain?
For lo! my love doth in herself contain
All this world's riches that may far be found.
If sapphires, lo! her eyes be sapphires plain;
If rubies, lo! her lips be rubies sound;
If pearls, her teeth be pearls both pure and round;
If ivory, her forehead ivory ween;
If gold, her locks are finest gold on ground;
If silver, her fair hands are silver sheen.
But that which fairest is, but few behold:
Her mind, adorned with virtues manifold.

In addition to the categories of imagery discussed above, numerous other semantic figures exist. These include euphemism (reference to something by means of a milder, more positive expression), pleonasm (superfluous stringing together of words with the same meaning), oxymoron (combination of two logically or thematically contradictory words) and personification (presentation of an abstract or concrete entity as if it were alive or human). Definitions and examples of the most important semantic figures are given in the table below.

Other semantic figures

Semantic

Tropes
Figures of similarity
Simile: one thing is likened to another by means of a comparative particle *My love is like a red, red rose* (ROBERT BURNS, "A Red Red Rose")
Metaphor: the characteristics of a particular vehicle are transferred to a tenor without being mediated by a comparative particle (see figure 3.3.) *The apparition of these <u>faces in the crowd</u>;* *<u>petals on a wet, black bough</u>.* (EZRA POUND, "In a Station of the Metro")
Synaesthesia: vehicle and tenor allude to different sensory perceptions *And the hapless soldier's <u>sigh</u>* *<u>Runs in blood</u> down palace walls.* (WILLIAM BLAKE, "London")
Personification: a concrete or abstract element is presented as if it were alive or human *<u>Fair Science frowned</u> not on his humble birth,* *And <u>Melancholy marked</u> him for her own.* (THOMAS GRAY, "Elegy, Written in a Country Churchyard")
Figures of contiguity
Metonymy: replacement of one term with another to which it is ontologically, logically or causally connected *When I consider how my <u>light</u> [= vision] is spent,* (JOHN MILTON, "Sonnet XIX")
Synecdoche: replacement of a part with a whole or vice versa *Fair stood the wind for France,* *When we our sails [= ships] advance,* (MICHAEL DRAYTON, "The Battle of Agincourt")
Antonomasia: replacement of a generic term with a proper name, or of a proper name with an epithet *A <u>Daniel</u> come to judgement [...]* *O <u>wise young judge</u>, how I do honour thee!* (WILLIAM SHAKESPEARE, *The Merchant of Venice*)
Other Tropes
Periphrasis/Circumlocution: description of an element by making reference to its characteristics *the bleating kind [= sheep]* (JAMES THOMSON, "The Seasons: Winter")
Euphemism: reference to something by means of a milder, more positive term *You can't believe that British troops '<u>retire</u>'* (SIEGFRIED SASSOON, "Glory of Women")
Hyperbole: use of (excessive) exaggeration *An <u>hundred years</u> should go to praise* *Thine eyes [...]*. (ANDREW MARVELL, "To His Coy Mistress")

Irony: meaning the opposite of what is said *Two vast and trunkless legs of stone / Stand in the desert. [...] / And on the pedestal these words appear: / 'My name is Ozymandias, King of Kings: / Look on my works, ye mighty, and despair!' / Nothing beside remains.* (Percy Bysshe Shelley, "Ozymandias")	

Litotes: reference to an element or quality by negating its opposite *Words at once true and kind, Or <u>not untrue</u> and <u>not unkind</u>.* (Philip Larkin, "Talking in Bed")

Other semantic rhetorical figures

Oxymoron: trenchant combination of two apparently contradictory terms *O <u>heavy lightness</u>! <u>serious vanity</u>!* (William Shakespeare, Romeo and Juliet)
Paradox: an apparently contradictory statement which, on closer inspection, is found to be true *<u>We die and rise the same</u>* (John Donne, "The Canonization")
Antithesis: juxtaposition of two logically opposed elements *Resolved to win, he meditates the way, / <u>By force to ravish</u>, or <u>by fraud betray</u>;* (Alexander Pope, "The Rape of the Lock")
Hendiadys (from Greek for 'one by means of two'): an idea that would usually be expressed by a single noun phrase is represented by two words joined by a conjunction *From <u>rest</u> and <u>sleep</u> [...].* (John Donne, "Holy Sonnet X")
Paronomasia/pun: a play on words using two identical or similar sounding words with different and perhaps contradictory meanings *Therefore I <u>lie</u> with her, and she with me, / And in our faults by <u>lies</u> we flattered be.* (William Shakespeare, "Sonnet 88")

Table 3.7.: Semantic rhetorical figures

A very good synopsis of the fundamentals, problems and categories of the analysis of poems can be found in Hans-Werner Ludwig's *Arbeitsbuch Lyrikanalyse* (1981/1994). First-rate introductions are also provided by Christoph Bode's *Einführung in die Lyrikanalyse* (2001) and Tom Furniss' and Michael Bath's *Reading Poetry: An Introduction* (1996). Eva Müller-Zettelmann's *Lyrik und Metalyrik* (2000) is recommended to those who wish to inform themselves about the various approaches in lyric theory. A systematic overview of the diverse rhetorical figures is given in Heinrich F. Plett's *Systematische Rhetorik* (2000), and a good introduction to the bewildering plethora of analytical terms can be found in the terminological dictionary *Terminologie der Literaturwissenschaft. Ein Handbuch für das Anglistikstudium* (1998) by Rudolf Beck, Hildegard Kuester and Martin Kuester, a revised edition of which is due to appear soon. Peter Hühn's excellent two-volume *Geschichte der englischen Lyrik* (1995) gives a very good overview of the history of English poetry, providing a large number of exemplary analyses.

Further reading on the analysis of poetry

CHAPTER An Introduction to the Analysis of Drama

Suit the action to the word, the word to the action, with this special observance, that you o'erstep not the modesty of nature. For anything so o'erdone is from the purpose of playing, whose end, both at the first and now, was and is to hold as 'twere the mirror up to nature. WILLIAM SHAKESPEARE, *Hamlet*, III, ii, 17–22.

1 A Text Written for Performance: Fundamental Features of Dramatic Composition

Relationship between text and performance

When, in the passage quoted above, Hamlet advises the actors performing the play within a play in *Hamlet* to coordinate word and action, language and gesture, he highlights the close relationship between the written text of a drama and its performance in the theatre. Hamlet's comment that the first and ultimate goal of acting is *"to hold […] the mirror up to nature"* is admittedly historically determined and based on a particular conception of literature as imitation of nature; however, his reference to the interplay between word and gesture alludes to a central aspect of the theory of drama and identifies two important components of drama.

Aims and content of this chapter

The main goal of this chapter is to identify the fundamental features of the composition of drama, to give a preliminary overview of some of the fundamentals of the analysis of drama and to introduce the most important categories and transferable methods of drama analysis. Beginning with the tension between drama and theatre, we will examine some constitutive features of dramatic texts. Following this, a communication model for drama will be developed that also takes into account the specificities of the theatrical context. A short introduction will then be given to the basics of a semiotics of theatre, which has increased awareness of the part played by non-verbal theatrical codes. The remainder of the chapter will be devoted to a summary of the most important terms and models used to describe the various elements and structures of dramatic texts.

The dramatic text as script and the play

Dramatic texts differ from other literary genres in their communication situation. It is important to remember that, in contrast to an essay or a poem, a dramatic text is not primarily written to be read, but rather as a script for a theatre performance. Dramas are therefore texts that are written to be performed as plays, and this performance requires not only a script, but also the entire

Geist, Apparat

apparatus of theatre production, which often includes considerable resources in terms of personnel and organisation.

It is true that dramatic texts are generally written by an author and
read by individual recipients; however, when a play is performed,
the communication situation is entirely different. Several individuals (for example, director, dramatic advisor, set-designers and
actors/actresses) are involved in the production of a play; performances are usually attended by large audiences. This phenomenon
is referred to as *"[t]he collective nature of production and reception"*
(PFISTER 1988: 11). The few dramas that are produced primarily as
reading material do not change the fact that watching, and not
reading, is the most appropriate mode of reception for drama.

Collective nature of production and reception

The process of preparing a drama for performance represents a
form of literary adaptation, in that it involves substituting another
medium for the literary text (see chapter 6.3.). While dramatic
texts only exist in written form, theatre performances use non-
verbal as well as verbal modes of communication: the theatrical
realisation of a dramatic text involves an acoustic (voices, noises,
music) and an optical dimension (set, presentation of the characters, gesture, facial expression), as well as occasionally engaging
other modes of sensory perception. We can describe a theatre performance as a *"multimedial form of presentation"* (PFISTER 1988: 6),
because the performance of a play draws on a wide repertoire of
verbal and non-verbal signs and codes, as well as on a variety of
modes of perception or communication channels.

Theatre performances as multimedial forms of presentation

Drama and theatre are therefore closely related; the dramatic text
functions as the script on which a performance is based. Given
that text and performance are valued equally as artistic works, it
is perhaps most appropriate to regard the dramatic text *"as a text
to be performed, as a literary artefact conceived with a view to its performance"* (HÖFELE 1991: 11). This avoids ascribing greater value
to either text or performance, and instead does justice to both as
distinct modes or media of artistic expression.

Interaction between drama and theatre

As many features of a dramatic work can be varied in performance and the actors generally have considerable scope for individual interpretation, every performance should be regarded as
an independent 'theatrical work of art'. A comparison of the various performances of any individual drama illustrates this capac-
ity for variation, which affects in particular the presentation of
characters, gesture and setting, whereas the outlines of the action
and the temporal structure of a drama tend to be prescribed by
the text. Theatre performance differs in various ways from drama
as written text, the most obvious difference being that the performance is a transient event that can never be exactly reproduced.

Variations in performance and production

Theatre studies vs. English literary studies	Although theatre studies and English and American literary studies are both concerned with the broad field of drama and theatre, their objectives and methods differ considerably. Since theatre studies became established as an independent discipline, the following distinction between the two disciplines has become widely accepted: theatre studies focuses primarily on the 'theatrical work' or the 'theatrical text', i.e. on the various aspects of the performance and production of plays in a theatre. It is therefore primarily concerned with the analysis of actual performances on the basis of a semiotics of theatre (see chapter 4.3.). English and American literary studies, on the other hand, are concerned primarily with the analysis and interpretation of dramas as printed texts, and thus focus particularly on the written sources of theatre performances, on the generic characteristics of dramatic texts, and on the interpretation and thematic as well as formal characteristics of individual dramas.
Performance criticism	Since the 1980s, however, interpretative approaches that are concerned primarily with performance and known as 'performance criticism' have gained in currency within English literary studies. Performance criticism encompasses a variety of approaches, which focus primarily on the 'implied production' already inherent within a dramatic text, or on the analysis of actual performances. Thus drama is analysed with a view to its production potential. ANDREAS HÖFELE (1991: 18f.) describes the *"implied performance [...] as the ensemble of instructions that a drama offers for its production: the pointer that is written into the dramatic text towards the 'text' that is to be produced – the text of the performance – but not towards the performance itself"*.
Stage forms	The character of each theatre production is determined to a large degree by the individual stage form, which also influences the audience's experience of the production, the distance between actors and audience and the acting style. In Ancient Greece, plays were performed in amphitheatres, closer in terms of size to today's football stadiums than to our modern play-houses. The audience sat in a semicircle around the stage, and the lack of stage set and the distance from the audience made a realistic performance impossible. Theatre in Shakespearean times, by contrast, was characterised by close contact between the actors and the audience, with the audience packed closely on various levels around three sides of the stage. The stage and the seating were 'lit' by natural daylight, and the set was minimal, thus encouraging the audience to use their imagination to embellish what they saw. Certainly, the physical features of Shakespearean theatre were not conducive to a realistic imitation of reality. Today's most common stage form with its box-like structure, lighting, curtains and other

props is far more suited to the creation of aesthetic illusion. The actors can act as if an invisible 'fourth wall' separated events on stage from the audience. However, the experimentation with stage forms that is common in today's theatre, and that frequently harks back to old models, is indicative of dissatisfaction with this convention.

2 A Communication Model for Dramatic Texts: Special Features of Theatre Communication

As we saw in our examination of the dramatic genre, the communication situation of a dramatic text is fundamentally different from that of a lyric text. Admittedly, in the case of both genres a distinction can be made between external communication involving the historical author and recipient, and communication within the text. However, in addition to the collective nature of the production and reception of theatre performance (and also of film), there are significant differences between the internal communication situations of dramatic and lyric texts.

Communication structure of lyric and dramatic texts

A communication model for drama enables us to represent in graphic form some of the main differences between dramatic texts and other literary genres. This communication model highlights three main communicative peculiarities of dramatic texts: firstly, on an internal level, dramas comprise several speakers and addressees in the form of the various characters. Secondly, these characters can move between the roles of addresser and addressee as often as they like, as indicated in the diagram by the arrows pointing in both directions. This leads on to the final major peculiarity of dramatic communication, which is that dialogue is the most important medium for the transmission of information. We should note, however, that a number of lyric texts also incorporate dialogues, and that various forms of monological speech occur frequently in dramas.

A communication model for dramatic texts

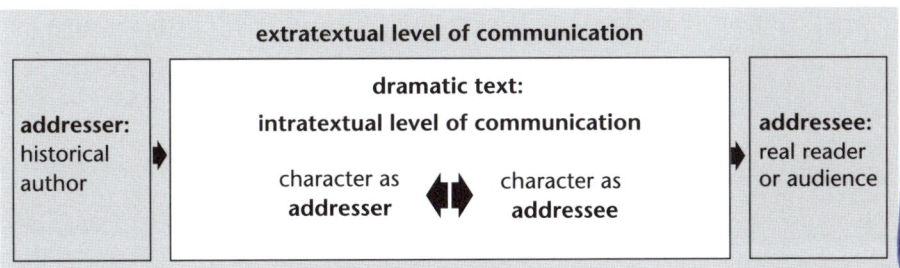

extratextual level of communication		
addresser: historical author	dramatic text: intratextual level of communication character as **addresser** ◀▶ character as **addressee**	addressee: real reader or audience

Figure 4.1.: A communication model for dramatic texts

Communication situation in dramatic and narrative texts	This model also demonstrates that, in the majority of dramas, internal communication takes place on only one textual level, the level of the characters. In narrative texts, by contrast, the events which take place on the level of the characters are mediated by a narrator (see chapter 5.2.). The lack of a mediating level of communication is generally considered to be one of the most important differences between dramatic and narrative texts and is referred to as "*the absolute nature of dramatic texts*" (PFISTER 1988: 4).
Communication situation in drama and in the theatre	In addition to these major differences between dramatic and narrative texts, we should also take into account the communication situation of the theatre performance. The situations that frame the act of reading a dramatic text on the one hand, and the theatre performance on the other, are presented schematically in the model below.

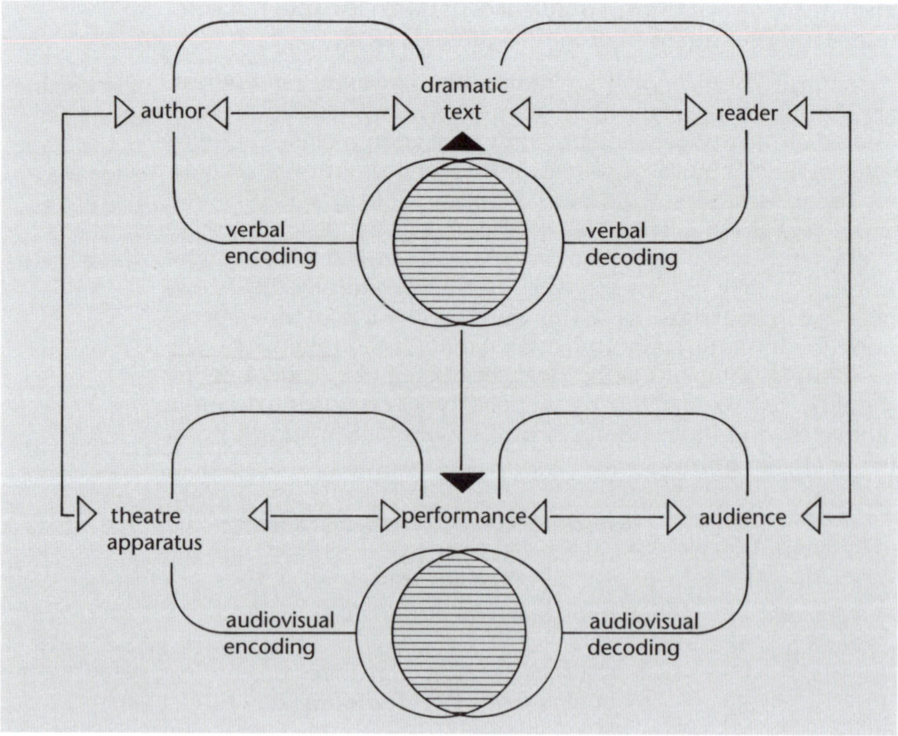

Figure 4.2.: Communication models for drama and theatre performance (see PLATZ-WAURY 1978: 41)

In the case of the act of reading a drama, the author functions as the addresser, the dramatic text as the message, and the reader as the addressee. In the case of a theatre performance, however, the entire theatre apparatus, consisting of the collection of individuals involved in its production, assumes the role of the addresser, the performance constitutes the message, and the audience assumes the role of the addressee, which is also collective. These two communication processes are, however, closely linked and influence each other mutually (in the figure above this reciprocal influence is indicated by the arrows between 'dramatic text' and 'performance').

Even more than the act of reading a drama, a theatre performance is a highly complex process of communication, in the course of which meaning is constituted simultaneously on a number of levels: "*a dramatic level (interaction between the characters on stage), a theatrical level (communication between the cast and the audience) and the level of everyday life (social communication about the production and its relation to everyday norms)*" (MAHLER 1992: 71).

Levels of meaning formation

Even the internal structure of dramatic texts anticipates performance. Dramatic texts comprise, firstly, a level of verbal communication that is composed of the characters' remarks, or the dialogue. However, they generally also contain more or less detailed information on how the text is to be performed, usually printed in italics. Whilst the characters' remarks constitute the 'primary text', which during the performance is to be spoken aloud by the actors, the stage directions are part of the 'secondary text'. These directions mainly concern the stage set as well as the characters' gestures and facial expressions, all of which can be prescribed to a greater or lesser degree by the playwright, but are ultimately realised in each individual performance. The secondary text includes all constituent parts of a dramatic text that are not part of the dialogue. In addition to the stage directions these include, for example, the demarcation of acts and scenes, information as to which character is speaking, and various other elements such as the title of the play, dedications, prefaces and the list of *dramatis personae* (characters) at the beginning.

Primary text and secondary text

Despite the aforementioned 'absolute nature of dramatic texts', there are also numerous instances that contradict the widely-held view that drama does not feature a communication level of narrative transmission or a narrator. Many dramas, especially from the 20th century, but also from earlier periods in the history of the genre, contain narrative elements, particularly at the beginning; in many plays a superordinate narrative frame to the action is constructed. Examples of this technique can be found in plays such as THORNTON WILDER's *Our Town* (1938) and PETER SHAFFER's

Narration and the narrator in drama

hugely successful *Amadeus* (1979). These plays are illustrative of certain structural characteristics and communication techniques which, thanks to their proximity to various characteristics of narrative (or epic) texts, are described as 'epic'. The character of the Stage Manager in *Our Town* and Salieri in *Amadeus* both appear in the dramas as mediating, narrating instances, with the result that the communication structure of these dramas is shifted closer to that of narrative texts (see chapter 5).

Introduction of epic elements by characters

The distinction between the introduction of epic elements by characters 'inside the action' and by characters 'outside the action' (see PFISTER 1988: 74ff.), is based on whether or not the narrating instance is involved in the action of the drama. SHAFFER's *Amadeus* is an example of a drama in which a character 'inside the action' assumes the role of a narrator. In contrast to what one might assume from the title, this play does not tell the story of Mozart's life and achievements; instead it offers a retrospective outline of the decisive episodes in Salieri's intrigues against his detested rival, presented in a succession of scenes and from Salieri's perspective. Salieri functions as a kind of first-person narrator, who not only recounts, comments on and evaluates the central episodes of his own life, which is overshadowed by his rivalry with Mozart; he also introduces himself and addresses his audience directly, in the hope of winning its understanding. The role of the narrator in WILDER's *Our Town*, by contrast, is occupied by a character 'outside the action', who is not involved on the communication level of the characters, instead presiding over events as a kind of director.

Further epic elements

Besides the introduction of a narrator, there are further epic elements to be found in drama. We can distinguish between verbal forms, for example stage directions involving commentary as well as projections and banners, and non-verbal forms of epic elements, the most important of which is the destruction of the theatrical illusion and exposure of its mechanisms, for example when a character steps out of his or her role. The techniques pioneered by BERTOLT BRECHT in his 'epic theatre' often serve as a means of producing the so-called 'alienation effect'. In contrast to this, the inclusion of narrative within drama – for example internal narrating instances or messenger speeches – often merely functions as a means of giving information; it therefore enhances rather than destroys the aesthetic illusion.

An Introduction to the Analysis of Drama

3 Semiotics of Theatre and Non-Verbal Theatrical Codes

As the main focus in English literary studies is generally placed on the analysis of drama as a written text, those aspects which are primarily or exclusively concerned with performance are frequently neglected. The main emphasis is usually placed on the analysis of textual characteristics, which is sometimes supplemented by watching the play performed in the theatre or on video. It is, of course, not possible to do justice to all aspects of performance analysis in the course of one short introduction; however, we hope to illustrate the aforementioned point that theatre communication differs considerably from the experience of reading a dramatic text, in terms of the medium and sign system as well as in terms of the reception process.

Analysis of dramatic texts

The study of the signs and codes of theatre communication is known as 'semiotics of theatre'. This area of enquiry takes account of the complexity of the various verbal and non-verbal sign systems of the theatre, which are also described as 'theatre codes'. New theories of drama and semiotics of theatre proceed from the premise that the spoken text is only one of the many dimensions or sign systems that contribute to a performance, and that the non-verbal codes are also of great importance for communication within theatrical performances.

Premises of semiotics of theatre

When devising a system for theatrical codes, we first must determine whether the sign is verbal or non-verbal. If it is non-verbal, we have to find out whether it is related to the actors, the stage or other aspects of the dramatic production. Further fundamental distinctions can be made between acoustic and optical or visual signs, and between 'durative' theatre codes that remain constant over an extended period of time (such as the stage set) and 'non-durative', temporary codes (for example, gestures and facial expressions). The following diagram, which is based on work by the Polish theatre semiotician TADEUSZ KOWZAN, provides a schematic and systematic overview of the most important theatre codes (see PFISTER 1988: 8; ASTON/SAVONA 1991: 105).

Systematization of verbal and non-verbal theatre codes

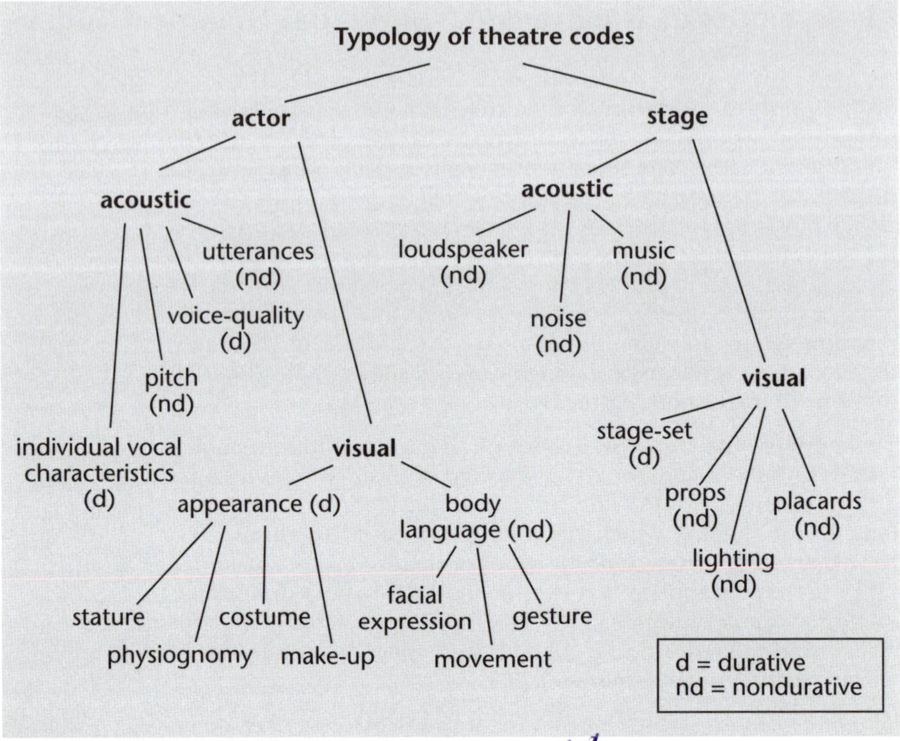

Typology of theatre codes

actor
- **acoustic**
  - utterances (nd)
  - voice-quality (d)
  - pitch (nd)
  - individual vocal characteristics (d)
- **visual**
  - appearance (d)
    - stature
    - physiognomy
    - costume
    - make-up
  - body language (nd)
    - facial expression
    - movement
    - gesture

stage
- **acoustic**
  - loudspeaker (nd)
  - music (nd)
  - noise (nd)
- **visual**
  - stage-set (d)
  - props (nd)
  - placards (nd)
  - lighting (nd)

d = durative
nd = nondurative

Figure 4.3.: Typology of theatre codes and sign systems  Kowzan

4 Transmission of Information and Verbal Communication

Transmission of information	As this typology of theatre codes illustrates, information can be transmitted in dramatic texts by means of both verbal and nonverbal codes and channels. In addition to propelling the action forward, verbal communication between the characters also conveys important information concerning the characters themselves, as well as time, place and all other aspects of the fictional world that are presented.
 **Exposition vs. dramatic introduction**	In both dramatic and narrative texts, the term 'exposition' refers to the transmission of introductory information necessary for an understanding of the initial dramatic events. 'Exposition' and 'dramatic introduction' differ (see PFISTER 1988: 86ff.) in that they perform different functions: the introduction serves primarily to establish a communication channel between the stage and the audience ('phatic function'), to awaken the interest of the audience

and to acclimatise it to the atmosphere of the play. The exposition, by contrast, has the function of informing the reader or audience about the history preceding the action and of introducing them to the time and place of the action, and the characters ('referential function', providing information). The dramatic introduction and exposition can occur simultaneously in the opening or the first act of the play; however, there are some famous examples of the two occurring in succession in SHAKESPEARE's dramas, for example, the witches' prelude in *Macbeth* (1605/06) and the shipwreck at the beginning of *The Tempest* (1610/11).

Although in classical and neo-classical drama the exposition generally takes place in the first act, this is by no means the only possibility. There are two basic varieties of exposition, which we will refer to as 'initial' and 'integrated' exposition. The former refers to the inclusion of all expository information in an isolated passage at the beginning of the text, separate from the action proper. In the case of the second, however, the expository information is distributed in small quantities throughout the text, woven into the action (see PFISTER 1988: 87f.). In classical drama, the prologue, a mainstay of epic theatre, is the most common form of exposition. However, in modern dramas the prehistory of the action is generally communicated in the form of an expository monologue (or soliloquy) or in the dialogue between the characters.

'Isolated' vs. 'integrated' exposition

An extreme variety of integrated exposition occurs in analytical drama, in which the exposition continues throughout the entire action or text. In analytical dramas (and similarly in analytical narratives), the action consists primarily in the gradual disclosure of the past events that have led to the initial situation.

Analytical drama

The various forms of monologue and dialogue represent further fundamental categories and areas of enquiry in the analysis of drama, and are therefore basic subject-matter in university courses on literary studies. We should bear in mind, however, that these categories are artificial constructs, conventions specific to the theatre, which are subject to historical change. Dialogue and monologue are important methods of transmitting information in many dramas, and can perform diverse functions. Other methods of conveying information that occur in drama are, for example, the messenger speech and the so-called 'teichoscopy' (whereby characters observe and simultaneously report events that are happening off-stage).

Dialogue and monologue

The term 'dialogue' refers to a succession of remarks and counter-remarks (or 'utterances') between two or more characters ('duo-logue' and 'polylogue'; see PFISTER 1988: 141). In a dialogue, the

Dialogue

characters exchange thoughts or opinions, discuss a topic or plot an intrigue. Dialogue is often referred to as the basic structure of drama, as it is a central constituent of the majority of dramas, and the progression of the action relies primarily on the characters' contributions in dialogue. Although dialogue is a central element of drama, it is by no means restricted to this genre; dialogue is also an important constituent of films and radio plays, and is frequently employed in narrative genres such as novels, short stories, fairy-tales and ballads.

Categories for the analysis of dialogue

The categories used in the analysis of dialogue are therefore applicable to a number of genres and media. When analysing dialogue, it is important to consider the length of individual utterances, the distribution of contributions among the characters, as well as the frequency with which the role of the speaker changes. The temporal relations between the various utterances can also yield important clues for interpretation: in addition to the more common model of linear succession of individual utterances in dialogue, interruption (which could be described as a partial simultaneity of utterances) is also common, and can function as a sign of malfunctioning communication. Consideration must also be given to the 'syntagmatics', or the logical coherence, of the dialogue; here, the three most important aspects for analysis are the structure of the logical interrelation between the individual parts of an utterance, the relationship of an utterance to previous ones by the same character, and to preceding remarks by other characters (see PFISTER 1988: chapter 4.6.4.).

Functions of dialogue

Although dialogues frequently appear to be very 'true to life', we should be aware when analysing them that they are in fact literary constructs that have been conventionalised to varying degrees and perform specific roles within the play. Whilst real conversations in everyday life primarily fulfil communicative and social needs, dramatic dialogues can serve quite different purposes. Dialogues set the action of a drama in motion and ensure its progression. They are also central to characterisation, and serve as a medium for conflict, for the clarification of opinions, and for expounding central themes. It should be taken into account, however, that the functions of dialogue are subject to historical change.

Wit

The 'artificiality' of dialogue is particularly evident in English comedies of the Restoration period (1660–ca.1700). From this period onwards, intellectual, artificial conversation came to be regarded as one of the typical features of the so-called 'comedy of manners'. This conversational style, known as 'wit', is exemplified by plays such as WILLIAM WYCHERLEY's *The Country Wife* (1675) and WILLIAM CONGREVE's *The Way of the World* (1700), as well as the

comedies composed in the 1890s by Oscar Wilde (1854–1900). The dialogue is not merely humorous; it comprises a verbal duel of a highly subtle, intellectual nature. The characters who are described as 'wits' make frequent use of certain rhetorical figures; the repetition of unusual similes and metaphors is particularly common. Wit also often uses the rhetorical figure of paradox, linking together terms that seemingly have nothing to do with one another, and may even be mutually contradictory.

We speak of a 'soliloquy' when a character is alone on stage while speaking, or is regardless of any hearers. The device is often used for the divulgence of innermost feelings. A 'monologue' is when a character speaks alone, but in the explicit presence of others. The two terms thus correspond to the German *Selbstgespräch* and *Monolog* respectively. (It is important to note, however, that in English usage 'soliloquy' and 'monologue' are often used interchangeably – see *Oxford English Dictionary*.) The information conveyed in monologues and soliloquies is often characterised by a high degree of subjectivity. Monologues and soliloquies do not, therefore, offer an 'objective' view of a situation; instead they bear the mark of the individual speaker's characteristics and perspective. Such speeches can range in length from several lines to a comprehensive commentary. Note that a 'dramatic monologue' is not a part of a drama but a poem (notably perfected by Robert Browning, see chapter 3.2.) or other non-dramatic composition in the form of a soliloquy.

Monologue and soliloquy

Monological speech is specific to the drama; there is no real parallel in everyday communication. As monological speech is based on the convention of a character thinking aloud on stage, it represents a specifically dramatic form of representing consciousness. Monologues and soliloquies, therefore, are only plausible in the context of the author's and the audience's shared acceptance of this convention. Realistic dramas, which aim to create the illusion that the events could genuinely occur as they are being presented, tend to avoid monological speech because of its obvious artificiality. In addition to informing the audience about a character's thoughts, feelings and plans, monological speech can also serve as a link between various appearances of characters and as a transition between scenes, as well as connecting episodes of the dramatic action by narrating events that are not presented on the stage.

Monological speech as a dramatic convention

The dialogue and the soliloquy naturally differ first and foremost in the number of characters present on stage; the solitary appearance of the soliloquist stands in contrast to the variable number of characters participating in a dialogue. A difference that also applies to monologues lies in the identity of the main addressee: whereas dialogues are addressed to an interlocutor on stage, mon-

Differences between dialogical and monological speech

ologues and soliloquies are directed towards the speakers themselves or the audience, rather than other characters in the performance. Monological utterances also differ from dialogues in that they are often more limited in terms of theme, but greater in terms of length, than dialogical utterances.

Monological tendencies in dialogue, dialogical tendencies in monologue and soliloquy

Despite these differences, there are some instances of overlaps between dialogical and monological speech. 'Monological tendencies' in dialogue occur when there is a considerable discrepancy between the length and frequency of the contributions, with the result that one character becomes dominant. When there is considerable consensus between two partners in a dialogue, this is also seen as a monological tendency. On the other hand, monologues and soliloquies are said to contain 'dialogical tendencies' when the speaker addresses an absent figure or object (see PFISTER 1988: 129ff.). A famous example of such an address is Macbeth's dagger soliloquy.

Introductory soliloquy in *Richard III*

The following soliloquy, addressed to the audience by the protagonist at the beginning of *Richard III* (1592/93), one of SHAKESPEARE's most important history plays, is illustrative of some of the peculiarities of monological speech and the functions it can perform. As this speech occurs at the beginning of the play, it is described as an 'introductory soliloquy'. In contrast to the soliloquies featured in SHAKESPEARE's tragedies, Richard's soliloquy shows none of the mental confusion and incoherence characteristic of Hamlet's or Macbeth's conflict-ridden consciousness. Instead, the thoughts and plans of the protagonist, Richard, Duke of Gloucester, are presented in an ordered, logical sequence.

Now is the winter of our discontent
Made glorious summer by this sun of York;
And all the clouds that loured upon our house
In the deep bosom of the ocean buried.
Now are our brows bound with victorious wreaths;
Our bruised arms hung up for monuments;
Our stern alarums changed to merry meetings,
Our dreadful marches to delightful measures.
Grim-visaged war hath smoothed his wrinkled front;
And now, instead of mounting barbed steeds
To fright the souls of fearful adversaries,
He capers nimbly in a lady's chamber
To the lascivious pleasing of a lute.
But I, that am not shaped for sportive tricks,
Nor made to court an amorous looking-glass;
I, that am rudely stamped, and want love's majesty
To strut before a wanton ambling nymph;
I, that am curtailed of this fair proportion,

  CHAPTER 4   An Introduction to the Analysis of Drama

Cheated of feature by dissembling Nature,
Deformed, unfinished, sent before my time
Into this breathing world, scarce half made up,
And that so lamely and unfashionable
That dogs bark at me as I halt by them;
Why, I, in this weak piping time of peace,
Have no delight to pass away the time,
Unless to spy my shadow in the sun
And descant on mine own deformity:
And therefore, since I cannot prove a lover,
To entertain these fair well-spoken days,
I am determined to prove a villain
And hate the idle pleasures of these days.
Plots have I laid, inductions dangerous,
By drunken prophecies, libels and dreams,
To set my brother Clarence and the king
In deadly hate the one against the other:
And if King Edward be as true and just
As I am subtle, false and treacherous,
This day should Clarence closely be mewed up,
About a prophecy, which says that G
Of Edward's heirs the murderer shall be.
Dive, thoughts, down to my soul: here Clarence comes.
(Richard III, I, i, 1–30)

Many of the functions exemplified by this introductory soliloquy from *Richard III* could not be performed to the same extent by dialogue. The following summary lists some of the most important functions of monological utterances:

Functions of monologues and soliloquies

- familiarizing the audience with the atmosphere of the play; description of the scenery or surroundings,
- providing expository information about preceding events and the initial situation, as well as introducing the action, characters, spatial and temporal context,
- commenting on previous events from the perspective of the speaker,
- introducing the protagonist and his or her self-characterisation,
- giving expression to the speaker's innermost thoughts and feelings, describing internal processes and conflicts,
- disclosing the speaker's plans, intentions and decision processes,
- introducing the audience to the personality of the hero/villain (means of eliciting sympathy/dislike),
- arousing expectations with regard to future developments (generating suspense).

| Aside | The 'aside' represents a further mode of speech specific to the drama. This convention also exemplifies the artificiality of many methods of transmitting information in drama. As in the case of monological speech, the aside is frequently addressed not to another character on the stage, but to the reader or the audience in the theatre. MANFRED PFISTER (1988: 137–140) differentiates between three different types of aside: |

- the 'monological aside', in which a character voices a thought, which is not expressed anywhere else, in such a way that only the audience understands (usually indicated by the stage direction 'Aside');
- the 'dialogical aside', in which, unnoticed by other characters on the stage, a group of initiated characters conduct a conspiratorial conversation in whispers (usually indicated by the stage direction 'Aside to X');
- the 'aside *ad spectatores*', in which a character addresses a comment directly to the audience (usually indicated by the stage direction 'Addressing the audience').

| Transmitting information to the audience alone | Monologues, soliloquies and asides represent a particularly interesting means of transmitting information in drama, as they make it possible to impart information to the audience (or reader) alone. Consequently, the aside provides the audience with an advantage over the other characters, from whom the information is withheld. Monological asides and asides *ad spectatores* therefore enable the author to control the distribution of information to the advantage of the audience and disadvantage of the other characters. |

| Discrepant awareness | The various forms of dialogical and monological speech are therefore important in determining to what extent the various characters and the reader or audience are informed about the dramatic events and the plans of the characters. If the audience is placed at an advantage or disadvantage in comparison with the characters, the situation is described as 'discrepant awareness'. 'Congruent awareness' occurs when characters and audience are provided with identical information. Even within the internal communication system, however, the levels of awareness of the various characters can vary considerably, with discrepant levels of awareness frequently leading to misunderstandings or communication difficulties between the characters. |

| Dramatic irony | Discrepant awareness is also a precondition for dramatic irony (which is not to be confused with verbal irony, where the speaker says the opposite of what he or she means). Dramatic irony is based on a discrepancy between the internal and the external communication systems, or between the level of awareness of the characters and that of the audience. For dramatic irony to occur, |

the audience or reader must be privy to information that is not available to the character concerned. This superior level of knowledge grants the audience or reader an insight into the character's errors of judgement, which imbues his or her remarks with an unconscious or unintentional additional meaning. In contrast to intentionally ironic remarks, in the case of dramatic irony the speaker him- or herself is the butt of the irony. Dramatic irony can be comic or tragic, depending on the individual situation.

5 Character and Action

In addition to time and place, character and action are the most elementary constituents of dramatic and narrative texts, as well as of films. Close examination of the portrayal of character and of the presented or narrated story is therefore central to the analysis of dramas, narrative texts and films. There are consequently numerous parallels between the analysis of dramatic and narrative texts, with regard to character and action as well as with regard to the presentation of time and place. However, the two genres also have individual specific characteristics. The following section will begin with general information on the terms 'action' and 'character' before going on to discuss the presentation of characters and action in dramatic texts. Although characters and action in narrative genres (for example novels and short stories) are subject to narrative mediation (see chapter 5), many of the categories introduced below are also relevant and useful for an analysis of both narrative texts and narrative genres in other media (see chapter 6).

Constituents of dramatic and narrative texts

In literary texts and films, the term 'action' in its widest sense implies a change or perpetuation of a situation brought about by the characters. Four factors influence the behaviour of the characters, and therefore the development of the action: abilities, needs, motivation and intention. The intentions of the characters are among the most important motors of the action, although in tragedy especially, the intentions of the individual characters are often frustrated by external powers. In comedy, the conclusion is generally brought about by chance occurrences and the misfiring of the opponent's plans, rather than by the success of the protagonist's plans.

Action

With specific reference to dramatic action, VOLKER KLOTZ makes a distinction between open and closed forms. The latter refers to an entirely self-contained story, which is brought to a definite conclusion. Units of action are composed of scenes and acts. The classical form of the tragedy corresponds to the ideal of a largely closed

Units and composition of the action

form consisting of five acts: I. introduction, II. development of the conflict, III. climax and beginning of the protagonist's tragic descent, IV. moment of delay and V. catastrophe (or dénouement).

Dramatic characters: concept and status

The anthropomorphic figures presented to the audience in literary texts and films are described as 'characters'. This term indicates that the figure is fictive and not to be confused with a real person. Whereas characters in a dramatic text are constituted only by their words and actions, in dramatic performance and film the physical presence and body language of the actor contribute to the characterisation. It is therefore important to differentiate between the (real) actor and the (fictive) role that he or she plays on stage.

Styles of staging characters

It is possible to distinguish between various styles of staging characters, depending on the degree of stylisation, or the extent to which they aim to preserve the illusion of performance. 'Neoclassical' styles are characterised by their adherence to rules and conventions, and their emphasis on the play's dignity and solemnity. 'Naturalistic' styles, on the other hand, aim to encourage the audience to empathise with the characters. BRECHT's 'epic theatre' famously strove to retain the distance between actors and audience with a range of 'alienating' techniques. A similar range of styles of staging characters can also be found in films, where the period or genre to which the film belongs plays an important role. We should be careful to differentiate, however, between the demands of the theatre, where gestures and facial expressions have to be more strongly emphasised because of the distance between actors and audience, and those of film, where it is possible to record details such as facial expressions and nuances of body language in close-ups.

Theories of 'character'

There are various different approaches to characterisation within literary studies, based on diverse understandings of what constitutes a character. In the majority of interpretations, characters are treated as real, existing individuals, with the major emphasis being placed on the psychologies of the characters and their relationships to one another; this is based on a realistic or mimetic understanding of literary characters which assumes that they are 'true to life' and 'imitate' real people. Structuralist theories of drama and narrative, on the other hand, stress the functional roles performed by characters. They consider characters as agents or functions of the plot rather than as 'psychological entities', and therefore refer to them as 'actants'. In his analysis of the Russian fairy-tale, VLADIMIR PROPP identified a number of plot functions, which he linked to the roles of particular actants or plot agents (for example, hero, helper, donor or villain). Both approaches are

ultimately one-sided, however, as character and plot are necessarily interdependent.

Ever since ARISTOTLE, drama has been defined as 'imitation of action'. The dramatic action arises from the dialogue between the characters, which sets and keeps the action in motion. There is a correlation between character and action: on the one hand, the characters act on the basis of their necessarily limited perspectives; on the other hand, the action affects the perspective of a character, because the knowledge, abilities and needs, as well as the motivation and intentions of a character can be changed by every action.

Interdependence of character and action

The expression *'dramatis personae'* is used to refer to all of the literary characters who appear in a play. The first act of a drama is usually preceded by a list of the *dramatis personae*. Depending on their importance in the play, a distinction is generally made between the main characters and the minor characters although the boundary between the two is permeable.

Dramatis personae

An important means of structuring the *dramatis personae* consists in the similarities and differences between the characters. These semantic equivalences and oppositions are referred to as 'correspondences and contrasts' (see PFISTER 1988: 163). The peculiarities of individual characters are highlighted by their difference from other figures. For example, the positive qualities of a heroine or hero are far more evident if he or she is juxtaposed with a villain than with another positive character.

Correspondences and contrasts

The structure of the *dramatis personae* in plays, narratives and films can be simplified by means of a graphic presentation of their relationships to each other, known as the 'character constellation'. This expression is used to describe the dynamic structure of the *dramatis personae* in a drama, novel or film. It does not merely refer to the traits of the various characters; it also encompasses the characters and their relationships throughout the text. The sources of impending conflict, and, therefore, of the dramatic action, can often be located in the constellations between the characters and the irreconcilability of their motives. Certain genres such as the comedy of manners are characterised by fairly conventionalised character constellations; many tragedies are based on a clear opposition between the protagonist and the antagonist. Within the wide variety of dramatic and narrative genres, the character constellations display a high degree of historical and cultural variability.

Character constellations

The most important criterion for the analysis of scenes is the entrance or exit of one or several characters. This alters the number of characters present on the stage, described as the 'configuration' of characters. By examining the structure of the character con-

Character configuration

figuration, we can ascertain how important a single character is within the play, as the number of configurations in which a character participates is an index of his or her status and of the relationship between the characters.

Character perspective

The expression *'Figurenperspektive'*, which was coined by Pfister (1977: 90), offers a range of further possible applications of the term 'perspective' when analysing characters in dramatic (and narrative) texts. 'Character perspective' can be used to describe the individual, more or less restricted view of reality of every character, as determined by three major factors: firstly, the character's level of knowledge; secondly, the character's psychological disposition; and thirdly, the character's ideological persuasions. The level of knowledge and the psychological disposition determine the spectrum of characteristics and the personality of a character. As the vague term 'ideological persuasions' is problematic, not least because of the diverse connotations of the term 'ideology', it can be replaced by the more precise concept of 'values and norms'. These terms are analytically more useful, as the character's values and norms generally appear explicitly in the text and are therefore easier to identify than his or her 'ideological persuasions'. The expression 'character perspective' therefore encompasses all those features that constitute a character and his or her subjective model of reality or view of the fictional world.

Perspective structure

In the theory of drama, the term *'Perspektivenstruktur'* or 'perspective structure' has been coined by theorists of drama (see Pfister 1974 and 1988) in order to describe the entirety of character perspectives and their relationship to each other. The expression has also proved useful in the analysis of narrative texts (see chapter 5.3.). As the perspective structure of a text is based on the selection and combination of character perspectives, two aspects are to be taken into consideration: the paradigmatic dimension, consisting of the selection of character perspectives, and the syntagmatic dimension, which refers to the combination of perspectives. Both are relevant for our evaluation of characters; in the context of 18th-century sentimental drama, which features a host of nearly ideal characters, even those with minor flaws appear to be far worse then they would, for instance, in one of the rather cynical Restoration comedies or in the plays of Oscar Wilde. The perspective structure in sentimental comedies is therefore much more homogenous than that of Wilde's comedies of manners or George Bernard Shaw's plays.

Closed vs. open perspective structure

The diverse categories used to analyse the relationship between the character perspectives can be subsumed beneath a broad, overall distinction between dramas (and also novels and films) with closed and open perspective structures (see Pfister 1988:

65ff.). In the case of a closed perspective structure, the diverse character perspectives ultimately converge on one point, conveying the impression of a unitary view of the world. An open perspective structure, by contrast, occurs when a drama presents no such convergence point and the individual character perspectives are divergent.

When considering the character conception, we should firstly ascertain whether characters remain unchanged throughout the drama, or whether they develop ('static' versus 'dynamic characters'). We should also consider whether a character is a one-dimensional 'type' characterised by a small, internally consistent collection of features, or a multidimensional character presented as an individual with a large number of characteristics. There is a broad spectrum of possible kinds of characterisation, comprising various degrees of individualisation. The two extremes of this spectrum are the 'personification', a figure who embodies or personifies a single characteristic, and the 'individual', who has so many different features that he or she seems to have as complex a character as a real human being. A large variety of characters exists between these two extremes.

Character conception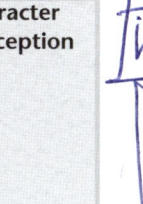

The terms 'individual' and 'type' are used to differentiate between two varieties of literary characters. 'Type' is used to refer to a character who has few specific human characteristics and individual features, or who is characterised, for example, as a representative of a social class. We can differentiate between various types: the psychological type embodies a particular mode of human behaviour (for example, the grouch or the skinflint), whereas the social type is based on a particular profession or social class (for example, the courtier, city-dweller or peasant). There is also a wide variety of ethnic, regional and national stereotypes, as well as gender stereotypes. A complex literary character, by contrast, is supplied with a large number of characteristics. The main emphasis is placed on the uniqueness and personal individuality of such characters; they are presented as multi-facetted and characterised by a large number of personal traits, and are therefore thought to resemble genuine human beings.

Individual and type

This distinction between type and character corresponds closely to E. M. FORSTER's differentiation between 'flat' and 'round', or one-dimensional and multi-dimensional, characters. In genres such as the novel or the tragedy, the individualised characters tend to be in the majority; the comedy and other genres such as satire, romance, and certain film genres such as the western, by contrast, tend towards character types. A genre in which the characters bear a conspicuously close resemblance to types is the English Restoration comedy, which usually includes such figures as the aristo-

Flat characters vs. round characters

cratic libertine, the lascivious, hypocritical and puritanical bourgeois, the dim-witted country bumpkin and the man-eating elderly woman among its *dramatis personae*.

Historical summary

In the course of literary history, we see a progressive tendency towards greater individualisation of characters. The *exempla* of the literature of Late Antiquity and of medieval morality plays generally embody an abstract concept, a vice or a virtue, and therefore function as personifications. The character types in the comedies of the Renaissance and of the 17th to the 20th centuries, by contrast, comprise a limited selection of psychological or sociological characteristics, rather than representing one single concept. In the late 17th and early 18th centuries, the representation of characters as types is even elevated to the status of a normative rule by neo-classical poetics. With its demands for 'appropriate' characterisation, described as 'decorum', the neo-classical school enshrines the categorisation of the human being according to age, gender, social status and nationality, which first appeared in ARISTOTLE's rhetoric and in HORACE's poetics. This neoclassical character typology has fallen increasingly into disuse since the Romantic period (ca. 1780–1830), however, and has been replaced by individualising and psychologising characterisation techniques, which stress the complexity and diversity of human identity.

Techniques of characterisation

In addition to constellation, configuration and conception, characterisation, or the conveyance of information concerning a character, is central to the analysis of drama (and also of narrative texts and films). Characterisation is concerned with the question of how characters are supplied with characteristics or semantic features. In drama there is a broad spectrum of characterisation techniques, which can be systematised with the aid of specific criteria (see PFISTER 1988: 183ff.). Firstly, a distinction is made between 'figural' and 'authorial techniques of characterisation', according to whether it is the author or the characters themselves who convey the relevant information. In the case of 'figural characterisation', the information is supplied primarily by the speech, gestures and actions of the characters, whereas character information is supplied by 'authorial' means if it derives from the structure of the entire play. A further criterion is based on the explicitness of the character information: in the case of explicit characterisation, the features and traits of a character are stated outright, whereas implicit techniques of characterisation present the traits and behaviour of a character and allow the recipient to draw his or her own conclusions.

Figural forms of characterisation include all those techniques in which the characters themselves supply the information. Characters can characterise themselves by means of 'explicit self-commentary', or they can characterise others; in both cases we should bear in mind, however, that the comments are distorted by the individual character's perspective and may therefore be unreliable. The *dramatis personae* also characterise themselves implicitly by means of their behaviour, actions and manners of speaking throughout the play. We should adopt the basic premise that every explicit characterisation of others is also an implicit self-characterisation, as the comments made by a character about others also enable us to draw conclusions concerning his or her own values, norms and personality traits.

Figural techniques of characterisation

Among the most common techniques of authorial characterisation are descriptions in the stage directions, and the use of telling names that impart implicit information. The similarities and differences, or the aforementioned 'correspondences and contrasts' between the characters, also contribute to characterisation. The following diagram provides an overview of the most important techniques of characterisation.

Authorial techniques of characterisation

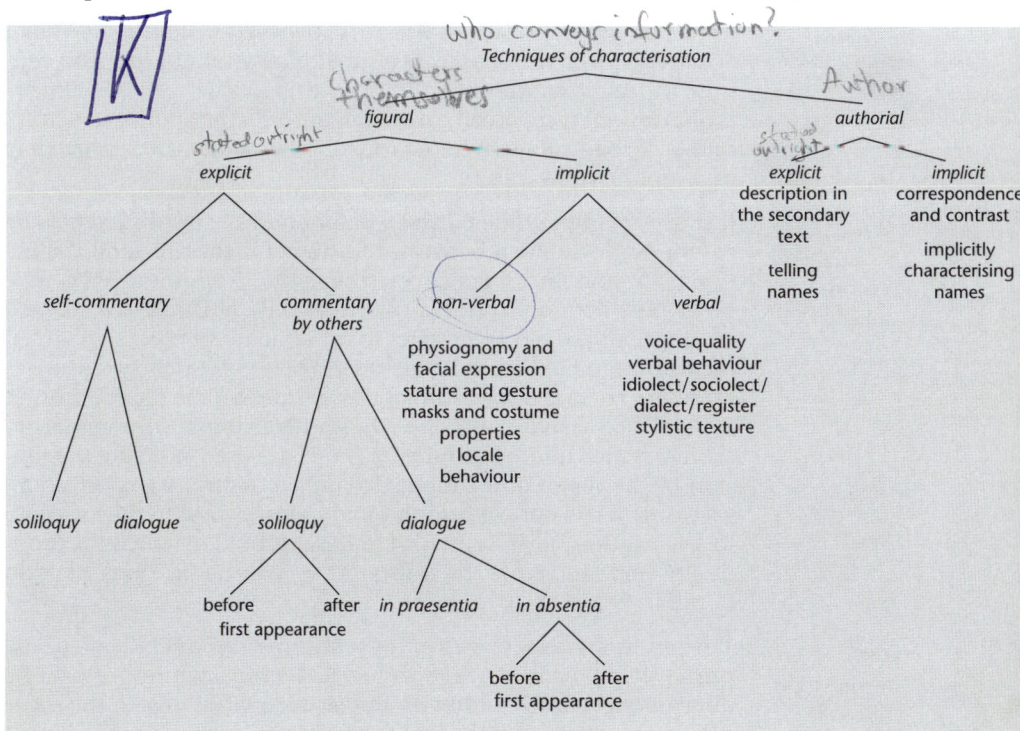

Figure 4.4.: Techniques of characterisation (PFISTER 1988: 185)

char)
action) constituents of
time) dramatic texts
place)

6 Representation of Place and Temporal Structure

Unity of time and place

For a long time, it was assumed on the basis of ARISTOTLE's poetics that dramas should observe the unity of time and place, despite the fact that ARISTOTLE's text actually only prescribes the unity of action. Neoclassical theorists insisted that these two unities were necessary to enable the audience to follow the play adequately in its imagination, and in order for the theatrical illusion to succeed. After all, the argument ran, there is no change in the real space during the performance, and the real time is also a continuum. Although the unities of time, place and action were generally grouped together as one requirement, they in actual fact represent three separate rules, which can be broken in different ways.

Closed vs. open temporal and spatial structure

In practice, drama and dramaturgy deviated from these classical norms considerably in the course of literary history. SHAKESPEARE's dramas, for example, have an open temporal and spatial structure: the setting changes frequently, and the time is not restricted to one day, as followers of ARISTOTLE believed it should be. When SHAKESPEARE was recognised as a great playwright in the 18th century, the predominant practice of writing plays changed: increasingly, dramas were given an open temporal and spatial structure, and a closed structure was no longer regarded as the *sine qua non* of dramatic composition.

Stage, theatre and fictional space

Just as we differentiate between actor and role, we should also be careful to distinguish between the stage (or theatre) and the fictional or imaginary space in which the dramatic events take place. The fictional space is generally only partially represented on stage; characters often refer to other fictional places, in which they claim to have been in the period between their appearances on stage. There is a spectrum of possibilities for the representation of the fictional space on stage, ranging from a realistic representation, in which a large number of props are used to create the illusion of the fictional location, through a neutral representation, with only a few optical signals giving plastic form to the location, to an anti-illusionist, symbolist representation, in which the props do not serve to create the illusion of a realistic fictional location at all.

Techniques of representation of place

The representation of place in theatre performances is achieved primarily by means of the set (curtains, props, lighting, etc.). The director is generally at liberty to decide to what degree the stage directions concerning the set are observed. There are other means of representing place, however, most significantly the device known as 'word-scenery', which attempts to engage the imagination of the audience. Word-scenery can be employed to describe the location of the action, or to refer to particular props or imaginary figures (for example, ghosts or similar apparitions), none of which are visible on stage. In contrast to the set, then, word-scenery is not an 'objective' means of representing place; rather, it is filtered through the perspective of the individual character who describes his surroundings. Moreover, word-scenery can convey information that could not be represented in concrete form on the stage.

The structure and presentation of the spatial context are important considerations when analysing this aspect of drama, as they are indicative of how place is 'semanticized', in other words, how space becomes a bearer of meaning in its own right. The preferred haunts of a particular character, for example, and the frequency with which he or she crosses boundaries between locations, can yield important information, as can the 'relationships within a single locale', the 'relationships between the stage and off-stage', 'the relationships between a number of different locales' and the relationship between the 'fictional locale [and the] real spatial context' (see PFISTER 1988: 257ff.).

Categories of representation of place

Various categories developed by theorists of narrative to describe temporal structures are also used in the analysis of drama and film. They include chronological and achronic representation, flashforwards and flashbacks, pauses and ellipses (see chapter 5.7.). A further distinction is made in the dramatic genres between actual performance time and fictional time. Actual performance time denotes the length of an individual film or a theatre performance; fictional time refers to the duration spanned by the staged events, with a further distinction being made between the period of time that is presented on stage and the period about which the audience is informed in the course of a performance (including, for example, the events summarised in the exposition or in the course of resolving mysterious plot elements). Periods of time are also frequently omitted from the fictional time structure between scenes, acts or film sequences.

Fictional time and actual performance time

Further information on all aspects of the analysis of drama, illustrated with numerous examples, can be found in MANFRED PFISTER'S introductory work Das Drama. Theorie und Analyse (1977/2000), which is also available in an English translation (The Theory and Analysis of Drama, 1988), and which develops a comprehensive repertoire for the systematic analysis of dramatic texts. This standard textbook on drama is indispensable for a thorough examination of the genre. Although none of the English introductions to the analysis of drama are nearly as comprehensive as PFISTER'S seminal book, ELAINE ASTON and GEORGE SAVONA'S Theatre as Sign System. A Semiotics of Text and Performance (1991) can be recom-

Further reading on the analysis of drama

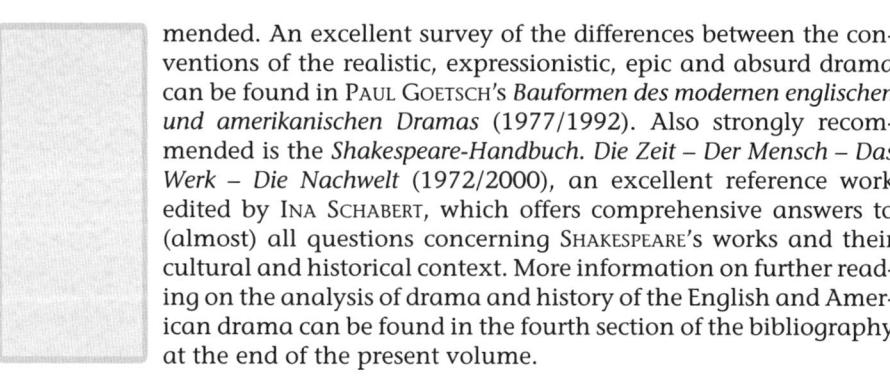

mended. An excellent survey of the differences between the conventions of the realistic, expressionistic, epic and absurd drama can be found in Paul Goetsch's *Bauformen des modernen englischen und amerikanischen Dramas* (1977/1992). Also strongly recommended is the *Shakespeare-Handbuch. Die Zeit – Der Mensch – Das Werk – Die Nachwelt* (1972/2000), an excellent reference work edited by Ina Schabert, which offers comprehensive answers to (almost) all questions concerning Shakespeare's works and their cultural and historical context. More information on further reading on the analysis of drama and history of the English and American drama can be found in the fourth section of the bibliography at the end of the present volume.

An Introduction to the Analysis of Drama

5 CHAPTER An Introduction to the Analysis of Narrative Texts

That cannibal, the novel, which has devoured so many forms of art, will by then have devoured even more. We shall be forced to invent new names for the different books which masquerade under this one heading.

VIRGINIA WOOLF, "The Narrow Bridge of Art"

1 The Novel as a Text Mediated Through Narrative: Basic Features of Narrative Composition

In her essay "The Narrow Bridge of Art", VIRGINIA WOOLF describes the novel metaphorically as a 'cannibal', which has 'devoured' many forms of art in the course of its history, and will doubtless integrate still more. This image effectively illustrates the remarkable mutability of this genre, which has enjoyed huge popularity since the 18th century. Thanks to the diversity of the genre, the novel is extremely difficult to define. It encompasses various subgenres classified according to subject-matter, such as campus, spy, adventure, war, artist, social and women's novel. Subgenres classified according to formal characteristics. These include the neopicaresque novel, the *bildungsroman*, the detective and crime novel, the thriller, and historical and science-fiction novels.

> Mutability and subgenres of the novel

The short story is characterised by a similar mutability, with such a variety of diverse manifestations that HANS BENDER once accurately described it as *"the chameleon among literary genres"*. However, there are a number of features that are generally regarded as characteristic of the short story. They include the formal principle of narrative economy, careful selection, reduction and compression in the presentation of characters and the spatial and temporal frame, concentration on the depiction of individual events, episodes, scenes or situations, and a tendency towards stylistic brevity and allusive prose.

> Diversity and generic features of the short story

Given the diversity and mutability of narrative genres, one of the most difficult tasks faced by literary studies is that of identifying the most essential elements and structural traits of narration. Of central importance, therefore, is the question of narrativity, that is, those characteristics that distinguish the narrative text from other genres. These mainly derive from the fact that narratives tell a story; and since this is also true of other genres, many of the categories that will be discussed in what follows also apply to films, comics and other narrative genres.

> The question of narrativity

Content and aims of this chapter	This chapter aims to give an introductory overview of some of the basics of the theory of narrative, and to present some of the most important categories, models and methods in the analysis of narrative texts. We will first summarise the most important generic features of narrative and present a communication model for narrative texts. The subsequent sections will comprise an introduction to the central considerations in the analysis of narrative texts (character, plot, narrative transmission, modes of presenting consciousness and the representation of time and space).
Narrative theory or narratology	The foundations of the analysis of narrative are supplied by the findings, categories and models of the theory of narrative, or narratology. This area of literary studies focuses on the complex structures that constitute the narration of a story. Narrative theory, which is rooted in structuralism, attempts to give a precise, systematic and rational account of textual structures, and, to this end, has developed a clearly defined terminology, as well as descriptive models and categories of analysis. The descriptive models of narrative theory are more than a mere conceptual aid; they provide us with the 'tools' for giving a precise, systematic and intersubjective account of the composite elements and structures of narrative texts and are thus the foundation for the interpretation of narrative texts.
 **Story vs. discourse**	Any analysis of the structure of narrative texts and films must begin by differentiating between the various levels of communication within the text. Various terms are used to refer to these levels; some approaches are based on a primary opposition between *fabula* and *sjuzhet* or 'story' and 'discourse', a binary distinction that goes back to Russian Formalism and Structuralism. Whereas the term 'story' refers to the chronological sequence of narrated events, 'discourse' refers to the shaping of this material by the narrator. This distinction is encapsulated in the basic questions: (1) What is narrated? (2) How is a story communicated narratively (or cinematically), i.e. mediated through narrative? This distinction between story and discourse takes account of the fact that the same story can be narrated in entirely different ways, depending on the events selected for representation and emphasis, the linguistic form, and the choice of narrative perspective as well as of specific kinds of plots and other narrative techniques.
Constituents of narrative texts	The distinction between story and discourse provides a framework for the analysis of the various constituents of narrative texts. The story can be further divided into 'events' and 'existents'; the latter term comprises the characters and the setting (see CHATMAN 1978: 19). The analysis of the discourse level begins with the questions of who is narrating, and from whose perspective the fictional world is presented.

The elements of form and content that characterise narrative texts and distinguish them from other genres are grouped together under the term 'narrativity'. Definitions of narrativity vary, however, according to whether the level of the content (the story) or the level of the narration (discourse) is taken as a point of departure. Structuralist narrative theory assumes that narrative texts (in contrast to descriptive, discursive and other types of texts) are characterised by a chronologically organised sequence of events, in which an event brings about a change in the situation. This means that narrative texts differ from lyric and other non-narrative genres in that they have a plot.

Story-oriented definition of narrativity

Approaches which focus on the level of discourse or narration, on the other hand, consider the most essential generic feature of the narrative text to be its 'mediacy' (see STANZEL 1984: 4ff.). Narrative transmission is therefore regarded as a constitutive characteristic of narrativity. According to these approaches, the fact that whatever happens is being recounted (in contrast, for instance, to pantomime or a play, which also tell a story) is the defining characteristic of narrative texts. For this and other reasons, the examination of the narrative perspective or 'point of view' is a central element of the analysis of narrative texts.

Discourse-oriented definitions of narrativity: mediacy

A third approach argues that the specifity of narrative texts lies in a feature that primarily concerns their content: the ability of narrative texts to give expression to human experiences by means of their narrative structure. MONIKA FLUDERNIK (1996: 12), for example, defines narrativity as *"experientiality"*, as the *"quasi-mimetic evocation of 'real-life experience'"*. This definition draws attention to the fact that stories are always accounts of experiences, and raises the question of the relation of narrativity to general considerations relating to the perception and representation of reality.

Experientiality

Rather than taking any one of these definitions as absolute, it seems more sensible to assume, as we did in the case of poetry and drama, that narrative texts are characterised by a collection of features. A narrative text must not necessarily manifest all three of the aforementioned features; instead one or the other feature can predominate in certain genres, periods or individual texts. In the case of the adventure novel, for example, the plot is of central importance; novels with a complex narrative structure, on the other hand, focus attention on the narrative transmission or mediacy; and in the psychological novels typical for the Modernist movement, the element of experientiality predominates.

Collection of features

2 A Communication Model for Narrative Texts: Story-Oriented Versus Discourse-Oriented Narratology

Structure of communication

Communication models provide a frame of reference for the analysis of narrative texts, as they encompass all elements, whether in the intratextual or the extratextual sphere, involved in the communication of a fictional text. The various models suggested by theorists, which identify up to five levels of communication, give a simplified overview of the communication structure of narrative texts by representing all instances of addresser and addressee on the various intratextual and extratextual levels of communication. Such models arrange the communication levels and various contextual functions into a hierarchy, as well as providing representations of the *"internal structure of the communication process"* (KAHRMANN et al. 1977: 38). The following representation offers a model for the communication structure of narrative texts.

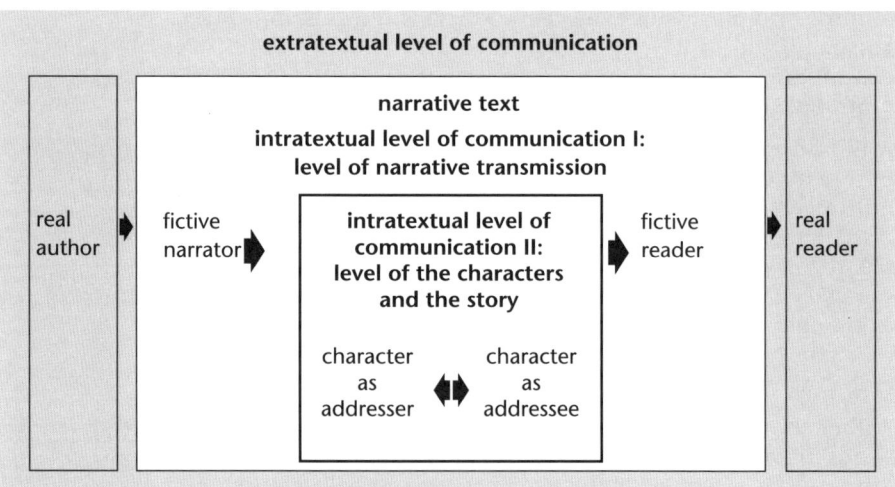

Figure 5.1.: A communication model for narrative texts

Levels and instances within the communication model

This communication model for narrative texts is compatible with the binary distinction between the content level (story) and the level of narrative transmission (discourse). The communication level of the fictional story, on which the speaker and addressee can exchange roles, consists – in dramatic and narrative texts as well as in film – of the dialogue between the characters. In contrast to drama (see chapter 4), however, the speech situation of the characters in narrative texts is embedded in the communication level of narrative transmission. On this level, a fictive narrator addresses a reader, or 'narratee', who is also fictive. In addition to these two intratextual, fictional levels of communication, a further, extratextual level of empirical communication can be identified, which includes the real author as addresser and the real reader as addressee. With the aid of these three levels of communication, we can distinguish between the narrator and the historical author, as well as between the fictive addressee and the real reader of a narrative text.

This model also illustrates what is meant by 'embedded' levels of communication. This term refers to a sequence of passages in which one narrative is inserted into another, superordinate narrative. Three basic criteria are used to identify an embedded narrative. Firstly, there should be a transition from a level of narration to the narrative embedded within it. Secondly, the inserted narrative should be subordinate to the other narrative level, so that the two levels can neither be considered equal, nor placed in a reverse hierarchy. Thirdly, the superordinate and embedded narratives should be homogeneous to the extent that they both belong to the same category, in the case of the novel, the category of fictional narrative. The communication model for narrative texts therefore provides an effective overview of the hierarchical and functional relations between the various narrative levels. The relationship between the extradiegetic level of narrative transmission and the diegetic level of the characters can be likened to a subject-object relationship, as the characters in the fictional world are the object of the narrator, the superordinate subject who recounts the events and comments on them. Among the most common types of embedded narrative are frame tales and interpolated tales, i.e. narratives that are inserted on the level of the story and involve characters assuming the role of narrator for several passages.

Embedded levels of communication

The diverse approaches to the study of narrative can be categorised according to the levels and constituent parts of narrative texts that they take as their focus; in other words, according to whether they are more concerned with the content of the narrative, or with the way in which the content is mediated by the narrative. Story-oriented narratological approaches are concerned with the structure of the narrated tale, or with the question of *what* the narrative text depicts. Approaches are classified as discourse-oriented, however, when they focus on *how* the level of narrative transmission, the structure of the plot or the temporal structure are fashioned in narrative texts.

Story-oriented vs. discourse-oriented narratology

❸ Character, Plot and Narrated World: Categories in Story-Oriented Narratology

Constituents of the narrated world

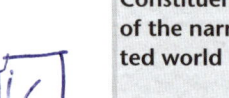

The narrated world is composed of temporal and spatial structures, together with the various objects which 'exist' within it and, last but not least, the characters. Story-oriented narratology has developed various categories in order to analyse these constituents. The most fundamental aspects of the analysis of the narrated story relate to the presentation of the characters, plot and spatial frame. When analysing the presentation of characters within a narrative text or film, we can draw on a broad variety of categories established by the theory of drama (see chapter 4). A very effective way to begin an analysis of the constituents of a story is to summarise the content of a narrative text, taking the character constellation and the relations of contrast and correspondence (see chapter 4.5.), as well as the division of the story into plot segments and sequences as the main points of departure.

'How sentences become characters (and narrated worlds)'

Although characters in narrative texts are actually only composed of textual elements, in the course of the reception process they frequently come to resemble real human beings. Reception-oriented and cognitive approaches have concerned themselves with the question of how people, or at least the impression of people, can be constructed by means of words and sentences on a page. Such impressions, which are part or the result of the process of creating aesthetic illusions, are generated not merely by the information contained in the text, but also by the presuppositions and general knowledge of the recipient. The recipient's implicit personality theories play a particularly important part in this process (see GRABES 1978; SCHNEIDER 2000).

Characterisation

Many of the concepts taken from drama theory require considerable modification when they are applied to narrative texts, as the additional level of narrative transmission has to be taken into account. Whereas the terms used to describe character constellations and conceptions (see chapter 4.5.) can be employed without difficulty in the analysis of narrative texts, many of the techniques used to analyse characterisation require some qualification. The terms used to describe explicit and implicit self-commentary and commentary by other characters in drama must be supplemented with categories that allow for further characterisation by the narrator, who frequently contributes diverse kinds of information, commentaries and evaluations to the characterisation, as well as steering the emotional response of the reader towards the various characters during the reception process.

When examining the techniques of characterisation used in a narrative text, our primary consideration must be from which textual speaker the information concerning a character originates. It is important to differentiate here between characterisation by the narrator or by another character. Further distinctions must be made between self-characterisation and characterisation by others, and between explicit and implicit characterisation, that is, whether a feature is directly specified or must be inferred indirectly from a character's behaviour. In addition, we must consider the reliability of the various instances of explicit self-characterisation or characterisation by others. We should bear in mind here that every explicit statement about another character is also an implicit (often subconscious) instance of self-characterisation, as the judgements made by a speaker about another character also enable us to draw conclusions about the speaker's own attitudes and values. We should also take careful note of whether characters express themselves directly (i.e., in direct speech), whether the stream of consciousness of a certain character is presented, and whether we are given information about the appearance and biographical background of a character.

The traditional enterprise of analysing literary characters can be made more precise by employing the concept of 'character perspective' explained in the previous chapter. This term refers to the spectrum of characteristics and attitudes of a particular character, and is composed of three elements: the knowledge of the character, his or her psychological disposition and his or her values and norms. By analogy, we can also consider the 'perspective' of the narrator, as the reader is granted insights into the psychological disposition as well as the values and norms of the narrating character by means of personal statements and attitudes (see chapter 5.5.). In contrast to the terms 'narrative perspective' or 'point of view', which are often used interchangeably with 'narrative situation', the concept of the 'narrator perspective' does not refer to the narrative transmission, but rather to the impressions formed by the recipient concerning the personality of the narrator on the basis of the information contained in the text. The narrator perspective is elucidated primarily through the values and norms adopted by the narrator within the text.

The 'perspective structure of a narrative text' is composed of the various individual perspectives within a text and their relation to one another. In contrast to the perspective structure of dramatic texts (see chapter 4.5.), which consists in the various relationships of contrast and correspondence between all the character perspectives, in the case of narrative texts perspective structure also encompasses the relationship between the norms and value systems of the various characters and the perspective of the narrator. The perspective structure is therefore fundamental to the analysis of such central phenomena as the text's underlying norm and value system and the way in which the emotional response of the reader is steered. The perspective structure is determined by the selection of individual perspectives presented in a text, the quantitative consideration of their number and the qualitative consideration of their variety (for example, the breadth of the social and cultural spectrum covered by the character perspectives), as well as the structure of the ensemble of perspectives (see NÜNNING/NÜNNING 2000).

Story vs. plot

Thanks to the interdependence of characters and action, as explained in chapter 4, characters also function as agents of the action. Various terms are used to describe the superordinate action, composed of the content of the text as a whole. E. M. FORSTER was the first to make the distinction between story and plot, which is now common currency. According to this distinction, the term 'story' is generally used to refer to the chronological sequence of events, without consideration of causal relations. A story is transformed into a plot, however, when the various events are also linked causally and logically to one another. To cite an illustrative example used by FORSTER (1927/1981: 93f.): *"A plot is also a narrative of events* [like the story], *the emphasis falling on causality. 'The king died and then the queen died', is a story. 'The king died, and then the queen died of grief', is a plot."* This two-sentence plot comprises two events, the second of which is causally dependent on the first.

Event

The plot sequence can be divided into segments of varying sizes. The smallest plot unit is known as an 'event', defined in structuralist narrative and drama theory as *"the smallest unit in the composition of the sjuzhet, which cannot be divided any further"* (LOTMAN 1972: 330). Events propel the action onward and bring about changes in the situation of the characters. In his semiotic approach, JURIJ LOTMAN (1972: 332) defines an event as *"the displacement of a character across the boundary of a semantic field"*. As can be seen from FORSTER's example, however, unintentional changes of situation are also classed as events. Yet although occurrences such as the gathering of clouds can be classed as events, a sequence of such occurrences alone does not constitute a narrative text. Narratives always contain agents (characters, or sometimes anthropomorphised, personified figures such as talking animals), who have a choice between diverse courses of action.

Kernels vs. satellites

In order to classify events according to their importance within the plot, ROLAND BARTHES (1966: 9f.) distinguished between 'kernels' or 'cardinal functions' on the one hand and 'catalysts' or 'satellites' on the other. 'Kernels' or 'cardinal functions' (also known as 'nuclei') play a constitutive, propelling role within the plot, and open narrative options. The terms 'catalyst' or 'satellite' refer to those events that merely embellish the central plot sequence and whose omission would not disrupt the logical sequence of the narrative. Events can follow one another in a 'chain', that is, directly on a single narrative level, or can be 'embedded', similar to an interpolated tale or a story within a frame narrative. The concept of the event, although easily applicable to many realist works, becomes problematic when we attempt to apply it to diverse works of modernism, which privilege mental 'events' by focusing on the characters' stream of consciousness (for example, in VIR-GINIA WOOLF's novels), and to many postmodernist works, which focus on the constructed nature of events.

It is also important to consider whether various plot sequences are based on the same deep structures. Particularly well known in this field is VLADIMIR PROPP's systematic investigation of the plot structures of Russian fairy-tales. PROPP demonstrated that these fairy-tales share a common plot structure consisting of 31 invariable elements or 'functions'. The individual functions, which are entitled, for example, 'The hero leaves the house', 'He is subjected to a test', 'The hero and his opponent begin to fight', and so on, do not appear in all fairy-tales; yet those that do occur always appear in the same sequence. As can be observed in, for example, James Bond novels and films, popular literature and films frequently follow such schemata, with only slight variations.

Plot structures and deep structures

As there are frequently considerable similarities between the plots of various texts, attempts have been made to develop plot typologies. An early attempt categorised plots according to types of action, that is, according to the relationship between 'external' and 'internal' action, distinguishing between the 'novel of action' and 'novel of character'. This scheme was later broadened to include the 'plot of thought'. There are now a great number of terms used to describe plots, some of the best known being 'court-ship plot', 'seduction plot', 'initiation plot' and 'quest'. Among the more specific designations are the generation plot and the coming-out-plot or mother-daughter plot (see GUTENBERG 2000).

Plot typologies

A further primary consideration in the analysis of narrative texts is the question of how the plot sequence is divided into strands of narrative. In narrative texts and films we differentiate between single-strand and multi-strand plots. The criteria for such a differentiation include the extent to which characters are divided into separate groups, changes in the character constellation, the juxtaposition of different spatial and temporal levels, changes of scene and the coherence and independence of the various identifiable plot sequences (see NISCHIK 1981).

Single and multiple plots

| | Of particular importance to the analysis of the action of narrative texts are the form of the beginning, the structure of the exposition and the manner in which the narrative is brought to a close. With regard to the numerous ways of structuring the beginning of narrative texts, a fundamental distinction is made between the detailed development of the plot with plenty of introductory and antecedent information, typically commencing with the birth of the protagonist (*ab ovo* beginning), and the launch of the narrative somewhere in the middle of the action (*in medias res*), as well as the analytical structure of beginning with the end of the story and gradually revealing the conditions of its beginning (*in ultimas res*). The exposition includes the information concerning time, place, characters and prehistory which is necessary for an understanding of the plot. Despite the particularities resulting from the fact that narrative texts feature a level of narrative transmission, the basic forms of exposition and giving information at the beginning of a novel correspond to those used in drama. In the novel (as in drama and film) we can therefore differentiate between 'isolated' and 'integrated' exposition (see chapter 4.4.). |

Beginning and exposition of novels

Endings

As in the case of dramatic texts, the primary consideration relating to the techniques for concluding narrative texts is whether the ending is 'closed', with all problems solved and the plot concluded in a logical manner, or whether it is 'open', with the conflict unresolved and the fate of the characters left open. An 'expected ending' occurs when 'poetic justice', or a fair allocation of reward and punishment, is brought to bear upon the characters. When the ending results from the unexpected intervention of an external agency, which has not been involved in the plot up to this point, it is referred to as a '*deus ex machina* ending'.

4 Characteristics of the Three 'Narrative Situations': Categories of Discourse-Oriented Narratology I

Terms for describing narrative transmission

In the following section of the chapter we will discuss the structure of narrative transmission, or the discourse. We will therefore be dealing with diverse aspects of discourse-oriented narratology. The question of how an event is mediated in narrative has probably been discussed more exhaustively than any other element relating to the analysis of narrative texts. The structure of narrative transmission is described as the 'narrative situation' of a text. The examination of the narrative situation is one of the central elements in the analysis of a narrative text, not least because the narrative transmission is one of the constitutive generic features of narrative texts. The term 'narrative situation', sometimes also

An Introduction to the Analysis of Narrative Texts

referred to as 'point of view', is among the most fundamental categories employed in the analysis of narrative texts. All are used to describe the way in which characters, events, plot elements or internal, psychological processes are presented in narrative texts.

FRANZ K. STANZEL's (1979) typological circle featuring 'three typical narrative situations', which describes the various possibilities of structuring the mediacy of narrative, has proven its analytical merit in this area. The typology is based on the three elements 'mode', 'person' and 'perspective', which can be divided further into the oppositions 'narrator/reflector', 'first person/third person' and 'internal perspective/external perspective'. In each of the three narrative situations, one of the poles of the binary opposition associated with it is dominant. The authorial narrative situation is characterised by the dominance of the external perspective; the crucial feature for the first-person narrative situation is an 'identity of the realms of existence of the narrator and of the rest of the characters', and the figural narrative situation is marked by the dominance of the reflector mode.

Stanzel's model of three typical narrative situations

In order to determine which narrative situation is present in a narrative text, we must first investigate the identity and explicitness of the narrator. A further important question is from whose point of view the narrated world is presented. With regard to the identity of the narrator, a significant aspect is whether or not he or she is involved in the action on the same level as the other characters. In order to answer this question, it is important to determine whether the narrated world is presented from the external perspective of the narrator, or from the internal perspective of one of the characters involved in the action.

Criteria for identifying the narrative situation

A narrator is a first-person narrator if he or she is involved in the narrated story. In the first-person narrative situation, events are relayed by a 'narrating I', who takes part in the action in the fictional world as a character or 'experiencing I'. The narrating and experiencing I are the same person, but they are often separated by temporal, and sometimes also moral, distance, as the narrator has gone through a process of reflection and maturation in the meantime. The first-person narrative situation differs from the authorial and figural narrative situations in that the first-person narrator is involved in the fictional events as a protagonist (I-as-protagonist) or a peripheral character (I-as-witness). Some of the typical characteristics of the first-person narrative situation can be found at the beginning of CHARLES DICKENS' *The Personal History of David Copperfield* (1849–50), a *bildungsroman* in which the eponymous hero is explicit about the fact that he is telling his own story:

First-person narrative situation

Example of the first-person narrative situation	*Whether I shall turn out to be the hero of my own life, or whether that station will be held by anybody else, these pages must show. To begin my life with the beginning of my life, I record that I was born (as I have been informed and believe) on a Friday, at twelve o'clock at night. It was remarked that the clock began to strike, and I began to cry, simultaneously.*
Limitations of the first-person narrator	The fact that the first-person narrator is part of the same world as the characters gives rise to a further characteristic of the first-person narrative situation: only the internal processes, thoughts and feelings of the narrating and experiencing I can be related. First-person narrators have no insight into the consciousness of the other characters; they can only surmise what the thoughts and feelings of others may be. First-person narrators are also restricted by the barriers of human cognition and physical limitations in further ways: those first-person narrators who present themselves as eye witnesses and vouch for the fictional accuracy of their account must be present at the scene of the events that they relate. When they are not present, they are reliant on information from other characters. Thus, although first-person narrators are not restricted to recounting only those events that they have witnessed personally, they are usually required to offer a legitimising explanation for accounts of fictional events that they did not personally witness. This means that the source of information must be named, and a plausible explanation given for the narrator's knowledge of the narrated events. A retrospective first-person narrator can generally review the entire past events leading up to the present of the narrating I, but unlike the 'omniscient' authorial narrator he or she is not able to look into the future.
Authorial narrative situation	In contrast to first-person narrators, authorial narrators, like the characteristically covert narrators in figural narrative situations, are situated outside the world of the characters. In the authorial narrative situation, the external perspective generally dominates. Authorial narrators appear as concrete, tangible speakers and present themselves as fictive individuals by means of personal interjections, comments and moral judgements on the events. Further typical features of the authorial narrative situation include addresses to the reader, flashforwards, generalisations and thematisation of the act of narration ('Erzählvorgang'). A good example for this type of narrative situation can be found at the beginning of the third chapter of Book 1 of HENRY FIELDING's novel *The History of Tom Jones. A Foundling* (1749):
Example of the authorial narrative situation	*I have told my reader, in the preceding chapter, that Mr. Allworthy inherited a large fortune; that he had a good heart, and no family. Hence, doubtless, it will be concluded by many that he lived like an honest man, owed no one a shilling, took nothing but what was his own,*

kept a good house, entertained his neighbours with a hearty welcome at his table, and was charitable to the poor, i. e., to those who had rather beg than work, by giving them the offals from it; that he died immensely rich and built an hospital.

And true it is that he did many of these things; but had he done nothing more I should have left him to have recorded his own merit on some fair freestone over the door of that hospital. Matters of a much more extraordinary kind are to be the subject of this history, or I should grossly misspend my time in writing so voluminous a work; and you, my sagacious friend, might with equal profit and pleasure travel through some pages which certain droll authors have been facetiously pleased to call The History of England.

A further difference between the authorial and the first-person narrator is that the authorial narrator is generally accredited with omniscience and omnipresence. These two, somewhat misleading, terms cover a large collection of privileges, which frequently characterise the authorial narrator, and which can be defined as follows:

Privileges of the authorial narrator

- the psychological privilege of insight into the internal processes of all characters and familiarity with their thoughts and feelings;
- the spatial privilege of invisible and fictive omnipresence, which includes presence in all places where characters are alone, as well as presence in several locations simultaneously;
- the temporal privilege of being able to survey the entire course of narrative events in the past, present and future.

Two dominant features are characteristic of figural narration. Firstly, in contrast to first-person and authorial narrators, in figural narrative situations the narrator generally recedes so far into the background that the traces of narrative transmission are barely noticeable. Secondly, the narrated world is presented from the perspective of a character who is involved in the action, a 'reflector', who functions as a medium or centre of orientation, whose perceptions and internal processes play a central role in determining what is narrated. In the figural narrative situation, the representation of subjective impressions and internal processes takes the place of accounts of events or action. The figural narrative situation therefore gives the reader the impression of having a direct insight into the sensory impressions and consciousness of the perceiving, thinking or feeling character. Whereas an authorial narrative situation features events presented from the external perspective of the superordinate narrator, then, in the figural narrative situation the internal perspective predominates. The term 'figural' refers not to the narrator, who is situated 'above' or

Figural narrative situation

'outside' the world of the characters, but to the reflector or 'centre of consciousness', i. e. the character from whose sensory or internal perspective the events are presented. The beginning of VIRGINIA WOOLF's novel *Mrs. Dalloway* (1925), in which the reader is plunged directly without any authorial exposition into the experiential perspective of the protagonist, is a typical example of a figural narrative situation.

Example of figural narrative situation

Mrs. Dalloway said she would buy the flowers herself. For Lucy had her work cut out for her. The doors would be taken off their hinges; Rumpelmayer's men were coming. And then, thought Clarissa Dalloway, what a morning – fresh as if issued to children on a beach.

What a lark! What a plunge! For so it had always seemed to her when, with a little squeak of the hinges, which she could hear now, she had burst open the French windows and plunged at Bourton into the open air. How fresh, how calm, stiller than this of course, the air was in the early morning; like the flap of a wave; the kiss of a wave; chill and sharp and yet (for a girl of eighteen as she then was) solemn, feeling as she did, standing there at the open window, that something awful was about to happen […].

Storytelling frame vs. viewing frame

The figural narrative situation conveys an entirely different impression from that created by the first-person and the authorial narrative situations. The latter two narrative techniques share the important similarity that, in both cases, the reader is given the impression of being told a story by a clearly identifiable speaker. As the act and process of narrating are foregrounded, the resulting cognitive schema is described as the 'storytelling frame', and typically creates the illusion of the presence and proximity of an individualised narrator who is telling a story and addressing a listener. The reflector mode of the figural narrative situation, in contrast, gives the reader the impression of following the events through the eyes or experiential perspective of one of the characters. Rather than creating the illusion of an individualised narrator, therefore, the text conveys the impression of immediate access to the perceptions and internal processes of a character. These cognitive frames of seeing, perceiving or experiencing are described as *"viewing frames"* (FLUDERNIK 1996: 345) or as a *"script of experiencing"* (FLUDERNIK 1993: 449). They represent the true hallmark of the reflector mode that is so characteristic of the figural narrative situation: *"[R]eflectoral narration […] structures narration around the script of experiencing or viewing, rather than telling events."* (ibid.). The two excerpts cited below – from the beginning of J.D. SALINGER's hugely popular bestseller *The Catcher in the Rye* (1951) and from ANITA BROOKNER's novel *Hotel du Lac* (1984) – should serve to illustrate the difference between the storytelling frame and the viewing frame:

If you really want to hear about it, the first thing you'll probably want to know is where I was born, and what my lousy childhood was like […] and all that David Copperfield kind of crap, but I don't feel like going into it.

| **Example of storytelling frame** |

Slightly more alert by now, she looked round the room, but there was little to see; the grey men were still absorbed in their conversation; two young couples, from the town, obviously, having a night out, had been placed near the windows, overlooking the invisible garden.

| **Example of viewing frame** |

Diverse hybrid forms exist, particularly between the authorial and figural narrative situations, whereas examples of combinations of the first-person and the authorial narrative situations are much rarer. The various intermediate stages between the authorial and the figural narrative situations can be classified according to the extent to which the narrator appears as speaker, as well as according to whether the external or internal perspective dominates in the presentation of the characters. Many novels begin with an authorial exposition, but then in the course of the narrative the narrator recedes gradually into the background to be replaced by one (or several) reflector(s). An example of a first-person narrator with authorial features can be found in the form of the talkative hero of LAURENCE STERNE's unique novel *The Life and Opinions of Tristram Shandy, Gentleman* (1759–67).

| **Hybrid forms** |

Narrative techniques are not atemporal, ideal types. They are historically determined and, like the choice of narrative theme, are subject to historical change. This is particularly evident when we examine the historical development of the narrative situations outlined above. The novels and narrative texts composed from the 16th through to the 19th century predominantly feature first-person and authorial narrative situations. Two models based on these two narrative techniques remained influential into the 20th century: firstly, the model of the fictional autobiography, based on the first-person narrative situation, the most famous early example of which is DANIEL DEFOE's novel *Robinson Crusoe* (1719); and secondly, the model of the authorial narrative situation introduced in England in the mid-18th century by HENRY FIELDING, which recurred in countless English and American novels of the 18th and 19th centuries. With the exception of certain important forerunners such as the novels of JANE AUSTEN, which were published in the early 19th century, the figural narrative situation developed out of the authorial narration at the end of the 19th century. The techniques of first-person and authorial narration, which predominated in the Victorian novel, and which correspond to the traditional 'telling' mode, were replaced in modernism by impersonal and scenic methods of representation (the 'showing' mode). The development of new modes for representing conscious-

| **Historical development of the narrative situation** |

ness was sparked by scepticism concerning the idea of the 'omniscient' narrator, as well as by the growth of interest in psychology (see chapter 5.6.).

Narrative situation and perception of reality

Investigation of the narrative situation can yield interesting insights into the representation of reality in narrative literature. Narrative techniques evolve from social and philosophical assumptions and serve to give expression to particular perceptions of reality, which are themselves subject to historical change. A brief glance at certain tendencies in the historical development of the typical kinds of narrative situation should serve to illustrate this. Numerous 18th-century novels feature a first-person narrator who guarantees the supposed authenticity of the narration, as he or she is reporting from personal experience. The omnipresence and omniscience characteristic of the authorial narrator, who stands apart from the action, suggest a belief in an ordered universe and in the possibility of explaining and evaluating human behaviour by reference to generally applicable criteria. The figural narrative situation characteristic of many modern novels, however, in which the narrated world is presented from the perspective of a reflector who is involved in the events of the narrative, can be considered the literary expression of an altered experience of reality (see chapter 5.6.). In addition to identifying and describing techniques of representation, we should therefore also consider the various functions performed by these techniques and the perception of reality to which they bear witness within a particular literary work.

Repertoire of other narrative forms

There are naturally many more possible ways of turning a story into a narrative text than the 'three typical narrative situations'. In what follows, a short description will be given of the most important among the broad repertoire of alternative narrative models.

Second-person narration

In addition to narratives in the first and third person, which are characteristic of the figural and authorial narrative situations, some texts are also narrated in the second person. These are described as 'second-person narratives'. *"The model of second-person narration has now been generally accepted as the use of the second-person pronoun throughout the text to address a character who is involved in the events of the narrative. This technique has far-reaching consequences for the character's relationship with the* histoire *and the narrating persona, and therefore enables a subtly disorienting address to the reader that fosters his or her involvement in the plot."* (WIEST-KELLNER 1999: 12) Examples of this technique include such diverse works as EDNA O'BRIEN's rites of passage novel *A Pagan Place* (1970) and SUNETRA GUPTA's novel *The Glassblower's Breath* (1993).

Novels that for the greater part avoid narrative transmission and consist almost entirely of conversations between the characters reported in direct speech are referred to as 'dialogue novels'. The novels of Ivy Compton-Burnett (1884–1969), who, thanks to her unconventional narrative style, is often credited with the 'invention' of the dialogue novel, are characterised by a relative scarcity of action and by stylised dialogues between the characters, which constitute the greater part of the text. The narrator's contributions are restricted to attributing comments to speakers and giving information on the spatial and temporal context and on the characters' body language.

Dialogue novels

The influence of film is clearly manifest in the camera-eye technique developed by Christopher Isherwood (1904–1986) and Ernest Hemingway (1899–1961). This technique, which is explained by the first-person narrator at the beginning of Isherwood's novel *Goodbye to Berlin* (1939), conveys the impression that the narrator functions as a passive observer: *"I am a camera with its shutter open, quite passive, recording, not thinking. Recording the man shaving at the window opposite and the woman in the kimono washing her hair. Some day, all this will have to be developed, carefully printed, fixed."* Despite the alleged authenticity and proximity to reality of the camera, the choice of *sujet*, camera setting and the subjective interpretations offered on the events of the narrative demonstrate that the camera-eye technique is by no means a neutral or even 'objective' representation of reality, and that the idea that such a representation can be offered by narrative texts or even by film is an illusion (see chapter 6.6.).

Camera-eye technique

As the example of the camera-eye technique demonstrates, the new media have considerably influenced the development of new narrative forms. A prime example is the experimental novel *Ulverton* (1992) by Adam Thorpe, which not only crosses generic boundaries, but also traces historical changes in systems of recording experience by switching between different forms of narration, which are modelled on different media. Each chapter of this novel represents a mode of experiencing and recording reality which is specific to a different historical period, with the last chapter taking the form of the post production script of a documentary film. By means of intermedial references, such novels provide a fictional demonstration of the effect of technical media, such as photography, typewriters, radio and film, and their specific modes of storing and processing data, on the perception and narrative presentation of reality.

New media, new narrative forms

⑤ The Structure of Narrative Transmission: Categories of Discourse-Oriented Narratology II

Genette's structuralist taxonomy	One of the most important contributions to discourse-oriented narratology in terms of terminology and systematization is GÉRARD GENETTE's (1980) structuralist taxonomy, which has since been further developed by other theoreticians. GENETTE replaces traditional terminological pairs such as the first-person narrator/third-person narrator with a systematic grid of analytical categories. Some time must be invested in order to be able to recognise and employ these terms, which were coined by GENETTE himself, but they provide clearly defined, differentiated and comprehensive models for describing the most important aspects of narrative texts.
Narration vs. focalization	A solution to the terminological and methodological problems arising from the imprecise terms 'narrative situation' and 'point of view' was supplied by GENETTE in the form of his distinction between 'narration' and 'focalization'. In making this distinction, GENETTE proceeded from the realisation that no typology based on the category of the point of view can provide a precise analysis of the narrative transmission of a text, as it will be unable to differentiate between the narrator and those observers from whose perspective the fictional world is represented.
'Who speaks?' and 'Who sees?'	In order to identify the narrative situation and the point of view of a narrative text, we must answer a number of questions. Firstly, 'Who speaks?', or 'Who narrates?'; secondly, 'Who sees?', or 'From whose perspective is the fictional world presented?'. Whilst the question 'Who speaks?' refers to the speaker who functions within the text as the narrating subject, 'Who sees?' refers to the question of the perspective from which the fictional events are presented (see GENETTE 1980: 186). The verb 'see' should not be understood in a purely literal sense, however, as it here refers to all sensory processes, as well as the processes of thinking, feeling and remembering. More recent studies of narrative texts therefore differentiate between those aspects related to the narration of a text, and those related to the focalization or refraction of the narrated world through the perspective of the observing or experiencing subject.
Narrator vs. focalizer	This terminological differentiation takes into account the fact that the narrator and focalizer perform different functions: narrating and perceiving or experiencing. The narrator gives a linguistic account of a fictional world. The focalizer, however, who corresponds to STANZEL's 'reflector', functions as a psychological centre of orientation through whose perceptions and consciousness the fictional events are filtered.

The distinction between narration and focalization also enables us to divide the process of analysing the point of view and the structure of narrative transmission into a number of easily comprehensible steps. The analysis of the structure of narrative transmission is based on the classification of various types of narrators and focalizers.

Structure of narrative transmission

When attempting to analyse and differentiate between narrating instances, we must begin by distinguishing between the various levels of a narrative text. The first question to be answered relates to the level of communication on which the speaker is located. 'Extradiegetic narrators' are located on the level of the narrative transmission and, together with the fictive addressee, constitute the narrative process. The term 'intradiegetic narrator', on the other hand, refers to those characters who are part of the narrated story and are located on the level of the story. However, it could be argued that the term 'narrator' is itself not entirely adequate when referring to characters who happen to narrate something to other characters on the level of the action. Perhaps we should instead refer to such characters as 'narrating characters', and reserve the term 'narrator' or 'narrating instance' for the instance which operates at the level of the narrative transmission.

Extradiegetic vs. intradiegetic narrators

If the narrator appears as a character within his own story, he or she is referred to as a 'homodiegetic narrator', a term that correlates with STANZEL's 'first-person narrator'. This is a difficult, but less confusing term than 'first-person narrator' because, as we have seen in the example for the authorial narrative situation, authorial narrators quite often refer to themselves as 'I' as well. A 'heterodiegetic narrator', by contrast, is located outside the narrated world. The critical question here is whether the narrator is one and the same as a character in the narrated world – whether he or she is personally involved in the story as a character. A homodiegetic narrator who is identical with the main protagonist and narrates his or her own life story, instead of being just an observer or witness, is known as an 'autodiegetic narrator'.

Heterodiegetic vs. homodiegetic narrators

In addition, narrating instances can be differentiated according to how explicitly they appear in a narrative text as speaker. The fundamental criterion here is to what extent the presence of a narrator can be discerned within the text. The degree to which a narrating instance is individualised can vary considerably. If a narrator appears on the level of the narrative transmission as an individualised speaker and concrete persona, he or she is described as an 'overt' (or 'explicit') narrator (see CHATMAN 1978). The reader is encouraged to attribute personal characteristics and value judgements to such a speaker. If, however, narrating instances take the form of anonymous voices, about which the readers are

Overt vs. covert narrator

given no information, then they are described as 'covert' (or 'neutral') narrators.

Fictive reader or narratee

An overt narrator generally speaks directly to a fictive reader, and consequently is often complemented by an equally overt narratee, who is also articulated in the text. This addressee is, like the narrator, a textual construct, which can considerably influence the reception process. An unidentifiable 'covert narratee', on the other hand, is generally the correlate of the covert narrator.

Functions of the covert narrator

The degree of explicitness of a narrating instance can also be determined by studying the functions that it performs. Generally, the functions of covert narrators are restricted to the neutral transmission of information about the constituent parts of the narrated world (i.e., time, place, characters and action). By describing the location and chronology of the action, giving expository information on the characters and reporting on the events, covert narrators create fictional worlds. As they serve primarily to provide information, they fulfil only the minimal narrative functions performed by every narrating instance, described by STANZEL (1984: 189) as the *"purely functional manifestations of the [...] narrator"*.

Functions of overt narrators

Overt narrators carry out a number of additional functions (see NÜNNING 1989: 124 or 1997: 342): they offer comments and value judgements on the perspectives and actions of the characters, and make further 'personal' contributions in the form of interpretations and generalising abstractions. With their commentaries, explanations, evaluations and generalisations, overt narrators can give information beyond that relating to the internal processes of the characters, and can establish links between the perspectives and actions of the characters. Overt narrators can also perform three further functions: they can give information about themselves (expressive function), they can address the fictive addressee directly (reader address, or conative function), and they frequently thematize aspects of the act of narration (metanarrative function). The greater the number of functions performed by a narrator, the more manifestly he or she will appear within the text as an individualised speaker.

Unreliable narration

A further important criterion for the differentiation and analysis of narrators within a text, which has consequences for the interpretation of the entire work, is the degree of their reliability, credibility or trustworthiness. Those narrators whose account or interpretation of events gives the reader cause for mistrust are described as 'unreliable narrators'. The reliability of a narrator is compromised most frequently by his or her limited knowledge, emotional involvement in the events and questionable norms or values.

An Introduction to the Analysis of Narrative Texts

Numerous signals for unreliable narration can be given on various levels of communication within a text. They include, for example, explicit contradictions within the narrator's comments, the inclusion of contrasting versions of the same event, discrepancies between the statements and the actions of the narrator, contradictions between the self-characterisation of the narrator and characterisation of the narrator by other characters, and discrepancies between his or her account and interpretation of events. A further signal is the repeated occurrence of subjective comments and addresses to the reader, by means of which the narrator deliberately attempts to manipulate the latter's response. Moreover, the narrator's insistence on his/her own credibility (or lack of credibility), references to memory lapses, a deliberately partisan attitude and various paratextual signals (for example, title, subtitle, preface) can all cause the reader to regard the narrator with scepticism and doubt his or her credibility (see NÜNNING/SURKAMP/ZERWECK 1998). The following citations, taken from the beginnings of EDGAR ALLAN POE's short story "The Tell-Tale Heart" (1843) and IAN MCEWAN's short story "Dead as They Come" (1979), should serve as illustrative examples of the most important textual signals for unreliable narration.

Textual signals for unreliable narration

True! – nervous – very, very dreadfully nervous I had been and am; but why will you say that I am mad? The disease had sharpened my senses – not destroyed – not dulled them. (POE, "The Tell-Tale Heart")

    I do not care for posturing women. But she struck me. I had to stop and look at her. The legs were well apart, the right foot boldly advanced, the left trailing with studied casualness. […] *Very artificial the whole thing, but then I am not a simple man.* (MCEWAN, "Dead as They Come")

Examples of unreliable narration

In addition to these textual signals, the question of whether certain extratextual frames of reference can compromise the credibility of a narrator represents a further important consideration. Among the most important extratextual frames of reference against which the textual world and the credibility of the narrator can be gauged, are general world knowledge, the relevant historical world view, theories of personality, and various socially accepted ideas concerning psychological normality and moral values. Together, these factors constitute the dominant system of norms and values within a society. Whilst, for example, the narrator in MCEWAN's "Dead as They Come" subjectively considers his love of a shop-window manikin as 'normal', his interpretation is at odds with the ideas concerning normality generally accepted in our society.

The role of extratextual frames of reference in identifying unreliable narration

The issue of the gender of the narrator was generally neglected by traditional theories of narrative. With the recent advent of femi-

| The gender of the narrator: feminist narratology | nist narratology, however, the gender of the narrators (and the focalizers), became a matter for consideration in both the approach to and the interpretation of literary texts (for an introduction to narratology at the intersection with feminist and gender studies, see NÜNNING/NÜNNING 2004). |

| Analytical categories for narrators | The following matrix offers a comprehensive overview of the most important analytical categories developed by narratology in order to identify and describe narrating instances. The basic criteria for the classifications appear on the vertical axis, whereas the horizontal axis features the analytical categories based on these criteria. |

Categories for the classification of narrators	Opposite ends of the spectrum	
communication level of the speaker	extradiegetic	intradiegetic
presence on the level of the characters	heterodiegetic	homodiegetic
degree of involvement in the narrated events	not involved	autodiegetic
degree of explicitness	covert (neutral)	overt (explicit)
degree of (un)reliability	reliable	unreliable
gender	female	male

Table 5.1.: Overview of the analytical categories applied to narrators

| Focalization | In contrast to the analytical considerations applied to the narrator, the term 'focalization' is used to refer to the non-verbal perception of the fictional world. It encompasses all perceptive, cognitive and emotional elements within the consciousness of the narrator or the characters, and therefore includes processes such as thinking, feeling and remembering, in addition to sensory perception. |

| Types of focalization | More recent typologies of focalization are based on the level of communication on which the focalizers are located (see RIMMON-KENAN 1983: 71–85). Focalization is 'external' if the focalizing subject is located on the level of narrative transmission and 'internal' if the focalizing subject is located on the same level as the characters, i.e. if the focalizer is part of the story. In cases of external focalization, then, the superordinate narrator and the focalizing subject are one and the same, and are therefore referred to as 'narrator-focalizers'. Internal focalization, on the other hand, refers to the refraction of perspectives that occurs when the characters in the fictional world function as 'character-focalizers'. If the fictional events are perceived consistently from the perspective of one specific character throughout the narrative, this is described as 'fixed focalization'. 'Multiple', or 'variable focalization', on the other hand, occurs when several characters in succession function as reflectors. |

In order to identify the focalizer in a particular text or section of a text, we must generally identify the subject of the verbs of perception, thinking, feeling and remembering. If these verbs refer to the narrator, who is observing the fictional world from a superordinate perspective, the focalization is external. Cases in which the perceptions, thoughts or feelings are attributed to a character, who then functions as an internal focalizer, can be identified by means of proper nouns and personal pronouns in the third-person singular. Further clues as to the identity of the focalizer can often be found in the subject-matter of the internal processes described in the text, as well as in the style used to relate the thoughts and feelings of a character (generally referred to as the 'mind style').

Criteria for the analysis of focalizers

The phenomenon of multiperspectivity is relevant to both narration and focalization, and refers to a form of narrative transmission in which a subject-matter – for example, an event, a period or a character – is presented from two or several different perspectives. Multiperspectivity occurs when the narrative events or the events presented on the level of the characters are recounted in several different versions. Such texts can usually be assigned to one (or more than one) of the following categories: firstly, narratives in which there are two or more narrators on the extradiegetic and/or intradiegetic levels of the narrative, with each narrator presenting the events from his or her own perspective; secondly, narratives in which the story is related from the perspective of two or more focalizers or reflectors; and thirdly, narratives with a narrative structure resembling a montage or collage, in which the observations of the characters are replaced or supplemented by other types of text (see NÜNNING/NÜNNING 2000).

Multi-perspectivity

The unmediated juxtaposition of different perspectives generally creates a broad scope for interpretation in the reception process, and requires the reader to make considerable efforts in order to reach a synthesis. Nonetheless, the technique does not always serve to problematize objectivity. In addition to serving as a reflection of what is known as 'epistemological scepticism', multiperspectivity can perform a variety of functions: the refraction of the story can heighten tension in a narrative (for example, multiple eye-witness accounts in a detective novel); it can serve as a medium for poetological or aesthetic reflection; or it can be used didactically to illustrate a philosophical position.

Functions of multi-perspectivity

6 Representing Consciousness in Narrative

Representation of consciousness	An issue that is closely related to the analysis of the narrative situation and to multiperspectivity is that of the techniques used to present consciousness, or the 'inner world' of the characters. When analysing this aspect, we must examine the way in which the thoughts, feelings, perceptions or memories of the characters are mediated in narrative. Literary narratives have at their disposal a considerably broader repertoire of techniques for representing the consciousness (and even the subconscious) of characters than do drama and film.
Representations of consciousness in the three narrative situations	The way in which the 'inner world' is represented differs from one narrative situation to the next. While in the first-person narrative situation the presentation of internal processes is typically subject to certain restrictions, due to the narrator's participation in the world of the characters, these restrictions do not apply to the authorial and figural narrative situations. Authorial narrators have access to the internal processes of all characters, and frequently analyse and comment on their thoughts rather than merely presenting them. Modes of representing consciousness are generally most highly developed and diverse in the figural narrative situation, whose potential was not fully exploited until the late 19th and, in particular, the 20th century.
Psychological realism	The shift in the history of narrative towards the representation of consciousness is a reflection of the increasing tendency toward psychologization and toward emphasising the subjectivity of experience which are characteristic of modernism. This development culminated in psychological realism and other modernist innovations. The techniques for presenting the 'stream of consciousness' enabled the apparently unmediated representation of a broad variety of sensory impressions and feelings. Illustrative examples of these techniques can be found in novels by various modernist writers, for example, WILLIAM FAULKNER, JAMES JOYCE, DOROTHY RICHARDSON, MAY SINCLAIR and VIRGINIA WOOLF.
Narrative modes for presenting consciousness	Narrative theorists differentiate between a variety of narrative modes for presenting consciousness, based on the degree to which the narrator appears as a mediator within the text. A basic distinction is made between three common *"narrative modes for presenting consciousness in fiction"* (see DORRIT COHN's book, 1978): 'psycho-narration', 'free indirect discourse' (or 'narrated monologue'), and 'interior monologue' (or 'quoted monologue'). These three main modes occur relatively frequently, and can generally be identified on the basis of certain characteristics of form and content, although there are admittedly various hybrid and cross-over types.

The term 'psycho-narration' describes a mode of representing internal processes characterised by a relatively high degree of compression and a high level of narrator participation. As in the case of free indirect discourse, the linguistic criteria are the use of pronouns for the third-person singular and the past tense. In contrast to free indirect discourse, however, in psycho-narration the narrator uses his or her own language (rather than the language of the character) to summarise a character's state of mind. This is illustrated by the following excerpt from HENRY JAMES' *What Maisie Knew* (1897): "*It took few hours to make the child feel that if she was in neither of these places she was at least everywhere else.*" Several hours of insecurity and agitation are thus summarised in one sentence, in which the narrator renders Maisie's style of mind from his own informed and elevated perspective.

Although the mode described as 'free indirect discourse' or 'narrated monologue' bears some formal resemblance to psycho-narration, the two techniques differ in that free indirect discourse attempts to convey the illusion of offering an immediate insight into the perceptions and internal processes of a character. It attempts to create this effect by using loose syntax and including questions, exclamations and other signals of subjectivity. The balance between the respective weight of the narrator and the character whose consciousness is presented can vary; however, the character's thoughts and feelings are generally reported in his or her own language. The following quotation from OSCAR WILDE's *The Picture of Dorian Gray* (1890/91) should serve to illustrate the salient characteristics of free indirect discourse: "*Was it true that the sense could cure it? Innocent blood had been spilt. What could atone for that? Ah! for that there was no atonement.*" Here the character's agitation is rendered in a language close to Dorian's thought processes.

The term 'interior monologue', or 'quoted monologue', refers to a highly mimetic form of presenting consciousness, in which the thoughts and feelings of a character are 'quoted' without any discernable mediating instance. These monologues, which can stretch over pages, aim to create the impression of complete immediacy in their representation of internal processes. In contrast to psycho-narration and to free indirect discourse, the interior monologue, which was first used by the French author EDOUARD DUJARDIN (1861–1949) in his novel *Les Lauriers sont coupés* (1887), makes extensive use of the first-person singular and the present tense. The widely-used expression 'stream of consciousness technique' is somewhat misleading, as the 'stream of consciousness' actually refers to the content of the interior monologue, which is itself only one of several possible modes of presenting consciousness. A rela-

Psycho-narration

Free indirect discourse

Interior monologue

tively extreme example of presenting the stream of consciousness can be found in JAMES JOYCE's novel *Ulysses* (1922), whose concluding chapter consists entirely of a forty-page interior monologue. As can be seen from the following short extract from the end of the novel, the technique is characterised by a number of peculiarities of form and content.

Example of the interior monologue

[...] *and Gibraltar as a girl where I was a Flower of the mountain yes when I put the rose in my hair like the Andalusian girls used or shall I wear a red yes and how he kissed me under the Moorish wall and I thought well as well him as another and then I asked him with my eyes to ask again yes and then he asked me would I yes to say yes my mountain flower and first I put my arms around him yes and drew him down to me so he could feel my breasts all perfume yes and his heart was going like mad and yes I said yes I will Yes.*

Characteristics of the interior monologue

As this example demonstrates, the interior monologue plunges the reader directly into the mental processes of a character. Time, place and the external world are only present as elements of these mental processes, filtered through the perspective of the subject. Among the formal characteristics of the interior monologue are the omission of all verbs of thinking and feeling, the complete removal of any mediating instance from the narrative, the presentation of the character's mental processes in his or her language or 'mind style', grammatical and stylistic idiosyncrasies, as well as elliptical syntax and the omission of punctuation. In terms of content, the interior monologue differs from the other modes of representing consciousness in the directness with which it relates perceptions and mental processes, in the central role played by free association as an organisational principle, in its reduction of linguistic and thematic coherence, as well as in the illusion of immediacy it aims to create.

7 Categories for the Representation of Time and Space

Literary representation of time and space

Time and space are included among the central components of fictional representations of reality. Literary theory has developed a number of categories for the representation of space in a literary work. Although these categories are relatively sophisticated, they are not as systematic as those categories used to analyse the narrative transmission. Representation of time, by contrast, has been analysed in a very detailed and precise manner by narratology.

Categories of representation of time

Analyses of the temporal structure of narrative texts or films generally differentiate between three different aspects: the narrative 'order' of events, the 'duration' or 'speed' of the narration and 'frequency' (see GENETTE 1980).

The category 'order' refers to the various possibilities of arranging the events that constitute a story. In chronological narrative, for example, the order of the narrative corresponds to the natural temporal sequence of the events. This is not the case in anachronic narrative, however, where the chronology can be interrupted by a flashback ('analepsis'), which describes events that occurred before the events currently being depicted in the narrative, or by a flashforward ('prolepsis'), which gives information about events that occur later in the chronological sequence.

Order

'Discourse time' refers to the period of time required in order to narrate or read a text (or to watch a film). The term 'story time', by contrast, denotes the temporal duration of the action that is described in the course of a narrative text or film. It is, in other words, the time that passes within the narrated world.

Discourse time and story time

The main concern when analysing the category of 'duration' is the relationship between discourse time and story time. An instance where there is a match between story time and the time of the discourse is known as a 'scene'; this occurs in dialogue and other forms of 'scenic presentation'. In a 'stretch' or 'slow-down', by contrast, the discourse time is 'stretched' to cover a greater expanse than the story time, whereas a passage where the discourse time or narration of the fictional events is shorter than their duration in the narrated world is known as a 'summary' or 'speed-up'. A period of time that is left out between events is referred to as an 'ellipsis' or 'omission', while 'pauses' in the narration occur when the story time stands still while the discourse time continues. The latter takes place, for example, if the narrator interrupts the progression of the story in order to hold forth about general problems, to comment on the characters' behaviour, or to reflect on the act of narrating. The following table presents an overview of the various relationships that are subsumed under the category of 'duration'.

Duration

	Discourse time	Story time
summary	<	
scene	=	
stretch	>	
ellipsis	0	1
pause	1	0

Table 5.2.: Categories of duration

Categories of duration

The category of 'duration' can also help us to determine which of the typical narrative modes we are dealing with in a particular part of a text (see BONHEIM 1982). Whereas the term 'report' generally refers to a summarising account of a series of events given by

Duration and narrative modes

the narrator, 'descriptions' of fictional spaces or objects and 'comments' by the narrator on fictional events generally bring about interruptions or 'pauses' in a series of events. The 'scenic report' or 'scene', in which the discourse and story times are congruent, generally features direct speech or a detailed description of remarkable events.

Frequency

With regard to the 'frequency' with which events are narrated, we distinguish between three basic possibilities. Individual events can be depicted once ('singulative narration') or several times ('repeating narration'). If an event occurs regularly or several times in a similar manner, but is only narrated once, it is referred to as 'iterative narration', which constitutes a form of summary (see GENETTE 1980: 113–160).

Conceptions of time

The categories of the representation of time discussed above all relate to measurable time. There are, however, other conceptions of time. In many modernist novels, for example, the characters' subjective experience of time, or 'mind time', is more important than the external 'clock time'. By thus privileging the subjective experience of time, modernist novels (for example, by VIRGINIA WOOLF, JAMES JOYCE and WILLIAM FAULKNER) emphasise the discrepancy between the 'time on the clock' and 'time in the mind'. Among the further conceptions of time are 'rhythmic time' and 'cyclical time', the latter of which makes use of, for example, the sequence of seasons. The experimental temporal structures of postmodern novels take into account that time is a social construct, which is relative because it is dependent on the perception of the individual.

Presentation of place/ space

'Place' and 'space' are general expressions which encompass the conception, structure and presentation of such elements as locations and objects, scenery and the natural world within the various genres. 'Place' is used primarily but not exclusively for drama, 'space' primarily but not exclusively for the novel. When analysing the spatial dimension of a fictional story we must firstly consider what kinds of locations, objects, situations and aspects of reality are presented within a narrative text and how they are narratively constructed or reconstructed. A further important consideration is whether the spatial context is described by a heterodiegetic narrator, or whether it is filtered through the perceptions of a character and correspondingly coloured by his or her subjective impressions. The 'setting' of a scene or episode in a drama or novel is its specific location in space and/or time.

Categories of space

Narratological examinations of the representation of space generally focus on three areas: firstly, theories, conceptions and typologies of literary space; secondly, the structure, presentation and poetics of space in the various genres; and, thirdly, the function-alization and semanticization of space in literature (see chapter 4.6.). There is a broad spectrum of possible conceptions of space, ranging between 'closed' and 'open' spatial and temporal structures and between *"abstract neutrality [and] a sharply focussed realistic type of scenic enactment"* (PFISTER 1988: 262).

More recent studies of the representation of literary space draw on diverse theoretical approaches. Some studies are based on the assumption that, as part of the aesthetic illusion created by a text, the constitution of literary space only takes place during the reception process; this principle is also applied to the concept of 'narrative space' in film analysis (see chapter 6.6.). Other approaches stress that every representation of literary space is a constituent part of a fictional model of reality, and that the presentation of scenery, nature and the objective world is an important mode of literary presentation, which fulfils particular functions. We should therefore differentiate between literary spaces and real locations outside the work of art, however close a resemblance the literary representation may bear to historical reality.

Basic
assumptions

A variety of modes can be used to represent space in narrative texts. Among the most common are description, modes of presenting consciousness (narrative situation, focalization) and the use of various figurative tropes, such as metaphor, metonymy and synechdoche (see chapter 3.6.).

Narrative
techniques
for representing space

The consideration that the settings of narratives or films are not merely ornamental, but fulfil a 'narrative function', and that *"spatial opposites are construed as models for semantic opposites"* (PFISTER 1988: 257), is crucial for their interpretation. The way a particular setting is structured, as well as the juxtaposition of different locations (for example contrasts between town and country), can yield important conclusions concerning the semanticization of space. Particular attention should be paid to the boundaries between the various locations within literary spaces, and to the crossing of these boundaries. Literary presentations of space do not, therefore, serve a merely decorative function; like other modes of presentation, they should be regarded as carriers of meaning within complex sign systems, which are subject to change.

Semanticiza-
tion of space

The functions of fictional space also constitute an important analytical and interpretative consideration. In his detailed typology, GERHARD HOFFMANN (1978: 55–108) differentiates between three basic types: 'mood-invested space', in which spaces and objects serve expressive (atmospheric or symbolic) functions; 'space of action', which primarily functions as a context or setting for the action (the locations provide a framework for the characters and

Functions of
space

their actions); and the predominantly static 'observed space', which supplies a panoramic overview.

Further reading on the analysis of narrative

A good overview of the fundamentals and categories of structuralist narrative theory can be found in SHLOMITH RIMMON-KENAN's introductory work *Narrative Fiction: Contemporary Poetics* (1983/2002), MICHAEL TOOLAN's useful book *Narrative: A Critical Linguistic Introduction* (1988/2001), MANFRED JAHN's article "Narratologie: Methoden und Modelle der Erzähltheorie" (1995/1998), and *Einführung in die Erzähltheorie* (1999/2000) by MATIAS MARTINEZ and MICHAEL SCHEFFEL. FRANZ K. STANZEL's *A Theory of Narrative* (1984; German original *Theorie des Erzählens:* 1979) remains a classic. Those who wish to inform themselves in greater depth about recent approaches in narratology and the analysis of narrative texts or about the history of the English and American novel, should consult the information on further reading in the fifth section of the bibliography at the end of the present volume.

6

CHAPTER

An Introduction to the Analysis of Media Genres

What is at stake is not merely a disciplinary facelift, but rather the implementation of the insight that all areas of enquiry within literary studies, without exception, should give adequate consideration to the mediality and intermediality of their subject-matter.

SIEGFRIED J. SCHMIDT

❶ From Literary to Media Studies

Up to this point, we have based our discussion on the implicit assumption that the category 'literature' refers to written texts. Although this assumption naturally holds for the greater part of literary history, such a view of literature is now rather dated. The appearance of new audiovisual and digital media has led to the extension of the category 'literature', and new disciplinary areas devoted to these developments have appeared in English and American studies. Many universities now offer courses in media studies in addition to literary studies.

> **Extension of 'literature' to include audiovisual media**

The development of English and American studies into an inter-disciplinary field incorporating cultural and media studies reflects the fact that we live in a media society. Rather than clinging to the concept of 'high-brow literature', many scholars now adopt a broad conception of culture, which does not privilege 'high-brow culture' or any individual medium. The inclusion of audiovisual media as a subject-matter creates new, productive opportunities for the modernisation of literary studies and their transformation into cultural and media studies.

> **Inclusion of media studies**

Media studies proceed from the assumption that we live in a soci-ety in which not only the entertainment industry, but also knowl-edge and communication, perceptions and feelings, memory and the processing of information, and even the socialisation of the individual, are influenced by the media. The observation and anal-ysis of single kinds of media in media studies always takes into account the development of other kinds, as the proliferation of new kinds of media affects the entire media system as well as the func-tions performed by the individual media (see SCHMIDT 2000).

> **Media studies**

Media studies encompass an extraordinarily broad spectrum of fields of study and areas of enquiry. The areas of study range from the development and modernisation of media, through competi-tion between media and their influence on perception, to media ecology and questions relating to the use and interpretation of

> **Fields and areas of enquiry in media studies**

media (see LUDES 1998). There are also a number of theories devoted to single kinds of media (for example, film and radio theory), as well as overarching media theories concerned with the theory of communication and systems theory (see FAULSTICH 1991).

Focus and objectives of this chapter

Despite the diversity within the discipline, we will focus in what follows on interaction between literature and other media. There are two reasons for this: firstly, the choice of focus results from the simple fact that the present volume is intended as an introduction to English and American literary studies and not as an introduction to media studies. Secondly, theoretical questions relating to media are less relevant to the practice of English studies than the concrete examination of particular media genres. This chapter therefore aims to provide an introduction to the individual areas of enquiry, fields of study, media genres and analytical categories that have emerged from the developments sketched above; it will focus particularly on the areas and issues that have been of interest to English and American studies in the recent past. As this is only intended as a short and illustrative survey, we have included detailed information on further reading in each of the sub-chapters, so that those interested in particular topics and genres can add to their knowledge.

2 Literary Studies and Media History

Interaction between literature and other media

As the example of the 'camera-eye' narrative technique in the previous chapter illustrated, changes in literary genres and literary modes of expression can often only be adequately understood if literature is examined in the context of changes in other media. It would exceed the scope of a short introduction to give an outline of the entirety of media history; we should, however, be aware of the continuous interaction between literature and other media.

Media-oriented interpretations of literature

One literature-centred approach which takes this interaction into account is media-oriented interpretation, which examines literature in the context of media development. This approach investigates the thematization of other media and the relationship between media within literary texts, as well as the influence of technological innovations and the appearance of media such as photography, radio, film and television on literature. Genres such as the literary screenplay, or phenomena such as 'the book of the film' have only appeared since the diversification of the media landscape. The rapid growth of the internet has led to the development of new literary forms such as hypertexts, and the increasing use of video recorders and DVD players has resulted in a *"literarization of film viewing"* (PAECH 1992: 371), meaning that the viewer can now 'read' a film like a book, 'leafing through' and marking particular sequences for another viewing. The technical advances of digitalisation and networking, which are currently thriving in the internet environment, have also opened the door to forms of interactive production, which, at least in their specific areas, change the relationship between author, text and reader and call into question the conception of authorship that has been in currency since the Romantic period. Media-oriented interpretations of literature proceed from the assumption that the content of a message will be determined to some extent by the nature of the media-specific techniques employed in order to transmit it.

From orality to literacy

The importance of the available media in determining the form and content of literature is illustrated by the transition from orality to literacy, whose starting point was HOMER's composition of the *Odyssey* in the 8th century BC. The advent of literacy opened up an array of possibilities for preserving literature as text, although these possibilities were only exploited gradually, due to the persistence of old traditions and the high cost of transcribing or reproducing texts. Literacy resulted in various changes to the form of literary works, for example, the gradual disappearance of (now redundant) memory props such as metre, rhyme and the repetition of formulae. A further consequence was the enlargement of the circle of recipients, which could now include readers from other regions and later periods as well as listeners. The importance of the oral tradition dwindled as that of the technical reproduction of literature grew. The written, and subsequently the printed, word became *"a medium for storing language"* (VOGT 2001: 265).

'Notation systems'

The written or printed word is admittedly not the only medium for storing information and conveying it to a recipient. In the recent past, the status of the printed and written medium has been challenged by increasing numbers of other media. FRIEDRICH KITTLER's analysis of this phenomenon introduced the term 'Aufschreibesysteme' (which literally means 'notation systems') to refer to such institutions or the *"network of technologies and institutions that allow a given culture to transmit, record and process relevant data"* (KITTLER 1990: 369).

Beyond the Gutenberg galaxy

For a considerable period of time, however, printing played such an important and influential part in the transmission of messages that HERBERT MARSHALL MCLUHAN's frequently cited reference to the 'Gutenberg galaxy' is no exaggeration. JOHANNES GUTENBERG's invention of the printing press with movable letters in the 1450s was the starting point of this important development; as a result, books – and, increasingly, also newspapers – could be made accessible to an ever-growing readership. From the early 18th century onwards, a constant interplay between increasing literacy rates, rising school attendance culminating in compulsory schooling from 1880, and escalating supply and demand made book production grow astronomically. Books assumed an important role in the process of socialisation, and printing was instrumental to such processes as scientific development, industrialisation and the formation of national identity. The monopoly of the printing medium began to come to an end in the late 19th century, however, and today, a variety of audiovisual media such as the telephone, radio, film, television, fax and computer all serve to store and transmit information.

Media competition and media convergence

As can be seen from the development of the media, old media are not merely replaced by new. Letters, fax and telephone conversations have not become superfluous now that we also have the possibility of transmitting messages via e-mail or SMS; instead the functions of the older media have been redefined. The format and functions of existing media have been altered by the appearance of new technological possibilities, whilst the new media have been influenced by the old in terms of content. Thus concerts are broadcast on the radio, dramas adapted as films, and films shown on television. As a result of the interdependence between the various kinds of media, an increasingly complex, interlacing contemporary media scene has appeared (see ROLOFF 1995: 270), in which the traditional boundaries can barely be discerned. This is also due to the fact that many authors write for a variety of media, market their products via diverse media and know how to take advantage of these media for the presentation of their public image. The influence of the new media on literature on the one hand and the importance of literature as a source of material and of aesthetic modes of representation on the other has led to a convergence between diverse media forms, particularly literature, theatre and film. This convergence is expressed by the various forms of hybridisation in our contemporary culture.

Hybrid cultures and hybrid forms

Hybrid forms, i. e. combinations of elements from areas that were originally separate, have become an important characteristic of modern culture (see KREWANI 2001). Whether combinations of attributes that are traditionally regarded as male and female, between diverse materials, styles and colours in the fashion industry, or between the private and public spheres in architecture or television, we can find instances of hybridisation in almost all areas of contemporary reality. The tendency towards hybridisation is particularly evident in television, in terms such as 'infotainment' and formulae such as 'reality TV', or magazine programmes that offer a collage of diverse genres and topics. Hybridisation does not stop at national boundaries; the distinction between the British *dramadoc* and the American *docudrama* is becoming increasingly blurred. Thanks to the influence of new media and habits of perception *"the hierarchy of high and low culture* [has been] *displaced* [...] *by the formation of other modes of experience, which exist beside and are* equal in status *to high-brow and low-brow culture"* (SCHNEIDER 1994: 22).

It is also impossible for us to apply the usual literary models to the new genre of internet literature. In 'hyperfictions', or fictional hypertexts that can be found on CD-ROM or the internet, the linearity of the text is dissolved, and the roles of the author and reader have changed by the empowerment of the recipient in the reading process. Unlike the author of a printed book, the author of a hypertext does not dictate the sequence of episodes within the text. The reader is free to decide in what order he or she wishes to read the individual parts of the text, to choose between a variety of alternatives and to decide which options he or she wishes to pursue. The 'text' therefore offers a variety of readings rather than a single story. The most important characteristics of hyperfictions are non-linearity and interactivity; they can also incorporate intermedial features such as images or film excerpts. Interactive cybertexts (such as adventure games, multi-user dungeons, online-fictions) offer even more possibilities for participation. Like hypertexts, such narrative forms offer *"a variety of alternative courses of action, from which the reader/user creates individual situations and worlds"* (MARTINEZ/SCHEFFEL 1999: 132). The empowerment of the recipient in cybertexts has also had an effect on literary works; some dramas by ALAN AYCKBOURN, for example, offer the audience a considerable amount of latitude in deciding how the play will continue (see BERNINGER 2000).

Hypertexts and internet literature

3 Inter-Art Studies/Intermediality: Literature and Other Art Forms

The crossing of boundaries between different genres, art forms and media is a phenomenon of long standing in many national literatures. Lately, however, there has been such a rapid increase in the hybridisation of genres from different media that WERNER WOLF's (1999: 2) use of the term 'intermedial turn' seems highly appropriate. The most striking example of this tendency is probably the phenomenon of virtual reality, made possible by the new media; but references to and the use of conventions from diverse media in art, literature and music have by now become important characteristics of postmodernism. The boom in such boundary crossings has contributed considerably to the increase of activity in the field of 'inter-art studies'.

Intermedial turn and inter-art studies

Inter-mediality

One of the most interesting areas that has come into focus with the inclusion of questions of mediality in English studies is the study of relations between literature and other forms of art such as music, painting, photography, film and television. These areas of study are subsumed under the term 'intermediality'. Although the discipline of literary studies has always encompassed such issues as 'interaction between art forms', the new area of study based on the concept of intermediality is the first to offer a comprehensive, systematic and historical approach to the broad issue of the interaction between literature and other media.

Fields of study

The investigation of various forms and functions of intermediality is not merely of interest for English and American studies; it is also an important field within general and comparative literary studies. Analyses of intermediality are primarily concerned with the question of how literary works react to and incorporate the conventions used in other media. Among the most common topics are the thematization and formal representation of music, painting, photography and film within literature. In addition, intermedial analyses are made of adaptations of literary works in other media, for example, electronic media such as television, radio or video. The various areas of enquiry can be grouped according to the forms of expression and media that are combined in any given case. In what follows, we will be considering relations of interaction and mutual influence between music and literature, art and literature, photography and literature, film and literature as well as the new media and literature.

Music and literature

The study of the interaction between music and literature, which is situated at the intersection of literary studies and musicology, has proved a particularly productive area within intermediality. It focuses on the ways in which poems, novels and other genres render the conventions of representation specific to music, and on the ways in which music incorporates references to literature. Three main areas of enquiry can be identified: literature in music (for example, programme music), combinations of music and literature (for example, vocal music), and thematic and formal references to music in literature (for example, the thematization of music and musicians, verbal music, word music, formal and structural parallels with music) (see ZIMA 1995: 69).

Music in literature

Music can appear in literature in a variety of ways: musical notations, the thematization of musical works, composers or musicians and covert intermedial interaction between the two genres. 'Word music', for example, is based on the verbal imitation of acoustic characteristics and the acoustic qualities of words. Formal and structural parallels with music in literature, based on the imitation of specific techniques of musical composition (for example, the *leitmotif*) or on the structure of particular musical genres (for example, the sonata) are rather more difficult to identify. The term 'verbal music' refers to the evocation of particular musical works by means of the aforementioned techniques or by the representation of individual reactions to performance. A survey of the diverse ways in which music can be rendered in literature is given by WOLF in his pioneering study *The Musicalization of Fiction* (1999).

Musical settings of literature

Settings of literature, i.e. adaptations of poems to music, are a combination of music and literature, and fall into the category of vocal music. There are diverse varieties of settings, some of which accord equal value to both components, whilst others allow one component to dominate. As far as the poetry of Antiquity and the Middle Ages is concerned, one usually thinks of word and music as inextricably connected. This connection can be seen in the activities of the so-called 'minnesingers', and their vocal performance of lyrics which were subdivided into verses and stanzas. This unity of words and music was replaced in the Early Modern period by the setting of texts which were first recorded in writing. This type of setting culminated in the form of opera established in Florence around 1600. These performances were based on dramatic texts written specially for musical adaptation; less frequently, prose texts were set to music

Rock, pop and folk as paradigms of popular culture

A phenomenon that is also located at the intersection of literature and music, and which has attracted increasing amounts of attention over the last thirty years, is that of popular music. This genre includes the rock, pop and folk music produced since the 1960s, as well as the various forms of rap and hip hop. This area of English and American media and cultural studies represents a central phenomenon in popular culture, and is of particular interest to studies in intermediality, as many of the texts of pop songs can be described as *"modern (mass) poetry"* (FAULSTICH 1978: 62). When analysing these texts, we should not focus exclusively on an interpretation of the language, but also compare the results of this investigation with those of musical analysis. The latter includes such categories as rhythm (with beat as a means of emphasising elements), melody and harmony, as well as sound (see ibid.: 32–60). The production and marketing strategies are also important considerations, particularly in the case of pop music, where the media presentation and star cult are central features of the industry.

Art and literature

There are also diverse varieties of interaction between literature, painting and other graphic arts. Structural correspondences exist between various artistic and literary procedures (for example in the case of the collage). There are also frequent instances of coincidental convergence between art and literature when artists and authors react to specific cultural topics and incorporate similar perspectives and motifs into their works, although there is no evidence of direct interaction. Images can also be based on texts – for example representations of biblical or mythical material or historical paintings based on works of historiography – and art can be adapted in literature in a variety of ways. Descriptions of images ('ekphrasis') play a significant role in some contemporary literature, for example in MICHAEL FRAYN's novel *Headlong* (1999) or PETER ACKROYD's *Chatterton* (1987), in which the representation and interpretation of fictive and real paintings have an important function. There is also a long tradition of text-image combinations; 'emblems', consisting of a title, an image and a short text describing the image and its relation to the title, were particularly popular in the Early Modern period. The relationship between illustration and text in novels is subject to numerous variations: text and image can complement each other, or one can serve as an interpretative key for the other. In that respect, comics, for instance, present a particularly interesting area of investigation (see SCHÜWER 2002).

Photography and literature

The relationship between photography and literature is structurally similar to that between painting and literature. Photography can also adapt literary material, and literature can incorporate references to photography. In some novels, for example ANITA BROOKNER's *Family and Friends* (1985), the description of a few photographs even determines the content and structure of the work. Combinations of the two art forms became popular with the photonovel, and photographs have been used as illustrations since the mid-19th century. The specific characteristics of the relationship between the two art forms are in part a result of the particular nature of photography: photographs give the impression of representing immediate reality, although they in fact always depict past realities. Thanks to its precise and detailed reproduction of its object, photography, which was initially considered an extremely objective medium, has served as a model for narrative forms of representation in realistic and naturalistic novels. Photography also raised awareness among authors of the possibility of rendering visual perceptions in writing, and led to new forms of representation in literature such as the description of visual impressions in novels by HENRY JAMES.

Film and literature

The interaction between film and literature represents a further area of study in the theory and history of intermediality. One of the most important areas of investigation within this field concerns changes of media, i.e. the transferral of a work from one medium to another. This area includes film adaptations of literature, whether in the form of a more or less creative adaptation of a novel or drama, or a recording of a theatre performance, as well as instances of 'literarization' of films, such as the 'book of the film'. Another interesting topic within this area is the 'multimedial transposition' of material by one or several authors; illustrative examples are JOHN IRVING's adaptation of the material for *The Cider House Rules* as a novel (1985) and then screenplay (1999), or the adaptation of H. G. WELLS' novel *The War of the Worlds* (1897) as a radio play, feature film and television film. The second area of intermedial analysis focuses on the adaptation of individual motifs or structural techniques from film in the medium of literature, and vice versa. We have already given some examples of literary adaptations of filmic techniques (see chapter 5.4.); however, films have also exploited literary procedures. One of the great early film makers, DAVID W. GRIFFITH, claimed to have taken the narrative structure of his films (i. e., his editing techniques) from the novels by CHARLES DICKENS. A third area of investigation has been opened by various structurally-oriented studies, which undertake comparative analyses of the characteristics of filmic and literary codes and the conditions of production and reception specific to the two art forms.

Screenplays

Screenplays or film scripts, which frequently exist in numerous versions corresponding to the various stages of their genesis, are located at the intersection of filmic and literary analysis. The characteristics of the genre, which began to appear in print in the 1980s, result from their functional character: screenplays serve as the basis for a film, although they differ from dramas in that they are written with only one performance in view. As a result of the specific characteristics of the film, the dialogue is often of less importance than in drama, whilst detailed stage directions (descriptions of the setting, narrative perspective, camera settings) are more important. Despite the descriptions and directions, whose translation into images generally requires considerable cinematic skill and imagination, it is necessary to compare the screenplay and the end product, as directors frequently add, modify or omit elements. Additional cuts or changes may also be required by the broadcaster or production company. A distinction is generally made between such functional screenplays and literary screenplays, which are published after major cinematic successes, for example MARC NORMAN's and TOM STOPPARD's *Shakespeare in Love* (1998).

Film adaptations of literature

If only in quantitative terms, film adaptations of literature represent an important area of investigation, as they have, at certain points in time, constituted up to 50% of all feature films produced. The criterion of 'fidelity to the original', which always appeared in studies of film and dramatic adaptations in the past, is no longer considered a desideratum; filmic adaptation is now regarded as a creative process: *"the director has the opportunity to shine in the creativity of the transformation, the tension and discrepancy between text and image, rather than the proximity to the literary source"* (ROLOFF 1995: 305). The issue of the appropriateness of the adaptation has been replaced by *"the question of what media texts do with specific elements or concepts from the 'original' text"* (J. E. MÜLLER 1996: 17). The nature of the transformation is influenced not only by the director's 'signature', the preferences of the producers and the prospective cast, but also by the genre of film (for example, Western, thriller, melodrama, comedy) to which the adaptation is related. Intermedial analyses of literary adaptations are concerned not only with the content of a film, but also with various formal aspects such as character constellation, narrative perspective, spatial and temporal structure, dialogue, the distribution of the sections of narrative, as well as means of creating distance or an alienation effect (see ROLOFF 1995: 291).

Film adaptations of English classics

The film adaptations of novels by JANE AUSTEN und E. M. FORSTER demonstrate the lasting popularity of film adaptations of English classics. A number of other recent adaptations have been box office hits, for example the film adaptations of such Booker prize-winning novels as THOMAS KENEALLY's *Schindler's Ark* (*Schindler's List*, directed by STEVEN SPIELBERG, 1993), KAZUO ISHIGURO's *The Remains of the Day* (directed by JAMES IVORY, 1993) and, most significantly, MICHAEL ONDAATJE's *The English Patient* (directed by ANTHONY MINGHELLA), which won nine Oscars in 1996.

Other literary adaptations

The popularity of film adaptations of literature can cause us to overlook the sheer breadth of the spectrum of literary adaptations. The expression 'literary adaptation' refers to the transferral of a literary work into another medium. Narrative texts are frequently adapted for the theatre or opera, for musicals, radio, television or video; however, dramas, poems and radio plays are also frequently adapted to other media and types of performance. Nowadays, when analysing film and other literary adaptations, we no longer apply the criterion of fidelity to the original; instead we focus on the complex interaction between the different works and art forms. Although the expression 'literary adaptation' has become common currency, analyses are now increasingly using the term 'transformations' and stressing the intermedial nature of their approach.

4 New Media – New Media Genres

The study of the relationship between literary and media studies is by no means restricted to the various aspects of intermediality that are focused on literary texts. There are also a great number of other fields in which perspectives and angles of enquiry from media studies can give new impetus to literary studies. These perspectives and areas are related primarily to the wide variety of media genres that have emerged as a result of the rapid proliferation of audiovisual and digital media.

Media and literature

In addition to the diversification of genres of print media (here we need only think of the variety of genres in the field of journalism alone!) there has also been an increase in the variety of media genres in the field of acoustic and audiovisual media. It is true that mass media such as television are somewhat hesitant to exploit the potential for new genres opened up by technical innovation, preferring instead to invest their time and money in familiar genres such as the sitcom, docudrama and talk show. Nevertheless, more than 900 different generic designations of television programmes can be found in television magazines. The fact that the approximately 500 generic terms used habitually by television audiences do not completely correlate with those in the magazines is indicative of the difficulty of giving clear definitions of individual media genres. However, some criteria for a generic classification of individual programmes remain; the following list details a few of them (see S. J. SCHMIDT 1994: 189f.):

Diversity of media – diversity of media genres

- **medium**: print medium; acoustic medium; audiovisual medium
- **main function of medium**: report; reflection; appeal; game; reproduction (each to an informative and/or a recreational end)
- **relation of medium to reality**: with reference to people: credible/not credible (for example, news reader versus emotional witness); with reference to statements: true/false, factual/non-factual, fictitious; with reference to time: live, recorded or anticipatory presentation
- **thematic specifics**: thematizing a milieu (for example, hospital, drug scene); topic-/story-oriented (for example, crime, sport)

The various categories of media genres also perform a variety of additional functions, for example, they

Functions of media genres

- *guide the expectations of media users with regard to the relation of a medium to reality as well as with regard to the cognitive and*

emotional gratification derived from the use of media [for example, excitement, entertainment, education];
- *guide the expectations of media users with regard to the reliability and credibility of the communicating parties*
- *guide expectations as to whether a medium of communication best serves instrumental (for example, a news programme) or expressive (for example, a literary TV film) purposes*
- *divide the content of media into categories such as report, appeal, reflection, game or reproduction.* (Schmidt/Weischenberg 1994: 219)

In short, media genres serve to guide the recipient; they awake certain expectations and facilitate the recognition, classification and evaluation of different varieties of media presentations.

Theory of media genres

The theory of media genres is concerned with three main areas of investigation: genre designations, the expectations these awake in the individual user, and the effects and functions of employing a genre classification (see SCHMIDT/WEISCHENBERG 1994: 213). The most important questions asked in research on genre theory are the following: *"What is the relationship between the individual work and the genre? How can we explain changes in the generic system of a society? Why do new genres emerge? What is the relationship between generic concepts and genre designations?"* (ibid.: 220) More recent research into the theory of media genres is therefore less concerned with the identification and definition of genres, than with the function that they perform for the individual and within society.

⑤ Aspects of Radio Play Analysis

Particularities of the genre

Since its inception in the 1920s, the British and American radio play or radio drama has succeeded in establishing itself as a new media genre. Equating the British radio play with the German *Hörspiel* can cause some confusion, as there are permeable boundaries between the British and American 'radio play', the predominantly factual 'feature', and the entertaining 'radio show', the latter of which is entirely oriented towards the peculiarities of the medium. However, some characteristics can be identified that allow us to differentiate between the radio play and other literary genres; these characteristics are related primarily to the acoustic transmission of the radio play (by radio in the first place, subsequently by sound-carriers such as cassettes and CDs). Sounds, and their absence, are therefore the main modes of expression in the radio play. The acoustic dimension is a far more important factor in the reception of the radio play than in that of drama, because a very small number of radio plays (less than 1%) appear in print.

Due to this exclusively acoustic reception, which does not allow the addressee to leaf back, important statements within the play are frequently emphasised by means of music, background noise or repetition, although many of these techniques, and repetition in particular, would appear superfluous or even redundant to the reader of a radio play. As in the case of the other mass media, film and television, the requirements of the medium cause a tension between the two fundamental aims of the radio play, *"the aim of developing into an artistic genre, a mode of expression equal to elevated forms of literature, and the goal of reaching as many listeners as possible, as a genre of the mass medium radio"* (THOMSEN/SCHNEIDER 1985: 4).

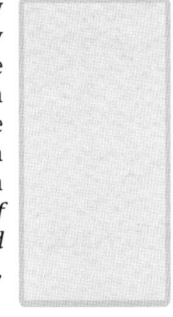

The majority of areas of enquiry in the analysis of radio plays focus not only on the spoken text, but also on the aforementioned characteristics that are specific to the medium and genre. The following table offers an overview of the various components of the radio play (see FRANK 1981: 78–100):

	Areas of enquiry in the analysis of radio plays

Word	in addition to denotative and connotative meaning, the capacity of the individual word to evoke images, and the acoustic quality of the word as a component of phonological tropes
Voice	serves to differentiate between individual speakers and types of speaker (by means of sociolect, dialect and information on the character), to express subjective emotions and evoke a particular atmosphere
Music	functions as a marker for internal organisation (for example, by signalling boundaries between scenes) and as a leitmotif; serves to accentuate details; also functions as an atmospheric soundtrack and sometimes also to evoke certain actions and events
Noise	employed as a marker for internal organisation and as a leitmotif; guides the listener and attunes him or her to the context of the action (background noise); sometimes used surrealistically
Silence	serves to express pauses of a grammatical or psychological nature in the dialogue; signals actions (which are presumably taking place during the pause); serves as a means of influencing audience response (heightening suspense or, in the case of an imaginative pause, giving the opportunity to visualise and digest content)
Stereophonic sound	acoustic quality which indicates the size of a space; changes in sound quality are used as a guide for the audience
Distance	used together with stereophonic sound in order to create an impression of authenticity by indicating movement; also employed to construct narrative perspective and in cuts between scenes
Radiophonic effects	sound effects produced with the aid of technical equipment, for example, 'telephone voices' produced with the assistance of a frequency filter or changes produced by accelerating or slowing the playback speed of a recording

Table 6.1.: Components of the radio play and their functions

Further reading

ARMIN PAUL FRANK's book *Das britische und amerikanische Hörspiel* (1981) is a very informative introduction to the peculiarities of the radio play. A standard companion to this genre is the volume *British Radio Drama* (1981), edited by JOHN DRAKAKIS, which can be supplemented with the interpretations of select radio plays in *Das englische Hörspiel* (1977), edited by HORST PRIESSNITZ.

6 Aspects of Film and Television Analysis

'Super-medium' audiovision

Although nowadays audiovisual media have an immense influence on our view of reality and experience as well as the process of socialisation, and although almost every child is able to use a television set (and perhaps even programme a video recorder) before he or she learns to read and write properly, the analysis of film and television has only gradually established itself as a field of English and American studies. In what follows, we group together many of the categories used in the analysis of film and television, because there are numerous parallels between films produced for the cinema, the television and video. In addition, many authors, directors and actors are active in all three genres. Indeed, the three media are so closely connected that they are sometimes placed under the umbrella category of a 'supermedium' called 'audiovision'. However, we should be careful not to overlook the particularities of each medium, which result primarily from differences in production mode: television and video are both produced electronically, while those films shown in the cinema are for the greater part still the outcome of a cinematic production process.

Television play

The 'television play' (or 'television drama') can serve to illustrate the many changes undergone by media genres under the influence of technical innovations and competition from other types of media. In the 1950s, the early days of nation-wide broadcasting, television plays were produced 'live', and this was initially seen as the main characteristic of the genre. The use of a studio set and the resulting presentation of interior spaces was to a degree dictated by technical factors, as the heavy cameras were not very mobile. Long takes were preferred, as editing was more cumbersome and technology did not allow the director to check on results and continuity in the course of filming. Although the action was followed by many cameras simultaneously and changes were made between cameras, this form of production was, on the whole, a good deal less flexible than cinematic filming methods. This situation changed – slowly – following the development of magnetic tape, which made possible the subsequent editing of recorded material, and thus dispensed with one of the most significant differences between television and cinematic production. Since then, the 'small screen' and the accompanying tendency towards close-ups and detail have been considered the main characteristics of television.

"The single play is dead. [...] The dominant form of TV drama today is a hybrid of the series and serial, aspiring to the soap form." (NELSON 2000: 111) The new conditions of production – extreme competition between channels and the necessity of broadcasting a large number of programmes every day and of securing the viewing loyalty of television audiences – have brought about the emergence of various new television genres. In general, a tendency towards serialisation can be observed. The various types of serial, often consisting of relatively discrete and independent episodes (as in the case of the crime series), can combine characteristics from a variety of genres. The appearance of new forms within this genre, and the new functions that they frequently perform, can be attributed to the cultural changes which have taken place over the past decades. Among the main characteristics of this hybrid genre are:

> **Television films as hybrid genres**

- concentration on acoustic/visual units of 30 to 90 seconds (sound-vision bytes)
- the integration of elements from a variety of genres (for example, the insertion of musical interludes, mostly pop songs, or the combination of dramatic and cinematic conventions in sit-coms)
- the incorporation of a variety of non-linear, overlapping plot structures; loose ends in the final episode of the series
- a relatively clear structure of episodes and plots as well as repeated transmission of the same information, which enable viewers who begin watching at a later stage to find their bearings quickly
- a carefully-timed alternation between periods of suspense and emotional climaxes
- focus on reception-oriented aesthetics (by hopping between channels, viewers frequently create a *bricolage* composed of units from various programmes) (see, for example, Nelson 2000: 112ff.).

The above discussion of the characteristics specific to the television programme should not cause us to overlook the similarities between the cinema and the television film. On the one hand, we should certainly take account of the fact that – as in the case of the radio play – programming considerations (broadcaster and broadcasting time) play a large part in determining the format, and that there are differences between the reception of the television and cinema film: video recorders enable us to integrate the

> **Television film – cinema film**

viewing of television films into our routine, and viewers tend to engage in other activities and to channel-hop whilst watching television. On the other hand, this is also true of those cinema films that are viewed via the medium of television. Few cinema films are produced without any funding from television companies, and many films are produced with a view to being screened on both media. Moreover, television films (in contrast to the earlier television play) are now produced cinematically, and aesthetic markers of difference are very hard to identify. With the development of high-resolution, (realflat) widescreens (16:9 format) that are accompanied by Dolby surround systems, the differences in quality have started to disappear – the experiential gap between television and the cinema is closing steadily. *"These television films now only differ from cinema films in that they are produced primarily for television and not for the cinema."* (HICKETHIER 2001: 162)

Areas of enquiry in the analysis of film and television

Some of the issues that are at the forefront of analyses of film and television have already been mentioned in the discussion of the relationship between film and literature and the phenomenon of film adaptations. However, film studies are also concerned with a number of further areas of enquiry. These include, firstly, the examination of production conditions (for example, the film industry, the structure of and competition between film companies and television companies, characteristics of public broadcasting corporations, and the issue of censorship), conditions of distribution, and questions relating to the composition of the audience (with respect to, for example, social stratum, age and gender). A second field of enquiry is the investigation of technical developments (for example, recording and storage techniques). Thirdly, the aesthetic features of individual films form the focus of studies of the œuvre of individual directors, examinations of the development of individual genres and subgenres (*film noir*, 'spaghetti western'), as well as analyses of individual films. Such analyses can take diverse approaches, which are fundamentally similar to those presented in chapter 2. Films can be interpreted biographically, psychologically and sociologically; structuralist examinations identify narrative and representational modes characteristic for a period or genre; hermeneutic approaches attempt to formulate a holistic interpretation; and more recent deconstructionist approaches emphasise the contradictions, differences and discontinuities within a film. Feminist studies are particularly concerned with gender-specific characteristics relating to the production, distribution and reception of films, and attempt to reveal patriarchal patterns within films by male directors and authors. There are also various approaches that can be grouped together under the heading 'film and television theory', although there are very divergent views concerning the existence or nature of a semiotics specific to film.

Four factors, and the interaction between these factors, are of particular importance when analysing film: image, sound, story and narrative mode. When analysing the action of the film, use is frequently made of elements from drama analysis (see chapter 4). Categories such as plot, character constellation, relations of contrast and correspondence, characterisation, open and closed form, the criteria for and functions of the dialogue and so on, can also be applied in film analysis. There are differences in other areas, however, for example, in the analysis of the representation of space. Film analysts differentiate between mechanical space (*'mechanischer Raum'*) and narrative space (*'narrativer Raum'*): 'mechanical space' refers to the space that is visible in the film, whereas 'narrative space' is constructed by the viewer on the basis of these fragments to form the location in the fictional world where the action takes place. Nevertheless, despite the different modes of representation employed in the two genres, the similarities between realistic and expressionistic dramas and films are considerable.

Main factors in film analysis

When analysing the auditory dimensions, we can draw on the categories that were outlined in the discussion of radio plays (see chapter 6.5.). Stereophonic sound, for example, is also an important component of film, as without it the visual images would not seem 'true to life'. When considering words and sounds, we must also take the relation of these elements to the image into account. A fundamental distinction is made between dialogue, commentary, or noises that occur 'on screen' (when the character or the source of noise is visible on the screen), and 'off screen'. Music can perform a wide variety of functions in film; in addition to serving to mark the boundary between scenes, to lend emphasis and as a general soundtrack. It can also imitate sounds and even evoke emotional states.

Sound-image relations

When analysing the composition of an individual frame, we must first examine the objects depicted in the image and their spatial relations. The filmic image is determined to a large extent by the camera settings. The four main factors that are to be considered when analysing film frames are listed in the table below (which is admittedly not exhaustive). They relate primarily to the type of shot, i.e. the distance between the camera and its object (or the proportions of the objects to the frame), the position and angle of the camera, its movements, and the speed of the frames. Interested readers should consult HICKETHIER (2001: 55–70) for a more detailed description of these techniques and further literature on the subject.

The filmic image

Shots	close up
	medium shot
	long shot
Camera angle	low angle
	eye-level shot
	high angle
Frame rate	24 images/second (frames per second = fps) is the normal projection speed; increasing the speed of the frame rate during filming creates the impression of deceleration (slow motion), whereas an impression of acceleration (fast motion) is created by decreasing the frame rate; freeze frame occurs when a single frame is repeated
Camera movements	pan (short for 'panorama'; rotation on a vertical axis)
	tilt (rotation on a horizontal axis)
	tracking shot (camera runs on a track; implies a change of position along the ground)
	crane shot (camera is mounted on a crane; implies a movement above ground level)
	zoom (not actually a movement of the camera, but evoking movement: variation of the lens to magnify the object while the camera remains stationary)

Table 6.2.: Criteria for the analysis of camera settings

New techniques for editing images

The digitalisation of electronically produced images has produced a wide range of new techniques for editing images; it is now possible to 'leaf through' images, to change their colour composition and perspective, to distort them and even to use them to produce new images. Digital technology also makes it feasible to generate figures that resemble people or actors on a computer and to insert them into an image. As a result of these new techniques, the boundary between the composition and processing or editing of images is becoming increasingly blurred.

The film as narrative: narratology and film

As films are also narratives, analytical categories from narratology are often applied to film, and some have even been developed on the basis of film techniques. Some knowledge of narratological concepts (see chapter 5) is therefore also extremely useful when analysing films. Categories for the representation of time are particularly relevant to film analysis. Variations in order and frequency can be achieved without too much difficulty by means of editing; alterations in duration can be brought about by changes in the frame rate which create the impression of deceleration ('slow motion') and acceleration ('fast motion'). These techniques are employed relatively rarely, however, as they impair the illusion of reality that films usually aim to create.

When analysing filmic narrative strategies, we must also take into consideration the editing techniques, or the arrangement of single shots into larger narrative units and sequences. Single shots are cut and arranged either seamlessly, or by means of other camera techniques such as the double take, dissolve or fade out, into new semantic units. The insertion of flashbacks or flashforwards, as well as the connection of various storylines by allowing them to run concurrently (parallel montage), are achieved by means of editing techniques. These techniques therefore represent *"a productive form of structuring time in film and television series"* and can indeed be described as *"the core of filmic narration"* (HICKETHIER 2001: 145). Specific editing techniques such as 'invisible editing' – very popular in Hollywood movies – can create the illusion that the cinema or television screen is a transparent window, allowing us an undistorted view of reality, while other techniques such as the 'jump cut' can destroy this illusion and remind us that film is a medium of representation. Jump cuts can also be used to create a specific viewing rhythm; a high-speed sequence achieved by frequent changes of shot can heighten suspense.

Editing techniques

The issue of narrative transmission in film has provoked a variety of divergent opinions among film analysts, as it is not easy to differentiate between narration and focalization in film. The fact that the position of the camera presupposes a particular perspective or point of view, has led several theoreticians to argue that the camera represents a kind of narrating instance; after all, an observing lens implies an observer (see HICKETHIER 2001: 130). Based on this premise, the camera can be considered an 'omniscient' narrator, as it frequently waits for characters at locations where future action is to take place or observes the action from positions that would be inaccessible for a human narrator, or from which a human being would not be able to see anything. The camera also appears to address the audience directly on occasions when, for example, close-up shots are used to guide the reception of the viewer. First-person narrators occur only rarely according to these theoretical premises; techniques such as 'subjective camera' – for example, the camera which pursues its object or unsteady and blurred shots which are supposed to be indicative of the subjectivity of the observer – are considered inadequate to the task of invoking the individual and restricted perspective required for this type of narrator.

Camera and point of view

In contrast to approaches which regard the camera as a narrator, SEYMOUR CHATMAN argues that, as in narrative texts, it is possible to distinguish between focalization and narration in films. The 'subjective camera' or the impression, created by editing techniques, that the viewer is looking 'through the eyes' of one of the

Narrator and modes of presenting consciousness

characters at a particular object, should be regarded as instances of focalization and therefore be differentiated from narrative, in which various events are described by a character. Difficulties arise when considering the fine distinction between report and interior monologue; the fact that a character's voice can be heard although his or her lips are not moving is not necessarily indicative of an interior monologue. Depending on the context, the character can also be giving a report of past events. This technique, known as the 'voice-over', is one of the most important modes of representing consciousness in films; other techniques include modes of suggesting or symbolically representing internal processes (for example, by using music) and figurative tropes such as metaphor and metonymy.

Word, image, and unreliable narration

Word and image can be linked in a variety of ways. They can mutually reinforce and complement each other, restrict or modify each other, offer the same information in two parallel forms, and diverge from or contradict one another (see RAUH 1987: 75ff.). Connections between word and image also make it possible to represent consciousness in a specifically cinematic manner; thus the thoughts of a figure can be relayed in a voice-over and simultaneously represented visually. In the case of unreliable narration (see chapter 5.5.), a character's account frequently does not correlate with the visual information, thus suggesting to the viewer that a character is, for example, idealising or repressing past events. A famous example of unreliable narration occurs in ALFRED HITCHCOCK's film *Stage Fright*, in which Johnny is exposed only late in the film as an unreliable narrator, when the version of the murder that he gives in a voice-over at the beginning of the film proves false.

Narrator and multi-medial modes of communicating information in films

Summarising, generalising or commenting voice-overs, which cannot be attributed to characters involved in the action, are generally classed in narratological film theory as contributions by nameless, impersonal heterodiegetic narrators. The question of whether we should postulate a narrator in film, even if such an instance does not appear or speak explicitly (as they do in the novel) has proved contentious. CHATMAN (1990: 135) has composed the following models of modes of representation; they give some indication of the complexity of the various multimedial channels used for communicating information in film.

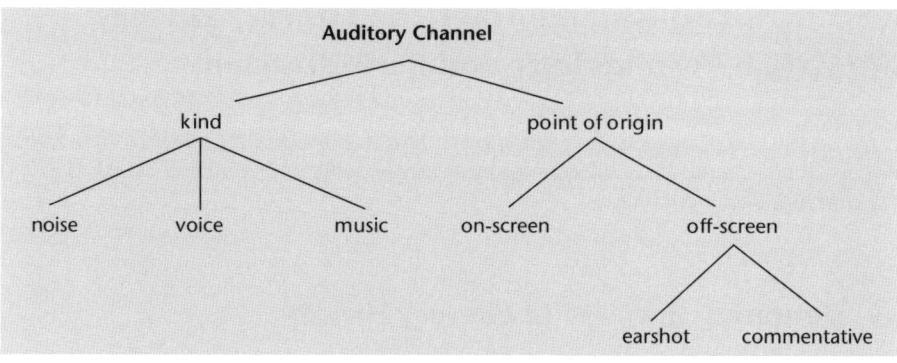

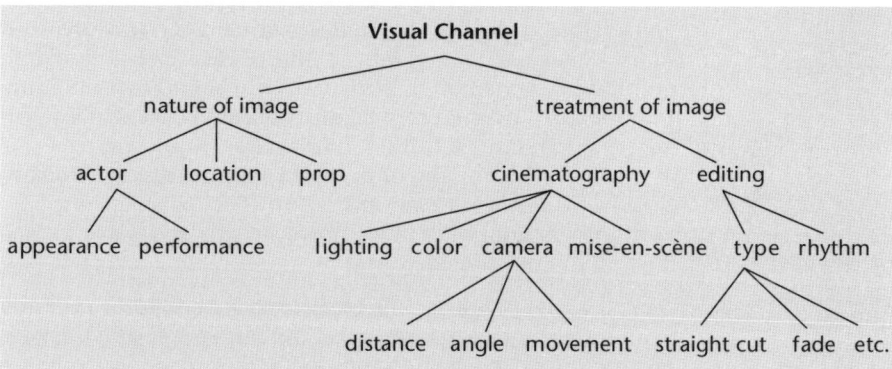

Figures 6.1. and 6.2.: Channels for communicating information in film
(CHATMAN 1990: 135)

KNUT HICKETHIER's *Film- und Fernsehanalyse* (2001) is an excellent introduction to the peculiarities of film and television analysis. LOUIS GIANNETTI's *Understanding Movies* (1972/1998) and ROBIN NELSON's *TV Drama in Transition: Forms, Values and Cultural Change* (1997) can be highly recommended as introductions in the English language.

Further reading

7

CHAPTER

English and American Literary History: Terminology and Periodization

If literary-historical 'objects' [...] are constructed, not given or found, then the issue of how such objects are constructed, in particular the genre of discourse in which they are constructed, becomes crucial.

BRIAN MCHALE

1 Definition and Use of Literary History

Ahistorical and historical understanding

The preceding chapters have focused primarily on systematic questions relating to literary studies, with literary history as a secondary consideration. However, the ability to analyse and interpret literary texts from a variety of genres and media is only one requirement – albeit a central one – within courses in English and American Studies. A further, and no less important aspect is literary history, which to the uninitiated may appear to be a confusing mass of names, titles and dates. If we wish to attain a historical understanding of texts, however, it is necessary to take their historicity into consideration.

Use of literary-historical knowledge

A historical understanding of literary texts presupposes not only sufficient knowledge of the history of the language, which is particularly important when studying works from earlier periods. We must also be aware of the fact that the full potential of meanings of a text only emerges when we study it in its historical and literary context. The importance of literary-historical and historical knowledge for an understanding of literary texts was stressed in the first chapter; it becomes particularly important when we are confronted with satirical allusions to political events and socioeconomic problems, as well as intertextual references to other works within the international literary canon. In addition, we can only hope to evaluate and appreciate the particularity of an individual work, its position within the genre system and any formal innovations that it may contain, if we possess broader literary-historical knowledge.

Objectives of this chapter

There are two main preconditions that we must fulfil if we are to tell the wood from the trees in the literary-historical forest: a familiarity with some of the fundamental terms of literary historiography, and a preliminary overview of the development and the most important periods of English and American literary history. This concluding chapter aims to assist the student in attaining both of these, and to offer some insight into the problems attendant on literary historiography, as well as introducing the student to the central categories with which literary historiography operates.

Although some knowledge of the most important dates of literary history is naturally indispensable, it is much more important to become conversant with some of the fundamental concepts of literary historiography. Literary theory and literary history are mutually interdependent rather than opposing fields, as literary history is underpinned by numerous theoretical presuppositions.

Theoretical nature of literary history

It is now widely accepted that literary histories are the result of a theory-based process of construction. Literary histories do not offer an objective representation of the literary past; they produce models and narratives of this past with the assistance of literary-historical categories. It is also generally agreed that the categories used by literary historians – period and genre designations, for example – are also constructs. As a consequence of the constructed nature of literary histories, we should replace the notion of 'one' history of English or American literature with the premise that there can be numerous 'histories' of any one national literature and any one period.

Literary histories as constructs

If periods, genres and literary currents are to be regarded as literary constructs, rather than real, existing objects, then the question of what criteria and methods function as principles of construction merits consideration. In the quotation at the beginning of this chapter, BRIAN MCHALE (1992: 3) succinctly points out that the question of *how* these objects are constructed is of central importance. After all, the parameters used for the selection and arrangement of texts in a literary history determine to a large extent the way in which a period or genre is presented. The question of what 'history' of a national literature, period or genre is narrated, then, is generally decided by the preferences of the literary historian and the concepts he or she works with. Careful application of literary categories is required in order to be able to record and characterise the diverse generic manifestations of, for example, the English drama of the Shakespearean era or the 20th-century American novel.

Literary-historical principles of construction

We should therefore firstly be aware of the distinction between literary-historical occurrences and phenomena (for example, the publication of literary works, changes in the book market, the lives of authors, thematic and formal characteristics of texts) and the presentation of these occurrences, that is to say, the literary histories in printed form. The ambivalent designation 'literary history' refers both to the subject-matter, that is to say, the historical development of literature, and its reconstruction and presentation in

Definition of literary history

literary historiography. As it is self-evident that the literary histories which stand on the bookshelf are quite distinct from the literary objects that they describe, questions arise concerning the relationship between the retrospective representations of literary-historical facts and actual literary-historical events.

Literary histories as maps

The status and use of literary-historical representations are best summarised by using the metaphor of a map, by means of which a territory consisting of literary texts from earlier periods is charted. This metaphor of a map indicates that literary histories are models rather than true-to-life representations of the textual landscapes of earlier periods. Like all models, then, literary histories abstract from the individual instance, are concerned with only a limited number of relevant aspects, and attempt to represent complex information by means of generalisation and simplification. Literary histories cannot claim, therefore, to be objective or complete representations of the complex terrain of past stages of literary production – whatever the period under consideration.

Use of literary histories

Moreover, the metaphor of the relationship between map and territory sheds some light on the potential uses of literary histories. They offer first and foremost a means of analytical differentiation and orientation within the otherwise bewildering diversity of literary production. Just as we run the risk of getting lost if we venture into an unfamiliar town or region without a map, we would similarly have problems finding our feet in the literatures in English without literary histories.

Selection and organisation

The metaphor of the model or the map also draws attention to two fundamental questions concerning literary historiography: the paradigmatic issue of selection and the syntagmatic question of combination. Which elements of the literary terrain (i. e., which literary-historical texts or events) are included in each respective map? According to which aspects are the selected objects structured or combined within each individual literary history? The question of what is included in individual literary histories points us toward the specific criteria which underpin the selection process. These criteria are rarely made explicit; however, they can be deduced from the genres, authors and works that appear within a literary history, as well as from those that are excluded. As we will see in the following section of the chapter, the task of judiciously selecting and structuring dates, facts and contexts presents literary historians with a number of problems.

2 Problems of Literary Historiography I: Selection, Evaluation, Canon Formation, and the Debate on the Canon

A decisive factor in determining which works of literature are included within a literary history, and what story is told, is the definition of literature used in each case (see chapter 1.3.). Literary histories that are based on a broad definition of literature attempt to take into account all written or printed material. British literary histories such as *The Cambridge History of English Literature* and *The Oxford History of English Literature*, to name two of the best known examples, include, in addition to the three main genres, other genres such as travel literature, essays, children's literature, pamphlets, ballads and other forms of popular literature, as well as non-fictional or semi-fictional text types such as autobiographies, biographies and works of historiography, philosophy and even science. By using such an extended definition of literature, literary histories can take a larger number of genres and text types into consideration. Literary histories that adopt a narrower definition of literature in order to focus on the pinnacles of literary achievement will of course neglect such non-fictional or semi-fictional text types.

Broad vs. narrow definitions of literature

The issues of selection and evaluation are closely related to the definition of literature employed in a particular literary history. Every literary history is the result of a selection process, which determines which authors, works and events are sufficiently important to be included. It is not a question of *whether* literary historians make a selection, but rather, of how consciously and explicitly they apply their selection criteria. The question of what aesthetic and other criteria form the basis of the selection process becomes all the more urgent when we consider that there can be no selection without evaluation. Yet this question is frequently neglected by literary histories, even though the selection criteria and underlying value judgements determine the nature and object of the history.

Selection and evaluation

Literary histories therefore play an important part in the cultural process known as 'canon formation'. The term 'canon' refers to all those texts that are regarded as particularly important or artistically superior. Texts included among the 'great works' of the canon therefore have the status of classics. Although the positive functions of the canon, which include securing the continuity of literary tradition and providing a framework for the study of literature, should not be overlooked, the problematic aspects of canon formation have attracted a good deal of attention and

Definitions of 'canon' and 'canon formation'

criticism in recent years. Literary works are not, after all, part of a canon *per se*; they are gradually canonized, i.e. organised into a canon, by means of selection procedures which involve a variety of institutions (for example, literary reviews, literary prizes, the book trade, academia and literary historiography). ALEIDA and JAN ASSMANN describe the process of canon formation, which necessarily entails the exclusion of the greater part of literary works, by means of a vivid metaphor: *"Every canon represents a reduction of the preceding tradition. This is achieved by, to use a metaphor, fencing in a particular area of a varied and extensive landscape, whose horizon is mostly concealed by fog. All attention is then focused on this sacred, circumscribed territory."* (ASSMANN/ASSMANN 1987: 11)

Historicity of canons

Processes of selection and canonisation are generally conducted on the basis of categories that are considered important at the time a particular literary history is written. The historical author's and reader's understanding of literary and generic conventions, as well as the prevailing consciousness and aesthetic norms of the day, are generally disregarded. Like the definition of literature itself, the value judgements and preferences underlying literary historiography are subject to historical change. A glance at older literary histories will yield numerous examples of changes in the assessment of the majority of 'great' authors. SHAKESPEARE, for instance, was not valued highly in the 17th century and acquired his fame as one of the greatest British authors only during the course of the 18th century.

Debate on the canon

For a long time, there was general agreement on the subject of which texts should be included in the canon of great works of English literature. Over the past three decades, however, considerable controversy has been sparked by the question of what works merit a place in histories of 'English' literature. Although the finer points of the discussion, whose effects can be observed in the syllabi and reading lists of a large number of institutes for English and American studies, cannot be discussed in detail here, students of literature should be aware of the problems and issues relating to canon formation.

Revision of the canon

Research into minority literatures and feminist demands for adequate consideration of literary works by women have increased awareness of the problems attendant on any canon and of the need for revision. Demands for revisions of the canon are based on the view that, to retain the previous metaphor, older maps of literary history offer a one-sided and distorted representation of the literature of bygone periods. The multicultural nature of American literature has been affirmed, for instance, by the inclusion of contributions on Native American, Afro-American, American Jewish, Asian-American and Chicano literature in more recent literary histories (see Zapf 1997). The process of revision is equally manifest in feminist-oriented literary histories, which employ other principles of selection, organisation and periodization and devote particular attention to forgotten female authors.

3 Problems of Literary Historiography II: Periodization and Contextualisation

Processes of selection and canonisation are only the prerequisites for a literary history, as they merely supply the basic material from which literary histories are produced. Structural and representational criteria then determine the way in which the selected works and dates are organised. The majority of literary histories are based on three basic organisational categories: authors, periods and genres.

Periods, genres and authors as organisational categories

Authors and their works are among the most important organisational principles of literary history, as is demonstrated by the fact that the names of important authors are frequently employed as period designations and as chapter headings. Many histories of English literature (for example, *The Cambridge History of English Literature*, *The Pelican Guide to English Literature* and the *Sphere History of Literature*) include chapters on particular periods which are named after famous authors such as Geoffrey Chaucer (ca. 1343–1400), William Shakespeare (1564–1616), John Dryden (1631–1700) and Samuel Johnson (1709–1784) and thus have titles such as 'The Age of Chaucer', 'The Age of Shakespeare', 'The Age of Dryden' and 'The Age of Johnson'. Moreover, a surprisingly large number of literary histories (for example, numerous volumes of the famous *Oxford History of English Literature*) content themselves with a mere chronological presentation consisting of single literary works by so-called 'major authors'. Evaluations and value judgements are implicit in the size of the passage devoted to each individual author, as 'major' authors usually receive an entire chapter, whereas so-called 'minor' authors are discussed summarily in other chapters. The compositional and organisational methods of this type of literary historiography are based primarily on the principles of chronological compilation and the presentation of facts about authors' lives and works.

Authors' names as organisational concepts

Two dimensions, generally referred to as 'synchrony' and 'diachrony', influence the processes of ordering and structuring literary histories. Literary phenomena that exist at the same time form the subject of the 'synchronic' dimension of literary histories. Synchronic studies thus focus on the literary production within, for example, a decade or a period. The diachronic dimension of liter-

Synchrony and diachrony

ary and generic histories, on the other hand, is based on period divisions; diachronic analyses focus on the description of historical change, for example, the development of genres and the transformation of aesthetic norms. A diachronic cross-section through English or American literature enables us to reconstruct its historical development along a temporal axis.

Genres and periods as organisational categories in literary historiography

The distinctions between various literary genres explained in the first chapter represent the most important means of structuring the synchronic dimension of literary history. A synchronic cross-section through a period encompasses the variety of text types and genres that are in existence within a particular period of time. Distinctions between periods, on the other hand, enable us to structure the diachronic dimension of literary and generic history. Periods are no more historical givens than genres; they are constructs or organisational categories, produced by literary historians when they engage in the process of periodization. The main purpose of generic and period designations for literary historiography is to facilitate the organisation of single texts into larger groups and to (re)construct literary-historical developments.

Periodization and period boundaries

The organisation of the diachronic dimension into various 'periods' of literary history is known as 'periodization', and relies heavily on significant changes or caesurae known as period boundaries. Some recent literary histories also take the historically situated awareness specific to the respective period into account, as this sheds light on the historical self-conception of a particular era.

Difficulties of periodization and period designations

The problems arising from periodization become apparent when we consider the variety of influences that can come into play, and the fact that periods frequently overlap. Some examples from English literary history should serve to illustrate these points. Many periods in English literary history have their origins in political history, with the reigns of the monarchs playing a particularly important part. This is illustrated by terms such as 'Elizabethan Literature' or 'Victorian Literature', which have become household words in literary histories; the term 'Restoration Literature' is also rooted in political history. It is true that due consideration should be given to the influence of political events on the development of literature; it is immediately evident in the case of 'Restoration Comedy', for example, that the restoration of the monarchy in 1660 was also an epochal event for literature, as it coincided with a revival in theatre. Yet, despite the fact that the beginning and end of the reign of QUEEN VICTORIA (1837–1901) cannot be considered important literary-historical events, we still speak of 'Victorian Literature'. Other period designations are based on criteria related to developments within the literary sphere itself, volume titles such as *The Age of Shakespeare* or *From Dryden to Johnson*

in *The Pelican Guide to English Literature* being cases in point. Still other designations are taken from the history of art or ideas and then applied to literature (for example, terms like 'Renaissance', 'Baroque', 'Impressionism', 'Enlightenment'), or are based on categories from the history of the English language (for example, Old English and Middle English literature). Chronological organisation of literary histories into centuries is also common.

Genre and period designations allow us to identify the characteristics common to literary works from a particular period, as well as the elements that distinguish them from texts from earlier or later periods. The most important functions performed by genre and period designations involve, firstly, structuring the objects of literary history according to specific criteria, and, secondly, situating literary works within their historical context. They function as organisational principles of literary history, highlighting contextual relations, supplying coordinates for diachronic analyses of developmental tendencies and offering typological categories as a foundation for synchronic analyses and classifications. They also perform descriptive and communicative functions: by referring to a literary work as a 'tragedy', a 'picaresque novel' or as typical of the Romantic or Modernist period, we implicitly allude to a (more or less well-defined) cluster of characteristics, without having to restate the thematic and formal specifics of the text with each new interpretation. Genre and period designations are also prerequisites for teaching and learning about literary history (whether in the context of the educational establishment or of private reading), as well as for communicating factual information (for example, in exams).

Functions of genre and period designations

A further central problem of literary historiography concerns the relationship between the literary texts and their context, and particularly their relationship to reality. There is no simple or general answer to the complex question of how the often charged relationship between works of art and their socio-cultural context is structured, primarily because this relationship is subject to historical and cultural variation. Marxist approaches proceed from the assumption that literature 'mirrors' reality; however, this theory is considered simplistic and misleading nowadays. The question of how we are to describe the relationship between literary texts and their contexts remains largely unsolved.

Relation to reality and contextualisation

When attempting to ascertain the relationship between a literary text and its historical context, we encounter three main problems (see PERKINS 1992: chapter 6). Firstly, the number of contexts that present themselves for consideration is potentially boundless (for example, political, social, economic, cultural and literary). Secondly, the selection of particular aspects of the socio-cultural con-

Problems of contextualisation

text for consideration, and the neglect of others, will always be hard to justify. Thirdly, it is also extremely difficult to prove the significance of a particular context for changes within the literary sphere. It may, for instance, be immediately obvious that the closure of theatres by the Puritan parliament in 1642 and the censorship of plays (known as the 'Theatre Licensing Act' (1737)) had serious consequences for English drama, as these measures almost resulted in the complete demise of the theatre. It is considerably more difficult, however, to assess the relevance of other contextual aspects that frequently feature in literary histories (for example, the reign of monarchs or currents in the history of art or of ideas).

Functions

Another issue relating to contextualisation, which is of considerable importance for cultural history, is the question of the functions performed by particular genres and works within individual periods. Historically, these have proved diverse: whereas courtly poetry, for example, mainly serves to offer an idealised representation of particular values and behavioural codes, English poetry from the First and Second World Wars functions primarily as an organ of propaganda or a medium for criticism of the meaninglessness of war. English and American literature from the 18th and 19th centuries, on the other hand, primarily fulfils moral and didactic functions, with the aim of educating and edifying the reading public. Many literary works have also served as a medium for the construction of English and American national identity.

4 Literary Historiography: Approaches and Forms

Literary histories rather than literary history

Rather than representing a definitive literary-historical 'reality', then, literary historians construct the model they consider the most plausible, and consistent with the literature from the period under consideration, on the basis of the texts selected for inclusion and their own preferred theories, concepts and literary criteria. The model produced by literary histories is determined, firstly, by the object (for example, the particular genre or period), and the areas of the literary system taken into consideration (for example, literary production or reception, the book market or relations between particular texts and contexts). In addition, literary histories can differ considerably in terms of their theoretical and methodological premises.

Text-oriented vs. context-oriented literary histories

A preliminary attempt to categorise the diverse approaches and forms found in literary histories can be made on the basis of their subject-matter. Histories of literature can focus on the history of a genre, the presentation of a period and of single 'currents', 'schools', social classes (for example, the history of the literature of the working class), and minority literatures, as well as the more common histories of the literature of a nation or region. A further distinction can be made between predominantly intrinsic, text-oriented and predominantly extrinsic, context-oriented approaches. The latter can be primarily production-oriented or primarily reception-oriented, or can encompass the entire literary system. There are, in the final analysis, as many forms of literary historiography as there are theoretical approaches (see chapter 2).

Thanks to the diversity of possible thematic and theoretical approaches, literary historiography can take a wide variety of forms: *"Its major modes have been Hegelian, naturalist, positivist, geistesgeschichtlich, Marxist, formalist, sociological and, paradoxically, postmodern. [...] The genre [literary history] includes works on the literature of nations, periods, traditions, schools, regions, social classes, political movements, ethnic groups, women, and gays, and these studies may foreground the genesis or production of texts, their effect on society or on subsequent literature, their reception, or all these moments synthetically."* (PERKINS 1992: 1)

Plurality of forms

From a diachronic perspective, interpretations of the nature and role of literary historiography, as well as its approaches and models, have been subject to frequent and fundamental change. The model of an encyclopaedic representation of a national literature in its entirety, which aimed to shed light on the national identity of a people, has been replaced by a large number of diverse forms of literary historiography. Although they fell into disfavour some time ago as a result of the popularity of the close reading of texts practised by proponents of the *New Criticism* and of the later theorization of literary studies, literary histories have recently experienced something of a Renaissance, thanks to HARALD WEINRICH's advocacy of a 'literary history of the reader'. Reception aesthetics and history of reception, which endow the reader with the status of a crucial 'factor within a new history of literature' and emphasise the dialogic character of the relationship between literature and reader, have sparked a renewed interest in literary-historical research which continues today. Of particular importance to this process was the realisation that literary history is a complex communication process, which cannot automatically be equated with the history of literary texts.

Changes in literary historiography

In addition to the approaches described above, which focus primarily on the literary texts themselves (i.e., on the symbolic system of literature), on the social context or on the social system of literature, a number of other innovative approaches exist. Common to all these approaches is a more explicit theoretical foundation, and a focus on the interaction between literature and its socio-cultural context. The social historiography of literature, for

New approaches in literary historiography

example, has established itself as an important method of studying literary history from a vantage-point that goes beyond a text-intrinsic perspective. It focuses primarily on extra-textual aspects like social structures (for example, differences between social classes), and the way in which they are thematised within literature. Discourse analytical, feminist, gender-oriented and new historical forms of literary historiography, as well as approaches related to the history of mentalities and of the function of literature, are also growing in popularity. These approaches no longer regard literature as the mirror of reality or of a society. They focus instead on the adaptation of social discourses and systems of knowledge within literature, as well as investigating the historically variable functions that can be performed by literature. An illustrative example of such approaches is Winfried Fluck's brilliant book *Das kulturelle Imaginäre* (1997), a pioneering 'history of the function of the American novel' from 1790 to 1900, which demonstrates what can be achieved when literary historiography is also open to cultural and historical insights.

5 Periods in English and American Literary History

Periodization in English and Irish literature

The following period designations, which recur in variant forms throughout literary histories, should suffice for a preliminary overview. This period structure supplies students with a useful framework for their studies: an overarching system within which individual courses, authors and works can be situated. The following table offers an abbreviated, schematic overview of the development of English and Irish literature. The following list of genres and authors is, of course, highly selective; it is not intended as a canon, but to offer preliminary orientation.

| Dates | Periods | *Genres* | | |
		Authors of lyric texts	*Authors of dramatic texts*	*Authors of narrative texts*
500– 1150	Old English literature	*The Dream of the Rood*		*Beowulf*
1150– 1500	Middle English literature	*Brut*	*Mystery Plays, Morality Plays (Everyman)*	Geoffrey Chaucer, Thomas Malory
1500- 1649	Renaissance	John Donne, Sir Philip Sidney, Edmund Spenser	Ben Jonson, Christopher Marlowe, William Shakespeare	Thomas Morus, Sir Philip Sidney

1649–1660	Common-wealth and Protectorate	Andrew Marvell, John Milton		
1660–1700	Restoration	Samuel Butler, John Dryden, Earl of Rochester	William Congreve, John Dryden, William Wycherley	Aphra Behn, John Bunyan
1700–1780	Neoclassi-cism and Enlighten-ment	Thomas Gray, Samuel Johnson, Alexander Pope, Lady Wortley Montagu	Susanna Centlivre, John Gay, Oliver Goldsmith, Eliza Haywood, Richard B. Sheridan	Daniel Defoe, Henry Fielding, Samuel Richardson, Laurence Sterne
1780–1837	Roman-ticism	William Blake, George G. Byron, Samuel T. Cole-ridge, Percy B. Shelley, William Wordsworth		*Sentimental Novel, Gothic Novel,* Jane Austen, Edward Bulwer-Lytton, Maria Edgeworth, Walter Scott, Mary Shelley
1837–1901	Victorian era	Elizabeth Barrett Browning, Robert Browning, Gerard M. Hopkins, Chris-tina Rossetti, Dante Gabriel Rossetti, Alfred Tennyson	Henry Arthur Jones, Arthur Wing Pinero, Oscar Wilde	Charlotte Brontë, Charles Dickens, George Eliot, Elizabeth Gaskell, Robert L. Stevenson, William M. Thackeray, Anthony Trollope
1901–1914	Edwardian era	Thomas Hardy	John Galsworthy, G. B. Shaw, John M. Synge, William B. Yeats	Arnold Bennett, Joseph Conrad, E. M. Forster, H. G. Wells
1914–1945	Modernism	W. H. Auden, T. S. Eliot, Siegfried Sassoon, Stevie Smith, Dylan Thomas	Noël Coward, Sean O'Casey, J. B. Priestley	Elizabeth Bowen, Ivy Compton-Burnett, James Joyce, D. H. Lawrence, Virginia Woolf
1945-2004	Post-war era	Eavan Boland, Wendy Cope, D. J. Enright, Seamus Heaney, Ted Hughes, Philip Larkin, Paul Muldoon, R. S. Thomas	Samuel Beckett, Caryl Churchill, Sarah Daniels, Pam Gems, Sarah Kane, John Osborne, Louise Page, Harold Pinter, Peter Shaffer, Tom Stoppard, Tim-berlake Wertenbaker	Peter Ackroyd, John Banville, Pat Barker, A. S. Byatt, Angela Carter, John Fowles, Kazuo Ishiguro, Pene-lope Lively, David Lodge, Ian McEwan, Graham Swift, Jeanette Winterson

Table 7.1.: Periods in English and Irish literary history

| Permeable period boundaries | Those beginning a course in literary studies should be made aware of two things from the outset, however: firstly, it should be immediately obvious that these periods cannot be regarded as discrete, clearly differentiable units. The boundaries between the periods are permeable. The Victorian and Modernist eras, for example, should not be regarded as two opposing periods, separated by a clear caesura; we should rather regard the period from 1880 to 1920 as an age of transition, in which gradual changes took place within society and literature. |

| Synchronic variation and dia-chronic change | The second factor of which we should be aware is that individual periods of literary production can comprise considerable synchronic variation and diverse forms of diachronic change. We therefore generally subdivide periods into further units: in the case of the Renaissance period, for example, we draw on the names of ruling dynasties and individual monarchs to form internal period designations such as 'Early Tudor', 'Elizabethan Age' (1558–1603), 'Jacobean Age' (1603–1625), and 'Caroline Age' (1625–1649). As the synchronic and diachronic variation is at least as great in other periods (for example, in the Neoclassical and Enlightenment eras, or in the Victorian era), these are also frequently subdivided. The last decade of the 19th century, for instance, is often set apart as 'the nineties' or 'fin de siécle', since at this time dissatisfaction with Victorian literary forms as well as with aesthetic and moral norms and values was widespread. The period designations selected often emphasise particular aesthetic trends, to the disadvantage of other developments. |

| Periodi-zation in American literature | Historians of American literature proceed in a similar manner, although with other systems of classification and period designations. In the absence of ruling dynasties and regencies, other criteria are used in order to divide American literary history into periods. Political events and aesthetic trends, in particular, are employed as period designations; certain influential cultural-historical factors are also indispensable for an understanding of the history of American literature and the way it is taught in many universities. The following table offers a simplified, schematic representation of the various periods in American literary history. Again, this list is highly selective, merely intending to offer preliminary orientation. |

Dates	Periods	Genres		
		Authors of lyric texts	*Authors of dramatic texts*	*Authors of narrative texts*
17th – mid-18th century	Early (colonial) literature	Anne Bradstreet, Ebenezer Cooke, Edward Taylor		John Cotton, Thomas Morton
Mid-18th – early 19th century	Literature of the early republic	*Connecticut Wits* (Joel Barlow, Timothy Dwight, John Trumbull), William C. Bryant, Lydia H. Sigourney	James Nelson Barker, William Dunlap, John Howard Payne, Richard Penn Smith, Royall Tyler	Charles B. Brown, James F. Cooper, Washington Irving, Catharine Sedgwick
1830–1860	Romanticism and American Renaissance	Emily Dickinson, Ralph W. Emerson, Henry W. Longfellow, Walt Whitman, John G. Whittier	Dion Boucicault, William W. Brown, Anna C. Mowatt	Alice Cary, Nathaniel Hawthorne, Herman Melville, Edgar Allan Poe, Harriet Beecher Stowe
1865–1910	Realism			Charles W. Chesnutt, William Dean Howells, Mark Twain, Edith Wharton
1893–1914	Naturalism			Stephen Crane, Frank Norris, Jack London
1910–1945	Modernism	E. E. Cummings, H. D., Robert Frost, Langston Hughes, Marianne Moore, Ezra Pound, Wallace Stevens, William Carlos Williams	Susan Glaspell, Lillian Hellman, Arthur Miller, Eugene O'Neill, Elmer Rice, Thornton Wilder, Tennessee Williams	Djuna Barnes, William Faulkner, F. Scott Fitzgerald, Ernest Hemingway, Katherine Anne Porter, Gertrude Stein
1945–2004	Postmodernism to present day	Alurista, John Berryman, Charles Bukowski, Susan Howe, Denise Levertov Audre Lorde, Robert Lowell, Sylvia Plath, Adrienne Rich	Edward Albee, David H. Hwang, LeRoi Jones, David Mamet, Marsha Norman, David Rabe, Sam Shepard, Wendy Wasserstein, Lanford Wilson, Robert Wilson	Paul Auster, Saul Bellow, Louise Erdrich, Toni Morrison, Vladimir Nabokov, Joyce Carol Oates, Philip Roth, J. D. Salinger, John Updike

Table 7.2.: Periods in American literary history

Structure and use of models in literary history	The vertical axis in the table represents the diachronic dimension of literary history; the synchronic spectrum of literary production (restricted in this case to the three 'major genres') appears on the horizontal axis. Such models organise authors and literary works into synchronic groupings and diachronic sequences, and provide an overview of interrelations and overarching developments. Yet however useful such models are as study guides, we should take care not to be blinded by their clarity, or to mistake the model for the reality of literary developments. Such representations infuse the period divisions with an order and clarity that they naturally never had in reality.
Further reading on English literary history	Those who wish to inform themselves in greater depth about the history of English literature should consult one of the literary histories listed in the appendix. The best overview in German is *Englische Literaturgeschichte* (1991/1999), edited by HANS ULRICH SEEBER, which also contains a very informative chapter about new literatures in the English language. Taking the concept of modernisation as its guiding premise, this present volume is able to combine social history and the history of ideas productively, and to shed light on the functional relationship between literary texts and their social and ideological contexts. In addition, the concept of modernisation serves to focus attention on certain *"modernising forces"* such as *"rationalisation, secularisation, the formation of nation states, the industrial revolution, democratisation, a differentiation of functions within society and culture, individualisation"* (SEEBER 1991/1999: ix). The work effectively demonstrates that there is no meaning inherent in the development of English literature; meaning is rather created by those who write literary histories, who take particular approaches (for example, the theory of modernisation). A pioneering study of the history of English literature from the perspective of gender studies is INA SCHABERT's *Englische Literaturgeschichte: Eine neue Darstellung aus der Sicht der Geschlechterforschung* (1997), which more than supplements traditional literary histories. *Eine andere Geschichte der englischen Literatur: Epochen, Gattungen und Teilgebiete im Überblick* (ed. NÜNNING 1996/1998) offers an overview of the most important genres in each of the major periods, and provides a useful guideline for independent study. Of the great number of literary histories written in English, we recommend *The Routledge History of Literature in English: Britain and Ireland* (1997/2001), edited by RONALD CARTER and JOHN MCRAE.
Further reading on American literary history	By far the best overview of American literary history in German can be found in *Amerikanische Literaturgeschichte* (1997), edited by HUBERT ZAPF, which also takes Canadian literature into consideration. Again, the process of modernisation serves particularly well as the central recurring theme and principle of organisation, as it

can encompass such fundamental elements of American studies as the dream of the 'New World', the secularisation of Puritan traditions and the ideal of the self-made man, as well as the mythology of the frontier. The *Columbia Literary History of the United States* (1988), edited by EMORY ELLIOTT, can also be recommended. The volume *A History of British, Irish and American Literature* (2003) by PETER WAGNER provides a good introduction to American as well as British literary history.

6 From English/American Literary Studies to the Cultural Study of Literatures in English

The fundamental revision and extension of the 'canon of masterpieces' is only one aspect of a general broadening of focus, which has quite rightly been described as an 'explosion of the research domain' in English literary studies (BROICH 1995: 81). Whether we welcome the processes of internal differentiation and specialisation within English and American literary studies, or regard them with scepticism, depends primarily on our own personal perspective. *"This development can be summarised as a de-canonisation, a decentralisation and a de-literarisation of English literary studies. However, it can also be regarded positively as a process of opening the discipline to all forms of literature, to literatures in English from all over the world, and to diverse kinds of cultural phenomena."* (Ibid.)

Recent developments in English literary studies

The focus on English and American literature which was predominant until fairly recently is now untenable, thanks to the development of a new World Literature in the English language. The voices which – with good reason – advocate the inclusion of Anglophone literatures from outside Great Britain and North America have been growing steadily in number for some time. English studies have now shifted their focus to include those areas that were previously subsumed under the title 'Commonwealth Literature', and are now known as 'new literatures of the English language', 'literatures in English' or simply 'New English Literatures'. These categories encompass all Anglophone literatures produced in the former British colonies of Canada, Australia and New Zealand, as well as in Africa, India, South-East Asia and the Caribbean, which also enjoy considerable popularity in Great Britain. In a development analogous to that which took place some decades ago in American literary studies, Irish, Canadian, Australian, New Zealand, Anglo-African and Indo-English literatures have all become flourishing and expanding areas of research.

Inclusion of new literatures in English

Multicultu-ralism and regional conscious-ness	Among the most palpable legacies of the British Empire and migration resulting from decolonisation is the increasingly multicultural character of both English society and contemporary literatures in English. This development has established multiculturalism as a dominant theme in a great deal of prose writing and drama. However, there are other reasons why we should nowadays be wary of referring to 'one' English literature. For some decades now, regional consciousness has progressively been leaving its imprint on literature, a tendency that can be observed equally in the literature of Scotland, Wales and Northern Ireland. In the United States, increasing attention has been devoted to Native American, Afro-American, Jewish-American, Asian-American and Chicano literature.
Internatio-nalisation of English literature	The progressive internationalisation of English literature is also due to the fact that many authors from former colonial territories now have a well-established status within the English literary sphere as well as within a new kind of 'world literature'. Authors such as NADINE GORDIMER, SALMAN RUSHDIE and WOLE SOYINKA (to name just a few of the most significant) have been responsible for many important developments in 'English' literature over the last few decades. The Nobel Prize was awarded in 2001 to Trinidadian writer V. S NAIPAUL and in 2003 to the South African J. M. COETZEE. The fact that, since 1980, such names as RUSHDIE, THOMAS KENEALLY, COETZEE, KERI HULME, PETER CAREY, BEN OKRI, MICHAEL ONDAATJE, RODDY DOYLE, PATRICK MCCABE, JAMES KELMAN, ARUNDHATI ROY, MARGARET ATWOOD, YANN MARTEL and DBC PIERRE, not one of whom is English, have appeared among the ranks of the winners of the Booker Prize (the most prestigious English prize for literature), is also indicative of the internationalisation of 'English' literature.
Internal differentiation and intra-disciplinary comparative studies	English and American studies have reacted to these new trends with increasing internal differentiation and the development of intradisciplinary comparative studies. The latter approach focuses on literatures in English from outside Great Britain and America, and on relations between new literatures in English and the literature of the former 'mother country'. Although they differ in many ways, new literatures in English have two things in common: they bear the imprint of interaction between the native or indigenous tradition of the former colonies on the one hand and the Anglo-European tradition on the other hand, and they also bear witness to a complex and charged interplay with British literature: *"The old dialogue between coloniser and colonised [has] been succeeded by a polylogue between all parties, which manifests itself in the form of a multicultural intertextual patchwork."* (PRIESSNITZ 1995: 188)

This presents intradisciplinary comparative approaches with a number of new and fruitful angles of enquiry. Comparative studies are concerned with such issues as the following: *"the functions and achievements of literary nationalist movements; strategies of naming and mapping; the construction of identities; literary regionalisms; functions of literary quests; conflicts between the 'old' and the 'new' worlds; forms and manifestations of utopian ideologies; the modification of ideologies of the old world; effects of multiculturalism on personal and collective quests for identity [...]; literary images of Great Britain and Europe; European images of the Other, for example, in travel literature; the function of the author; founding myths and myths of conquest [...]."* (Ibid.: 191)

Issues in intra-disciplinary comparative studies

As this list demonstrates, intradisciplinary comparative studies are not merely concerned with the extension of the discipline to include other national literatures in the English language; the comparative approach also opens up a wide variety of new areas of study. In addition, the new approach does not merely involve the application of traditional methods to literatures in English; the new objects of study raise new questions, which in turn necessitate the expansion of the existing methodological repertoire.

New areas of study

The shift of attention onto new areas of study has been accompanied by the appearance of new approaches in the theoretical field, which are generally subsumed under the title 'postcolonial theory and criticism'. Among the new subjects and modes of writing with which postcolonial criticism is concerned are the critical study of the legacy of British colonialism, the problematisation of the traditionally high value placed on the British 'centre' as opposed to the colonial 'periphery', and the 'rewriting' of various classics of English literature. Works such as SHAKESPEARE's *The Tempest* (1611), DANIEL DEFOE's *Robinson Crusoe* (1719) and JOSEPH CONRAD's *Heart of Darkness* (1899) have proved particularly fascinating to authors from the former colonies, and inspired a series of intertextual adaptations.

Postcolonial literary criticism

The close dialogic relationship between many works from the 'new' literatures in English and the 'classics' of English literature, clearly illustrates that we should not throw out the baby with the bathwater and dismiss the canon of classics along with the imperialist view of the world. The subversive potential of intertextual adaptations such as JEAN RHYS' *Wide Sargasso Sea* (1966), SAM SELVON's *Moses Ascending* (1975) or PETER CAREY's *Jack Maggs* (1997), each of which is a rewriting of a famous novel from English literature from a postcolonial perspective – CHARLOTTE BRONTË's *Jane Eyre* (1847), DEFOE's *Robinson Crusoe* and CHARLES DICKENS' *Great Expectations* (1861) – is only obvious against the background of an acquaintance with the source texts, the knowledge of the latter

Intertextual adaptations

being a prerequisite for any attempt at getting to grips with the former.

Omni-presence of Shakespeare

Probably the best example of the omnipresence of the cultural heritage in contemporary literatures in English and cultures is the importance of a familiarity with the works of WILLIAM SHAKESPEARE (who else?), without which considerable parts of English-speaking culture, and even popular culture, are not intelligible. The film *Shakespeare in Love* (1998), whose screenplay was written by the renowned English dramatist TOM STOPPARD, and which won seven Oscars, is the most recent example of the centrality of SHAKESPEARE's dramas to the cultural memory. The film is composed of a dense tissue of intertextual allusions to his plays. In addition to theatrical performances of SHAKESPEARE's works, which can be seen all over the world, his *œuvre* has also been adapted, or at least alluded to, in a plethora of operas and musicals, in the visual arts and, more recently, in films. There has also been a variety of adaptations and literary reworkings (particularly of the plays *Romeo and Juliet* and *Hamlet*), two famous examples being LEONARD BERNSTEIN's musical *West Side Story* (1956) and TOM STOPPARD's drama *Rosencrantz and Guildenstern Are Dead* (1966).

Novels as 'echo chambers' of cultural history

A thorough familiarity with English and American literary history is therefore necessary both for an understanding of the New literatures in English, and for the study of contemporary English and American literature. Those who are interested primarily in contemporary literature and who are therefore dubious about the use or importance of a familiarity with literary history will soon be convinced otherwise when they learn that many 20th-century works – in particular, the literature of the so-called 'postmodernist' period – are only accessible if one is familiar with a broad historical spectrum of literary works. This is so primarily because many modernist and postmodernist works comprise such a dense network of intertextual allusions to the classics that their potential of meaning can only be realised if the reader is familiar with these texts and the representational techniques that are parodied by the modern or postmodern text. Prime examples of such works are JAMES JOYCE's centennial novel *Ulysses* (1922), VIRGINIA WOOLF's fictional biography *Orlando: A Biography* (1928), THOMAS PYNCHON's *Gravity's Rainbow* (1973), PETER ACKROYD's novels *Chatterton* (1987) and *English Music* (1992) and JULIAN BARNES' *England, England* (1998). Thanks to their numerous intertextual allusions, such novels can be regarded as literary 'echo chambers', in which the voices of English and American cultural history reverberate. These novels can naturally be read and enjoyed without an understanding of the allusions; however, for those who wish to carry out an academic analysis of their aesthetic innovations and to obtain an understanding of the cultural functions of these innovations, there is no alternative to the acquisition of a thorough knowledge of the literary traditions to which they allude.

Precisely this presence of the past in contemporary literature illustrates the importance of acquiring the broadest possible familiarity with literary history before deciding to specialise in one or more of the new literatures in English, or in a particular period of English or American literature. To neglect the canon and focus on one of the new literatures in English or on contemporary English or American literature is therefore to overlook the fact that pairings such as literary history and contemporary literature, or the canon and new literatures in English, do not represent alternatives. As these pairs are interdependent, and cannot be considered in isolation, familiarity with both is a necessity in order fully to understand the texts and to achieve all-round competence in English and American studies.

Use of literary-historical knowledge

The areas of study relating to postcolonial criticism and to the intertextual and intermedial adaptation of classics of English literature are just two examples of domains where English and American studies overlap with cultural studies. Further examples of the increasing affiliation of English and American studies with media and cultural studies are the growth of interest in the history of forms of communication, of the media and of intermediality (see chapter 6), as well as the emergence of new approaches to literature from the perspective of cultural history and the growth of interest in the relationship between literature and cultural phenomena such as national identity and alterity, encounters with the Other and collective memory (for an excellent introduction to cultural studies, see SOMMER 2003).

Literary history and cultural studies

A particularly fascinating and informative aspect of the study of the history of literatures in English is the light it sheds on cultural memory, on conceptions of national identity (for example, 'Englishness' and 'Americanness'), as well as on images of the homeland and of other nations. These cultural issues are of enormous importance in the current age of Europeanisation and globalisation; they are most effectively researched through the lens of a form of literary history with strong affiliations to cultural studies. This is one of the many reasons for the continuing appeal of English and American literary and cultural studies today.

Cultural memory, Englishness and Americanness

Further reading on other literatures in English

EBERHARD KREUTZER's chapter on "Die Neuen Englischsprachigen Literaturen" in the volume *Englische Literaturgeschichte* (1991/1999, ed. SEEBER) is highly recommended as an introduction to literatures in English. The chapter has been extended considerably for the third edition of the volume (note that in the first edition it appeared under the significantly different chapter heading "Commonwealth-Literatur"), and offers introductory information on new authors and literature for the reader with appetite. The volume *Companion to the New Literatures in English*, edited by CHRISTA JANSOHN, is also very useful, containing excellent chapters, for example on Indian and South African literature. There are also books devoted to each of the diverse literatures in English; MARIA and MARTIN LÖSCHNIGG's work *Eine kurze Geschichte der kanadischen Literatur* (2001) is particularly worthy of mention. A survey of these works can be found in the comprehensive bibliography in the appendix to the present volume.

Bibliography

(The books recommended in the paragraphs giving information on further reading, along with several other works which are recommended for frequent use, are marked with a ◆.)

1. Introductions and Reference Works

ABRAMS, M.H. (ed.): *A Glossary of Literary Terms.* 7th ed., New York: Rinehart 1999 [1957].

◆ ARNOLD, Heinz Ludwig & Heinrich DETE-RING (eds.): *Grundzüge der Literaturwissenschaft.* 5th ed., Munich: dtv 2002 [1996].

◆ BECK, Rudolf, Hildegard KUESTER & Martin KUESTER: *Terminologie der Literaturwissenschaft. Ein Handbuch für das Anglistikstudium.* Ismaning: Hueber 1998.

BÖKER, Uwe & Christoph HOUSWITSCHKA (eds.): *Einführung in die Anglistik und Amerikanistik.* Munich: Beck 2000.

BORCHMEYER, Dieter & Viktor ŽMEGAČ (eds.): *Moderne Literatur in Grundbegriffen.* 2nd, rev. ed., Tübingen: Niemeyer 1994 [1987].

BRACKERT, Helmut & Jörn STÜCKRATH (eds.): *Literaturwissenschaft. Ein Grundkurs.* 7th, rev. ed., Reinbek: Rowohlt 2001 [1992].

BRENNER, Peter J.: *Das Problem der Interpretation. Eine Einführung in die Grundlagen der Literaturwissenschaft.* Tübingen: Niemeyer 1998.

BROGAN, T.V.F. (ed.): *The New Princeton Handbook of Poetic Terms.* Princeton, NJ: Princeton University Press 1994.

BROICH, Ulrich & Manfred PFISTER (eds.): *Intertextualität. Formen, Funktionen, anglistische Fallstudien.* Tübingen: Niemeyer 1985.

DRABBLE, Margaret (ed.): *The Oxford Companion to English Literature.* 6th ed., Oxford: OUP 2000 [1985].

DRESCHER, Horst W.: *Lexikon der englischen Literatur.* Stg.: Kröner 1979.

EICHER, Thomas & Volker WIEMANN (eds.): *Arbeitsbuch Literaturwissenschaft.* 2nd, rev. ed., Paderborn: Schöningh 1997 [1996].

◆ ENGLER, Bernd & Kurt MÜLLER (eds.): *Metzler Lexikon Amerikanischer Autoren.* Stg., Weimar: Metzler 2000.

◆ FABIAN, Bernhard (ed.): *Ein anglistischer*

Grundkurs. Einführung in die Literaturwissenschaft. 9th, rev. ed., Bln.: Schmidt 2004 [1971].

FOWLER, Alastair: *Kinds of Literature. An Introduction to the Theory of Genres and Modes.* Oxford: Clarendon 1982.

FRICKE, Harald & Rüdiger ZYMNER. *Einübung in die Literaturwissenschaft. Parodieren geht über Studieren.* 4th, rev. ed., Paderborn: Schöningh 2000 [1991].

FRICKE, Harald et al. (eds.): *Reallexikon der Deutschen Literaturwissenschaft.* Vol. 2: H-O. Neubearbeitung des *Reallexikons der Deutschen Literaturgeschichte.* 3rd, rev. ed., Bln., New York: de Gruyter 2003 [2000]. [Vol. 1 cf. WEIMAR 1997; Vol. 3 cf. MÜLLER 2003]

GRABES, Herbert: "Literaturinterpretation als Wissenschaft." In: *Methodenprobleme der Literaturinterpretation.* Eds.: Herbert MAINUSCH et al. Tübingen: Deutsches Institut für Fernstudien 1981a. 21–47.

GRABES, Herbert: *Fiktion – Imitation– Ästhetik. Was ist ‚Literatur'.* Tübingen: Deutsches Institut für Fernstudien 1981b.

HEMPFER, Klaus W.: *Gattungstheorie.* Munich: Fink 1973.

◆ HORNUNG, Alfred: *Lexikon amerikanische Literatur.* Mannheim: Meyers Lexikonverlag 1992.

JESSING, Benedikt & Ralf KÖHNEN: *Einführung in die neuere deutsche Literaturwissenschaft.* Stg., Weimar: Metzler 2003.

KARRER, Wolfgang & Eberhard KREUTZER: *Daten der englischen und amerikanischen Literatur.* Vol. 1: *Daten der englischen Literatur von 1700–1890.* 2nd ed., Munich: dtv 1983 [1979]; vol. 2: *Werke der englischen Literatur von 1890 bis zur Gegenwart.* 4th, rev. ed., Munich: dtv 1989 [1973].

Kindlers Neues Literatur Lexikon. 22 vols. Munich: Kindler 1988–1992, 1998.

KLARER, Mario: *Einführung in die anglistisch-amerikanistische Literaturwissenschaft.* 4th, rev. ed., Darmstadt: WBG 2004 [1994].

KORTE, Barbara: *The Short Story in Britain.* Tübingen: Francke, 2003.

KORTE, Barbara, Klaus-Peter MÜLLER & Josef SCHMIED: *Einführung in die Anglistik.* 2nd ed., Stg., Weimar: Metzler 2004 [1997].

KREUTZER, Eberhard & Ansgar NÜNNING (eds.): *Metzler-Lexikon englischsprachiger Autorinnen und Autoren: 631 Portraits, von den Anfängen bis zur Gegenwart.* Stg., Weimar: Metzler 2002.

LÖFFLER, Arno et al.: *Einführung in das Studium der englischen Literatur*. 6th, rev. ed., Wiebelsheim: Quelle & Meyer 2001 [1982].

LOTMAN, Jurij M.: *Die Struktur literarischer Texte*. 4th ed., Munich: Fink 1993 [1972].

LUDWIG, Hans-Werner & Thomas ROMMEL: *Studium Literaturwissenschaft: Arbeitstechniken und Neue Medien*. Tübingen et al.: Francke 2003.

MEYER, Michael: *English and American Literatures*. Stg.: UTB 2004.

MÜLLER, Jan-Dirk (eds.): *Reallexikon der Deutschen Literaturwissenschaft*. Vol. 3: P-Z. Neubearbeitung des *Reallexikons der Deutschen Literaturgeschichte*. Bln., New York: de Gruyter 2003. [Vol. 1 cf. WEIMAR 1997; Vol. 2 cf. FRICKE 2000]

NEUHAUS, Stefan: *Grundriß der Literaturwissenschaft*. Tübingen et al.: Francke 2003.

NÜNNING, Ansgar: *Uni-Training Englische Literaturwissenschaft. Einführung in Grundstrukturen des Fachs und Methoden der Textanalyse*. Stg.: Klett 1996.

NÜNNING, Ansgar & Andreas H. JUCKER: *Orientierung Anglistik/Amerikanistik. Was sie kann, was sie will*. Reinbek: Rowohlt 1999.

PECHLIVANOS, Miltos et al. (eds.): *Einführung in die Literaturwissenschaft*. Stg., Weimar: Metzler 1995.

PREMINGER, Alex & T.V.F. BROGAN (eds.): *The New Princeton Encyclopedia of Poetry and Poetics*. Princeton, NJ: Princeton UP 1993.

RICKLEFS, Ulfert (ed.): *Fischer Lexikon Literatur*. 3 vols. FfM.: Fischer 1996.

SALZMAN, Jack (ed.): *The Cambridge Handbook of American Literature*. Cambridge: CUP 1986.

SCHNEIDER, Ralf (ed.): *Literaturwissenschaft in Theorie und Praxis*. Tübingen: Narr 2004.

SCHWANITZ, Dietrich: *Literaturwissenschaft für Anglisten. Das neue studienbegleitende Handbuch*. Munich: Hueber 1985.

SCHWEIKLE, Günther & Irmgard SCHWEIKLE (eds.): *Metzler Literatur Lexikon. Begriffe und Definitionen*. 2nd, rev. ed., Stg.: Metzler 1990 [1984].

SOMMER, Roy: *Grundkurs Cultural Studies. Kulturwissenschaft Großbritannien*. Barcelona et al.: Klett 2003.

STRUBE, Werner: *Analytische Philosophie der Literaturwissenschaft. Untersuchungen zur literaturwissenschaftlichen Definition, Klassifikation, Interpretation und Textbewertung*. Paderborn: Schöningh 1993.

◆ THIES, Henning (ed.): *Hauptwerke der amerikanischen Literatur. Einzeldarstellungen und Interpretationen*. Munich: Kindler 1995a.

◆ THIES, Henning (ed.): *Hauptwerke der englischen Literatur. Einzeldarstellungen und Interpretationen*. Vol. 1: *Von den Anfängen bis zum Ende des Viktorianischen Zeitalters*. Vol. 2: *Das 20. Jh. und die neuen Literaturen außerhalb Englands*. Munich: Kindler 1995b.

TITZMANN, Michael: *Strukturale Textanalyse. Theorie und Praxis der Interpretation*. 3rd ed., Munich: Fink 1993 [1977].

VOGT, Jochen: *Einladung zur Literaturwissenschaft. Mit einem Hypertext-Vertiefungsprogramm im Internet*. 2nd, rev. ed., Munich: Fink 2001 [1999].

VOSSKAMP, Wilhelm: "Gattungen." In: BRACKERT & STÜCKRATH, 253–269.

WEIMAR, Klaus et al. (eds.): *Reallexikon der Deutschen Literaturwissenschaft*. Vol. 1: A-G. Bln., New York: de Gruyter 1997. [Vol. 2 cf. FRICKE 2000; Vol. 3 cf. MÜLLER 2003]

WILPERT, Gero von: *Sachwörterbuch der Literatur*. 8th, rev. ed., Stg.: Kröner 2001 [1955].

ZIMA, Peter V.: *Komparatistik. Einführung in die vergleichende Literaturwissenschaft*. Tübingen: Francke 1992.

2. Introductions to Literary Theories, Models and Methods

BAASNER, Rainer & Maria ZENS: *Methoden und Modelle der Literaturwissenschaft. Eine Einführung*. 2nd ed., Bln.: Schmidt 2001 [1996].

BELSEY, Catherine: *Critical Practice*. 2nd, rev. ed., Ldn.: Routledge 2002 [1980].

BERTENS, Hans: *Literary Theory. The Basics*. Ldn.: Routledge 2001.

BOGDAL, Klaus-Michael (ed.): *Neue Literaturtheorien. Eine Einführung*. 2nd, rev. ed., Opladen: Westdeutscher Verlag 1997 [1990].

BONHEIM, Helmut: *Literary Systematics*. Cambridge: Brewer 1990.

◆ CULLER, Jonathan: *Literary Theory. A Very Short Introduction*. Oxford, New York: OUP 1997.

CULLER, Jonathan: *Literaturtheorie. Eine kurze Einführung*. Transl. by Andreas MAHLER. Stg.: Reclam 2002. [Transl. of *Literary Theory. A Very Short Introduction*]

◆ EAGLETON, Terry: *Literary Theory. An Introduction*. 2nd ed., Oxford: Blackwell 1996 [1983].

EAGLETON, Terry: *Einführung in die Literaturtheorie*. Transl. by Elfi BETTINGER and Elke HENTSCHEL. 4th, rev. ed., Stg.: Metzler 1997 [1988]. [Transl. of *Literary Theory. An Introduction*]

FRANK, Manfred: *Was ist Neostrukturalismus?* FfM.: Suhrkamp 1983.

GEISENHANSLÜKE, Achim: *Einführung in die Literaturtheorie. Von der Hermeneutik zur Medienwissenschaft*. Darmstadt: WBG 2003.

HAWTHORN, Jeremy (ed.): *A Glossary of Contemporary Literary Theory*. 4th ed., Ldn.: Arnold 2000 [1992]. (German translation: *Grundbegriffe moderner Literaturtheorie. Ein Handbuch*. Tübingen: Francke 1994)

KIMMICH, Dorothee et al. (eds.): *Texte zur Literaturtheorie der Gegenwart*. Rev. ed., Stg.: Reclam 2003 [1996].

◆ MAKARYK, Irena R. (ed.): *Encyclopedia of Contemporary Literary Theory. Approaches, Scholars, Terms*. Toronto: University of Toronto Press 1993.

MILLER, Joseph Hillis: *Reconsiderations of Literary Theory, Literary History and Cultural Authority*. Baltimore, MD: Johns Hopkins UP 2002.

MOI, Toril. *Sexual/Textual Politics. Feminist Literary Theory*. 2nd ed., Ldn.: Routledge 2002 [1985].

MOI, Toril. *Sexus, Text, Herrschaft: Feministische Literaturtheorie*. Transl. by Elfi HARTENSTEIN et al. Bremen: Zeichen + Spuren 1989. [Transl. of *Sexual/Textual Politics. Feminist Literary Theory*]

◆ NÜNNING, Ansgar (ed.): *Literaturwissenschaftliche Theorien, Modelle und Methoden. Eine Einführung*. 3rd, rev. ed., Trier: WVT 1998 [1995].

◆ NÜNNING, Ansgar (ed.): *Metzler Lexikon Literatur- und Kulturtheorie. Ansätze – Personen – Grundbegriffe*. 3rd, rev. ed., Stg., Weimar: Metzler 2004 [1998].

NÜNNING, Ansgar (ed.): *Grundbegriffe der Literaturtheorie*. Stg., Weimar: Metzler 2004.

NÜNNING, Ansgar & Vera NÜNNING: *Konzepte der Kulturwissenschaften. Theoretische Grundlagen – Ansätze – Perspektiven*. Stg., Weimar: Metzler 2003.

◆ PAYNE, Michael (ed.): *A Dictionary of Cultural and Critical Theory*. Oxford: Blackwell 1996.

RENNER, Rolf Günter & Engelbert HABEKOST (eds.): *Lexikon literaturtheoretischer Werke*. Stg.: Kröner 1995.

◆ SELDEN, Raman & Peter WIDDOWSON: *A Reader's Guide to Contemporary Literary Theory*. 4th ed., Hemel Hempstead: Harvester Wheatsheaf 1997 [1985].

SEXL, Martin (ed.): *Einführung in die Literaturtheorie*. Stg.: UTB 2004.

WELLEK, René & Austin WARREN (eds.): *Theory of Literature*. 3rd ed., Ldn., Harmondsworth: Penguin 1993 [1949].

WOLFREYS, Julian: *Critical Keywords in Literary and Cultural Theory*. Basingstoke, Hampshire et al.: Palgrave Macmillan 2003.

◆ ZAPF, Hubert: *Kurze Geschichte der angloamerikanischen Literaturtheorie*. 2nd ed., Tübingen: Francke 1996 [1991].

ZIMA, Peter V.: *Die Dekonstruktion. Einführung und Kritik*. Tübingen: Francke 1994.

3. Introductions to the Analysis of Poetry

BEACH, Christopher: *The Cambridge Introduction to Twentieth-Century American Poetry*. Cambridge: CUP 2003.

◆ BODE, Christoph: *Einführung in die Lyrikanalyse*. Trier: WVT 2001.

BURDORF, Dieter: *Einführung in die Gedichtanalyse*. 2nd, rev. ed., Stg., Weimar: Metzler 1997 [1995].

CARPER, Thomas & Derek ATTRIDGE: *Meter and Meaning. An Introduction to Rhythm in Poetry*. New York et al.: Routledge 2003.

FENTON, James: *An Introduction to English Poetry*. Ldn. et al.: Viking 2002.

FRIEDRICH, Hugo: *Die Struktur der modernen Lyrik. Von der Mitte des 19. bis zur Mitte des 20. Jh.s*. 23rd ed., Reinbek: Rowohlt 1996 [1956].

◆ FURNISS, Tom & Michael BATH: *Reading Poetry: An Introduction*. Ldn. et al.: Harvester Wheatsheaf et al. 1996.

◆ HÜHN, Peter: *Geschichte der englischen Lyrik. Vol. 1: Vom 16. Jh. bis zur Romantik*. Vol. 2: *Von der viktorianischen Epoche bis zur Gegenwart*. Tübingen: Francke 1995.

JAKOBSON, Roman: *Poetik. Ausgewählte Aufsätze 1921–1971*. FfM: Suhrkamp 1979.

JAKOBSON, Roman: "Closing Statement: Linguistics and Poetics." In: *Style in Language*. Ed.: Thomas A. SEBEOK. New York, Ldn.: Wiley 1960. 350–377.

KNÖRRICH, Otto: "Einleitung. Lyrik – Begriff und Theorie einer Gattung." In: *Lexikon lyrischer Formen*. Ed.: Otto KNÖRRICH. Stg.: Kröner 1992. Xii-l.

KURZ, Gerhard: *Metapher, Allegorie, Symbol*. 4th, rev. ed., Göttingen: Vandenhoeck & Ruprecht 1997 [1982].

LAUSBERG, Heinrich: *Elemente der literarischen Rhetorik*. 10th ed., Ismaning: Hueber 1990 [1949].

LEECH, Geoffrey: *A Linguistic Guide to English Poetry*. 20th ed., Ldn.: Longman 1999 [1969].

LINK, Jürgen: "Das lyrische Gedicht als Paradigma des überstrukturierten Textes." In: *Literaturwissenschaft. Grundkurs 1*. Eds.: Helmut BRACKERT & Jörn STÜCKRATH. Reinbek: Rowohlt 1981. 192–219.

LINK, Jürgen: "Elemente der Lyrik." In: *Literaturwissenschaft. Ein Grundkurs*. Eds.: Helmut BRACKERT & Jörn STÜCKRATH. 7th, rev. ed., Reinbek: Rowohlt 2001 [1992]. 86–101.

◆ LUDWIG, Hans-Werner: *Arbeitsbuch Lyrikanalyse*. 4th ed., Tübingen: Narr 1994 [1981].

MELLER, Horst: *Zum Verstehen englischer Gedichte*. Munich: Fink 1985.

MÜLLER, Wolfgang G.: *Das lyrische Ich. Erscheinungsformen gattungseigentümlicher Autor-Subjektivität in der englischen Lyrik*. Heidelberg: Winter 1979.

MÜLLER, Wolfgang G.: "Das Problem der Subjektivität der Lyrik und die Dichtung der Dinge und Orte." In: *Literaturwissenschaftliche Theorien, Modelle, Methoden. Eine Einführung*. Ed.: Ansgar NÜNNING. 3rd, rev. ed., Trier: WVT 1998 [1995]. 93–105.

◆ MÜLLER-ZETTELMANN, Eva: *Lyrik und Metalyrik. Theorie einer Gattung und ihrer Selbstbespiegelung anhand von Beispielen aus der englisch- und deutschsprachigen Dichtkunst*. Heidelberg: Winter 2000.

PLETT, Heinrich: *Systematische Rhetorik. Konzepte und Analysen*. Munich: Fink 2000.

◆ PLETT, Heinrich: *Textwissenschaft und Textanalyse. Semiotik, Linguistik, Rhetorik*. 2nd, rev. ed., Heidelberg: Quelle & Meyer 1979 [1975].

ROBERTS, Phil: *How Poetry Works*. 2nd ed., Ldn.: Penguin 2000 [1986].

4. Introductions to the Analysis of Drama

ASMUTH, Bernard: *Einführung in die Dramenanalyse*. 5th, rev. ed., Stg.: Metzler 1997 [1980].

◆ ASTON, Elaine & George SAVONA: *Theatre as Sign System. A Semiotics of Text and Performance*. Ldn.: Routledge 1991.

ELAM, Keir: *The Semiotics of Theatre and Drama*. London et al.: Routledge 2002 [1980].

ESSLIN, Martin: *The Theatre of the Absurd*. 3rd ed., Ldn.: Methuen 2001 [1962].

ESSLIN, Martin: *Das Theater des Absurden*. Transl. by Marianne FALK. Ffm: Athenäum 1964. [Transl. of *The Theatre of the Absurd*]

ESSLIN, Martin: *The Field of Drama. How the Signs of Drama Create Meaning on Stage and Screen*. Ldn.: Methuen 1987.

ESSLIN, Martin: *Das Zeichen des Dramas. Theater, Film, Fernsehen*. Transl. by Cornelia SCHRAMM. Reinbek: Rowohlt 1989. [Transl. of *The Field of Drama*]

FISCHER-LICHTE, Erika: *Semiotik des Theaters. Eine Einführung*. 3 vols. Vol. 1: *Das System der theatralischen Zeichen*. Vol. 3: *Die Aufführung als Text*. 4th ed., Tübingen: Narr 1994 [1983].

◆ GOETSCH, Paul: *Bauformen des modernen englischen und amerikanischen Dramas*. 2nd ed., Darmstadt: WBG 1992 [1977].

GRABES, Herbert: *Das amerikanische Drama des 20. Jh.s*. 2nd ed., Stg.: Klett 2003 [1998].

HÖFELE, Andreas: "Drama und Theater. Einige Anmerkungen zur Geschichte und gegenwärtigen Diskussion eines umstrittenen Verhältnisses." In: *Forum Modernes Theater* 6 (1991), 3–23.

KLOTZ, Volker: *Geschlossene und offene Form in Drama*. 14th ed., Munich: Hanser 1999 [1960].

KRIEGER, Gottfried: "Dramentheorie und Methoden der Dramenanalyse." In: *Literaturwissenschaftliche Theorien, Modelle und Methoden. Eine Einführung*. Ed.: Ansgar NÜNNING. 3rd, rev. ed., Trier: WVT 1998 [1995]. 69–92.

LENNARD, John & Mary LUCKHURST: *The Drama Handbook. A Guide to Reading Plays*. Oxford: OUP 2002.

KRIEGER, Gottfried: *Das englische Drama des 20. Jh.s*. Stg.: Klett 1998.

◆ MAHLER, Andreas: "Aspekte des Dramas." In: *Literaturwissenschaft. Ein Grundkurs*. Eds.: Helmut BRACKERT & Jörn STÜCKRATH. 7th, rev. ed., Reinbek: Rowohlt 2001 [1992]. 71–85.

MEHL, Dieter (ed.): *Das englische Drama. Vom Mittelalter bis zur Gegenwart*. 2 vols. Düsseldorf: Bagel 1970.

MÜLLER, Klaus-Peter: *Englisches Theater der Gegenwart. Geschichte(n) und Strukturen*. Tübingen: Narr 1993.

NÜNNING, Josefa (ed.): *Das englische Drama*. Darmstadt: WBG 1973.

PFISTER, Manfred: *Studien zum Wandel der Perspektivenstruktur in elisabethanischen und jakobäischen Komödien*. Munich: Fink 1974.

◆ PFISTER, Manfred: *Das Drama. Theorie und Analyse*. 11th, rev. ed., Munich: Fink 2001 [1977].

PFISTER, Manfred: *The Theory and Analysis of Drama*. Transl. by John Halliday. Cambridge: CUP 1988. [Translation of *Das Drama*]

PLATZ-WAURY, Elke: *Drama und Theater. Eine Einführung*. 5th, rev. ed., Tübingen: Narr 1999 [1978].

SCHABERT, Ina (ed.): *Shakespeare-Handbuch. Die Zeit. Der Mensch. Das Werk. Die Nachwelt*. 4th, rev. ed., Stg.: Kröner 2000 [1972].

5. Introductions to the Analysis of Narrative Texts

ABBOTT, Horace Porter: *The Cambridge Introduction to Narrative*. Cambridge, New York: CUP 2002.

BAL, Mieke: *Narratology. Introduction to the Theory of Narrative*. 2nd ed., Toronto: University of Toronto Press 1997 [1985].

BARTHES, Roland: *Introduction to the Structural Analysis of Narrative*. Birmingham: Birmingham University 1966.

BONHEIM, Helmut: *The Narrative Modes. Techniques of the Short Story*. Cambridge: Brewer 1982.

BOOTH, Wayne C.: *The Rhetoric of Fiction*. 2. ed., repr., Chicago, Ldn.: University of Chicago Press 1991 [1961].

BOOTH, Wayne C.: *Die Rhetorik der Erzählkunst*. Transl. by Alexander POLZIN. Heidelberg: Quelle & Meyer 1974. [Transl. of *The Rhetoric of Fiction*]

CHATMAN, Seymour: *Story and Discourse. Narrative Structure in Fiction and Film*. 6th ed., Ithaca, New York: Cornell UP 1993 [1978].

CHATMAN, Seymour: *Coming to Terms. The Rhetoric of Narrative in Fiction and Film*. Ithaca, New York: Cornell UP 1990.

COBLEY, Paul: *Narrative*. Ldn.: Routledge 2001.

COHN, Dorrit: *Transparent Minds. Narrative Modes for Presenting Consciousness in Fiction*. Princeton: Princeton UP 1978.

FLUCK, Winfried: *Das kulturelle Imaginäre. Eine Funktionsgeschichte des amerikanischen Romans 1790–1900*. FfM.: Suhrkamp 1997.

FLUDERNIK, Monika: *The Fictions of Language and the Languages of Fiction. The Linguistic Representation of Speech and Consciousness*. Ldn.: Routledge 1993.

FLUDERNIK, Monika: *Towards a 'Natural' Narratology*. Ldn.: Routledge 1996.

FORSTER, E.M.: *Aspects of the Novel*. Harmondsworth: Penguin 1981 [1927].

FORSTER, E.M.: *Ansichten des Romans*. Transl. by Walter SCHÜRENBERG. Bln. et al.: Suhrkamp 1949. [Transl. of *Aspects of the Novel*]

GENETTE, Gérard: *Narrative Discourse. An Essay in Method*. Transl. by Jane LEWIN. Oxford: Blackwell 1980. [Transl. of *Discours du récit*]

GENETTE, Gérard: *Narrative Discourse Revisited*. Transl. by Jane LEWIN. Ithaca, New York: Cornell UP 1988. [Transl. of *Nouveau discours du récit*]

GENETTE, Gérard: *Die Erzählung*. Ed.: Jochen VOGT. Transl. by Andreas KNOP. Munich: Fink 1994. [Transl. of *Discours du récit* and *Nouveau discours du récit*]

GRABES, Herbert: "Wie aus Sätzen Personen werden … Über die Erforschung literarischer Figuren." In: *Poetica* 10 (1978), 405–428.

GRÜNZWEIG, Walter & Andreas SOLBACH (eds.): *Grenzüberschreitungen. Narratologie im Kontext/Transcending Boundaries. Narratology in Context*. Tübingen: Narr 1999.

GUTENBERG, Andrea: *Mögliche Welten. Plot und Sinnstiftung im englischen Frauenroman*. Heidelberg: Winter 2000.

◆ HAWTHORN, Jeremy: *Studying the Novel. An Introduction*. 4th ed., Ldn.: Arnold 2001 [1985].

HELBIG, Jörg (ed.): *Erzählen und Erzähltheorie im 20. Jahrhundert. Festschrift für Willhelm Füger*. Heidelberg: Winter 2001.

HERMAN, David (ed.): *Narratologies. New Perspectives on Narrative Analysis*. Columbus, OH: Ohio State UP 1999.

HOFFMANN, Gerhard: *Raum, Situation, erzählte Wirklichkeit. Poetologische und historische Studien zum englischen und amerikanischen Roman*. Stg.: Metzler 1978.

ICKSTADT, Heinz: *Der amerikanische Roman im 20. Jh. Transformationen des Mimetischen*. Darmstadt: WBG 1998.

♦ JAHN, Manfred: "Narratologie. Methoden und Modelle der Erzähltheorie." In: *Literaturwissenschaftliche Theorien, Modelle, Methoden. Eine Einführung*. Ed.: Ansgar NÜNNING. 3rd, rev. ed., Trier: WVT 1998 [1995]. 29–50.

JAHN, Manfred & Ansgar NÜNNING: "A Survey of Narratological Models." In: *LWU* XXVII,4 (1994), 283–303.

KAHRMANN, Cordula, Gunter REISS & Manfred SCHLUCHTER: *Erzähltextanalyse. Eine Einführung. Mit Studien- und Übungstexten*. 4th ed., Kronberg: Athenäum 1996 [1986]. [New, rev. ed. of *Erzähltextanalyse. Eine Einführung in Grundlagen und Verfahren*, 1977]

KINDT, Tom & Hans Harald MÜLLER (eds.): *What is Narratology? Questions and Answers Regarding the Status of a Theory*. Bln.: de Gruyter 2003.

KORTE, Barbara: *Techniken der Schlußgebung im Roman. Eine Untersuchung englisch- und deutschsprachiger Romane*. FfM.: Lang 1985.

KORTE, Barbara: *Körpersprache in der Literatur. Theorie und Geschichte am Beispiel englischer Erzählprosa*. Tübingen: Francke 1993.

LÄMMERT, Eberhard: *Bauformen des Erzählens*. 8th ed., Stg.: Metzler 1991 [1955].

LANSER, Susan Sniader: *The Narrative Act. Point of View in Prose Fiction*. Princeton, NJ: Princeton UP 1981.

LANSER, Susan Sniader: *Fictions of Authority. Women Writers and Narrative Voice*. Ithaca: Cornell UP 1992.

LUDWIG, Hans-Werner (ed.): *Arbeitsbuch Romananalyse*. 6th ed., Tübingen: Narr 1998 [1982].

♦ MARTINEZ, Matias & Michael SCHEFFEL: *Einführung in die Erzähltheorie*. 4th ed., Munich: Beck 2003 [1999].

NISCHIK, Reingard M.: *Einsträngigkeit und Mehrsträngigkeit der Handlungsführung in literarischen Texten. Dargestellt insbesondere an englischen, amerikanischen und kanadischen Romanen des 20. Jh.s*. Tübingen: Narr 1981.

NÜNNING, Ansgar: *Grundzüge eines kommunikationstheoretischen Modells der erzählerischen Vermittlung. Die Funktionen der Erzählinstanz in den Romanen George Eliots*. Trier: WVT 1989.

NÜNNING, Ansgar: "Die Funktionen von Erzählinstanzen. Analysekategorien und Modelle zur Beschreibung des Erzählerverhaltens." In: *LWU* XXX.4 (1997), 323–349.

NÜNNING, Ansgar: *Der englische Roman des 20. Jh.s*. Stg.: Klett 2000 [1998a].

NÜNNING, Ansgar (ed.; with Carola SURKAMP and Bruno ZERWECK): *Unreliable Narration. Studien zur Theorie und Praxis unglaubwürdigen Erzählens in der englischsprachigen Erzählliteratur*. Trier: WVT 1998b.

NÜNNING, Ansgar & Vera NÜNNING (eds.): *Neue Ansätze in der Erzähltheorie*. Trier: WVT 2002.

NÜNNING, Vera: *Der englische Roman des 19. Jh.s*. Stg.: Klett 2000.

NÜNNING, Vera & Ansgar NÜNNING (eds.): *Multiperspektivisches Erzählen. Zur Theorie und Geschichte der Perspektivenstruktur im englischen Roman des 18. bis 20. Jh.s*. Trier: WVT 2000.

NÜNNING, Vera & Ansgar NÜNNING (eds.): *Erzähltheorie transgenerisch, intermedial, interdisziplinär*. Trier: WVT 2002.

NÜNNING, Vera & Ansgar NÜNNING (eds.): *Erzähltextanalyse und Gender Studies*. Stg., Weimar: Metzler 2004.

PRINCE, Gerald: *A Dictionary of Narratology*. Rev. ed., Lincoln: University of Nebraska Press 2003 [1987].

♦ RIMMON-KENAN, Shlomith: *Narrative Fiction. Contemporary Poetics*. 2nd ed., Ldn., New York: Methuen 2002 [1983].

SCHNEIDER, Ralf: *Grundriß zur kognitiven Theorie der Figurenrezeption am Beispiel des viktorianischen Romans*. Tübingen: Stauffenburg 2000.

♦ STANZEL, Franz K.: *Theorie des Erzählens*. 7th ed., Göttingen: Vandenhoeck & Ruprecht 2001 [1979].

STANZEL, Franz K.: *A Theory of Narrative*. Transl. by Charlotte GOEDSCHE. Cambridge: CUP 1984. [Transl. of *Theorie des Erzählens*]

STANZEL, Franz K.: *Unterwegs. Erzähltheorie für Leser. Ausgewählte Schriften.* Incl. an introduction and an appendix by Dorrit COHN. Göttingen: Vandenhoeck & Ruprecht 2002.

◆ TOOLAN, Michael J.: *Narrative. A Critical Linguistic Introduction.* 2nd ed., Ldn., New York: Routledge 2001 [1988].

WIEST-KELLNER, Ursula: *Messages from the Threshold. Die You-Erzählform als Ausdruck liminaler Wesen und Welten.* Bielefeld: Aisthesis 1999.

WOLF, Werner: *Ästhetische Illusion und Illusionsdurchbrechung in der Erzählkunst. Theorie und Geschichte mit Schwerpunkt auf englischem illusionsstörenden Erzählen.* Tübingen: Niemeyer 1993.

6. Introductions to Inter-Art Studies/ Intermediality, Media Studies and the Analysis of Media Genres

ALBERSMEIER, Franz-Josef: "Literatur und Film. Entwurf einer praxisorientierten Textsystematik." In: ZIMA, 235–268.

ALBERSMEIER, Franz-Josef & Volker ROLOFF (eds.): *Literaturverfilmungen.* FfM.: Suhrkamp 1989.

AMELUNXEN, Hubertus von: "Photographie und Literatur. Prolegomena zu einer Theoriegeschichte der Photographie." In: ZIMA, 209–234.

BERNINGER, Mark: "Children's Games and Children's Plays – Computer Adventures Meet the Stage in Alan Ayckbourne's *Mr A's Amazing Maze Plays* and *Callisto 5*." In: VOIGTS-VIRCHOW, 209–216.

BIGNELL, Jonathan: *An Introduction to Television Studies.* Ldn. et al.: Routledge 2003.

BORDWELL, David: *Narration in the Fiction Film.* Ldn.: Methuen 1985.

BRANIGAN, Edward: *Narrative Comprehension and Film.* Ldn.: Routledge 1992.

BURTON, Graeme: *More Than Meets the Eye: An Introduction to Media Studies.* 3rd ed., Ldn.: Arnold 2002 [1990].

CROOK, Tim: *Radio Drama: Theory and Practice.* Ldn.: Routledge 1999.

◆ DRAKAKIS, John (ed.): *British Radio Drama.* Cambridge: CUP 1981.

ERNST, Ulrich: *Intermedialität im europäischen Kulturzusammenhang. Beiträge zur Theorie und Geschichte der visuellen Lyrik.* Bln.: Schmidt 2002.

FAULSTICH, Werner: *Rock – Pop – Beat – Folk. Grundlagen der Textmusik-Analyse.* Tübingen: Narr 1978.

FAULSTICH, Werner: *Die Filminterpretation.* 2nd ed., Göttingen: Vandenhoeck & Ruprecht 1995 [1988].

FAULSTICH, Werner: *Medientheorien. Einführung und Überblick.* Göttingen: Vandenhoeck & Ruprecht 1991.

FAULSTICH, Werner: *Grundkurs Filmanalyse.* Munich: Fink 2002.

◆ FAULSTICH, Werner: *Einführung in die Medienwissenschaft.* Munich: Fink 2003.

◆ FRANK, Armin Paul: *Das englische und amerikanische Hörspiel.* Munich: Fink 1981.

◆ GIANNETTI, Louis: *Understanding Movies.* 9th ed., Upper Saddle River, NJ: Prentice Hall 2002 [1972].

GIER, Albert: "Musik in der Literatur. Einflüsse und Analogien." In: ZIMA, 61–92.

GOETSCH, Paul & Dietrich SCHEUNEMANN (eds.): *Text und Ton im Film.* Tübingen: Narr 1997.

GRIEM, Julika & Eckart VOIGTS-VIRCHOW: "Filmnarratologie. Grundlagen, Tendenzen und Beispielanalysen." In: *Erzähltheorie transgenerisch, intermedial, interdisziplinär.* Eds.: Vera & Ansgar NÜNNING. Trier: WVT 2002. 155–184.

HELBIG, Jörg (ed.): *Intermedialität. Theorie und Praxis eines interdisziplinären Forschungsgebietes.* Bln.: Schmidt 1998.

HELBIG, Jörg: *Geschichte des britischen Films.* Stg.: Metzler 1999.

HICKETHIER, Knut & Siegfried ZIELINSKI (eds.): *Medien/Kultur. Schnittstellen zwischen Medienwissenschaft, Medienpraxis und gesellschaftlicher Kommunikation.* Bln.: Spiess 1991.

HICKETHIER, Knut (ed.): *Fernsehen. Wahrnehmungswelt, Programminstitution und Marktkonkurrenz.* FfM.: Lang 1992.

◆ HICKETHIER, Knut: *Film- und Fernsehanalyse.* 3rd, rev. ed., Stg.: Metzler 2001.

HOWELLS, Richard: *Visual Culture. An Introduction.* Cambridge: Polity 2003.

KITTLER, Friedrich A.: *Aufschreibesysteme 1800/1900.* 4th, rev. ed., Munich: Fink 2003 [1985].

KITTLER, Friedrich A.: *Discourse Networks 1800/1900.* Transl. by Michael METEER & Chris CULLENS. Palo Alto: Stanford UP 1990. [Transl. of *Aufschreibesysteme 1800/1900*]

KREWANI, Angela: *Hybride Formen: New British Cinema Television Drama Hypermedia.* Trier: WVT 2001.

LACEY, Nick: *Narrative and Genre. Key Concepts in Media Studies.* Basingstoke: Macmillan 2000.

LISTER, Martin et al.: *New Media. A Critical Introduction.* Ldn., New York: Routledge 2003.

LUDES, Peter: *Einführung in die Medienwissenschaft. Entwicklungen und Theorien.* 2nd, rev. ed., Bln.: Schmidt 2003 [1998].

LÜDEKE, Roger & Erika GREBER (eds.): *Intermedium Literatur. Beiträge zu einer Medientheorie der Literaturwissenschaft.* Göttingen: Wallstein 2004.

MARRIS, Paul (ed.): *Media Studies. A Reader.* 2nd ed., Edinburgh: Edinburgh UP 2002 [1996].

MERTEN, Klaus, Siegfried J. SCHMIDT & Siegfried WEISCHENBERG (eds.): *Die Wirklichkeit der Medien. Eine Einführung in die Kommunikationswissenschaft.* Opladen: Westdeutscher Verlag 1994.

MÜLLER, Jürgen E.: *Intermedialität. Formen moderner kultureller Kommunikation.* Münster: Nodus 1996.

MÜLLER, Ulrich: "Literatur und Musik. Vertonungen von Literatur." In: ZIMA, 31–60.

◆ NELSON, Robin: *TV Drama in Transition: Forms, Values and Cultural Change.* Basingstoke: Macmillan 1997.

NELSON, Robin: "TV Drama. 'Flexi-Narrative Form' and 'a New Affective Order'." In: VOIGTS-VIRCHOW, 111–118.

PAECH, Joachim: *Literatur und Film.* 2nd, rev. ed., Stg.: Metzler 1997 [1988].

PAECH, Joachim: "Vom Feuilletonroman zum Fernsehspiel." In: *Literaturwissenschaft. Ein Grundkurs.* Eds.: Helmut BRACKERT & Jörn STÜCKRATH: 7th ed., Reinbek: Rowohlt 2001 [1992]. 360–374.

PAECH, Joachim (ed.): *Film, Fernsehen, Video und die Künste. Strategien der Intermedialität.* Stg.: Metzler 1994.

PAGET, Derek: "Acting the Real: Dramatic Practices in Television Dramadoc/Docudrama." In: VOIGTS-VIRCHOW, 101–110.

PRIESSNITZ, Horst (ed.): *Das englische Hörspiel.* Düsseldorf: Bagel 1977.

RAJEWSKI, Irina O.: *Intermedialität.* Tübingen: Francke 2002.

RAUH, Reinhold: *Sprache im Film. Die Kombination von Wort und Bild im Spielfilm.* Münster: MakS-Publikationen 1987.

RAYNER, Philip et al. (eds.): *Media Studies. The Essential Introduction.* Ldn.: Routledge 2001.

RAYNER, Philip et al. (eds.): *Media Studies. The Essential Resource.* Ldn.: Routledge 2004.

ROLOFF, Volker: "Film und Literatur. Zur Theorie und Praxis der intermedialen Analyse am Beispiel von Bunuel, Truffaut, Godar und Antonioni." In: ZIMA, 269–309.

SCHANZE, Helmut (ed. with Susanne PÜTZ): *Metzler-Lexikon Medientheorie, Medienwissenschaft: Ansätze, Personen, Grundbegriffe.* Stg., Weimar: Metzler 2002.

SCHATZ, Thomas (ed.): *Hollywood. Critical Concepts in Media and Cultural Studies.* 4 Vols. Ldn.: Routledge 2004.

SCHER, Steven P. (ed.): *Literatur und Musik. Ein Handbuch zur Theorie und Praxis eines komparatistischen Grenzgebietes.* Bln.: Schmidt 1984.

SCHMIDT, Siegfried J.: *Kognitive Autonomie und soziale Orientierung. Konstruktivistische Bemerkungen zum Zusammenhang von Kognition, Kommunikation, Medien und Kultur.* FfM.: Suhrkamp 1994.

SCHMIDT, Siegfried J.: *Kalte Faszination. Medien · Kultur · Wissenschaft in der Mediengesellschaft.* Weilerswist: Velbrück Wissenschaft 2000.

SCHMIDT, Siegfried J. & Siegfried WEISCHENBERG. "Mediengattungen, Berichterstattungsmuster, Darstellungsformen." In: MERTEN, SCHMIDT & WEISCHENBERG, 212–236.

SCHNEIDER, Irmela: *Der verwandelte Text. Wege zu einer Theorie der Literaturverfilmung.* Tübingen: Niemeyer 1981.

SCHNEIDER, Irmela: "Hybridkultur. Eine Spurensuche." In: THOMSEN, 9–24.

SCHÜWER, Martin: "Erzählen in Comics. Bausteine einer plurimedialen Erzähltheorie." In: *Erzähltheorie transgenerisch, intermedial, interdisziplinär.* Eds.: Vera & Ansgar NÜNNING. Trier: WVT 2002. 185–217.

THOMSEN, Christian W. (ed.): *Hybridkultur. Bildschirmmedien und Evolutionsformen der Künste. Annäherungen an ein interdisziplinäres Problem.* Siegen: Universität-GH-Siegen 1994.

THOMSEN, Christian W. & Irmela SCHNEIDER (eds.): *Grundzüge der Geschichte des europäischen Hörspiels.* Darmstadt: WBG 1985.

VOIGTS-VIRCHOW, Eckart (ed.): *Mediated Drama, Dramatized Media.* Trier: WVT 2000.

WALDMANN, Werner & Rose WALDMANN: *Einführung in die Analyse von Fernsehspielen.* Tübingen: Narr 1980.

WILLIAMS, Kevin: *Understanding Media Theory.* Ldn: Arnold 2003.

WOLF, Werner: *The Musicalization of Fiction. A Study in the Theory and History of Intermediality.* Amsterdam, Atlanta: Rodopi 1999.

◆ ZIELINSKI, Siegfried: *Audiovisionen. Kino und Fernsehen als Zwischenspiele in der Geschichte.* Reinbek: Rowohlt 1989.

ZIELINSKI, Siegfried (ed.): *Video – Apparat, Medium, Kunst, Kultur. Ein internationaler Reader.* FfM.: Lang 1992.

ZIMA, Peter V. (ed.): *Literatur intermedial. Musik – Malerei – Photographie – Film.* Darmstadt: WBG 1995.

ZIMA, Peter V.: "Ästhetik, Wissenschaft und 'wechselseitige Erhellung der Künste'. Einleitung." In: ZIMA, 1–30.

7. Literary Historiography and Histories of Literatures in English

ALEXANDER, Michael: *A History of English Literature.* Basingstoke et al.: Macmillan 2000.

ASHCROFT, Bill, Gareth GRIFFITHS & Helen TIFFIN: *The Empire Writes Back: Theory and Practice in Post-Colonial Literatures.* 2nd ed., Ldn.: Routledge 2002 [1989].

ASSMANN, Aleida & Jan ASSMANN: "Kanon und Zensur." In: *Kanon und Zensur. Archäologie der literarischen Kommunikation II.* Eds.: Aleida & Jan ASSMANN. Munich: Fink 1987. 7–27.

BENNETT, Bruce (ed.): *The Oxford Literary History of Australia.* Oxford: OUP 1998.

BERKHOFER, Robert F. Jr.: *Beyond the Great Story. History as Text and Discourse.* 2nd ed., Cambridge, CMA, Ldn.: The Belknap Press of Harvard UP 1997 [1995].

BLODGETT, Edward Dickinson: *Five-Part Invention. A History of Literary History in Canada.* Toronto: University of Toronto Press 2003.

◆ BORGMEIER, Raimund (ed.): *Die englische Literatur in Text und Darstellung.* 10 Vols., Stg.: Reclam 1982–1986.

BREUER, Rolf: *Irland. Eine Einführung in seine Geschichte, Literatur und Kultur.* München: Fink 2003.

BROICH, Ulrich: "Gegenstands- und Zielbestimmungen der anglistischen Literaturwissenschaft im Lichte fachinterner Entwicklungen." In: *Anglistische Lehre Aktuell. Probleme, Perspektiven, Praxis.* Eds.: Barbara KORTE & Klaus Peter MÜLLER. Trier: WVT 1995. 75–91.

◆ CARTER, Ronald & John MCRAE (eds.): *The Routledge History of Literature in English. Britain and Ireland.* 2nd ed., Ldn.: Routledge 2001 [1997].

◆ ELLIOTT, Emory (ed.): *Columbia Literary History of the United States.* New York: Columbia UP 1988.

FABIAN, Bernhard & Willi ERZGRÄBER (eds.): *Die englische Literatur.* Vol. 1: *Epochen – Formen;* Vol. 2: *Autoren.* 3rd ed., Munich: dtv 1997 [1991].

GRABES, Herbert (ed.): *Literary History/Cultural History. Forcefields and Tensions. REAL – Yearbook of Research in English and American Literature* 17 (2001).

HUTCHEON, Linda & Mario J. VALDÉS (eds.): *Rethinking Literary History. A Dialogue on Theory.* New York, Oxford: OUP 2002.

IMHOF, Rüdiger: *A Short History of Irish Literature.* Stg. et al.: Klett 2002.

◆ JANSOHN, Christa (ed.): *Companion to the New Literatures in English.* Bln: Schmidt 2002.

KOSOK, Heinz: *Geschichte der anglo-irischen Literatur.* Bln.: Schmidt 1990.

KRÖLLER, Eva-Marie (ed.): *The Cambridge Companion to Canadian Literature.* Cambridge: CUP 2004.

◆ LÖSCHNIGG Maria & Martin LÖSCHNIGG: *Kurze Geschichte der kanadischen Literatur.* Stg.: Klett 2001.

MCHALE, Brian: *Constructing Postmodernism.* Ldn.: Routledge 1992.

NÜNNING, Ansgar: "Kanonisierung, Periodisierung und der Konstruktcharakter von Literaturgeschichten. Grundbegriffe und Prämissen theoriegeleiteter Literaturgeschichtsschreibung." In: NÜNNING 1998 [1996], 1–24.

◆ NÜNNING, Ansgar (ed.): *Eine andere Geschichte der englischen Literatur. Epochen, Gattungen und Teilgebiete im Überblick.* 2nd, rev. ed., Trier: WVT 1998 [1996].

PECK, John & Martin COYLE: *A Brief History of English Literature.* Basingstoke et al.: Palgrave 2002.

PERKINS, David: *Is Literary History Possible?* Baltimore, MD: Johns Hopkins UP 1992.

PRIESSNITZ, Horst: "Wie kann man die verschiedenen englischen Literaturen in die anglistische Forschung und Lehre einbeziehen?" In: *Anglistische Lehre Aktuell. Probleme, Perspektiven, Praxis*. Eds.: Barbara KORTE & Klaus Peter MÜLLER. Trier: WVT 1995. 183–194.

PRIESSNITZ, Horst: *Die Terranglia als System. Literarische Kohärenz- und Dezentralisierungsmarkierungen in dominant anglo-europäischen Palimpsestkulturen*. Tübingen: Narr 1999.

SAMPSON, George (ed.): *The Concise Cambridge History of English Literature*. 3rd, rev. ed., Cambridge: CUP 1990 [1941].

SANDERS, Andrew: *The Short Oxford History of English Literature*. 2nd ed., Oxford: Clarendon 2000 [1994].

◆ SCHABERT, Ina: *Englische Literaturgeschichte. Eine neue Darstellung aus der Sicht der Geschlechterforschung*. Stg.: Kröner 1997.

SCHÄFER, Jürgen (ed.): *Commonwealth-Literatur*. Düsseldorf: Bagel 1981.

◆ SEEBER, Hans Ulrich (ed.): *Englische Literaturgeschichte*. 3rd, rev. ed., Stg., Weimar: Metzler 1999 [1991].

STURM, Terry (ed.): *The Oxford History of New Zealand Literature in English*. 2nd ed., Auckland: OUP 1998.

TOYE, William (ed.): *The Oxford Companion to Canadian Literature*. 2nd ed., Toronto: OUP 1997 [1983].

◆ WAGNER, Hans-Peter: *A History of British, Irish and American Literature*. Trier: WVT 2003 [includes CD-ROM].

◆ ZAPF, Hubert (ed.): *Amerikanische Literaturgeschichte*. Stg., Weimar: Metzler 1997.

8. Anthologies

ABRAMS, M.H. (ed.): *The Norton Anthology of English Literature*. 2 vols., 7th ed., New York, Ldn.: Norton 2000 [1968].

BAYM, Nina (ed.): *The Norton Anthology of American Literature*. 5th ed., New York, Ldn.: Norton 1998 [1979].

CLARK, Robert & Thomas HEALY (eds.): *The Arnold Anthology of British and Irish Literature in English*. Ldn.: Arnold 1997.

LAUTER, Paul (ed.): *The Heath Anthology of American Literature*. 4th ed., Lexington, MA: Heath 2002 [1990].

LÖFFLER, Arno & Eberhard SPÄTH (eds.): *English Poetry. Eine Anthologie für das Studium*. 4th, rev. ed., Wiesbaden: Quelle & Meyer 2003 [1976].

MELLER, Horst & Rudolf SÜHNEL (eds.): *British and American Classical Poems*. Emended Repr., Heidelberg: Winter 1999 [1966].

THIEME, John (ed.): *The Arnold Anthology of Post-Colonial Literatures in English*. Ldn., New York: Arnold 1996.

9. Bibliographies

ABELL Annual Bibliography of English Language and Literature (frequently updated bibliography; primary and secondary literature).

ABES: Annotated Bibliography of English Studies (summaries of selected publications from the fields of literatures in English, linguistics, cultural studies and film studies; available on CD-ROM).

MLA International Bibliography of Books and Articles on Modern Languages and Literatures (frequently updated, international bibliography of writings on linguistics and literary studies; also available on CD-ROM and online).

NCBEL: The New Cambridge Bibliography of English Literature, 5 vols., ed. George WATSON. Cambridge : Cambridge University Press, 1969–1977 (primary and secondary literature up to ca. 1965).

10. Periodicals on English/ American Literary Studies

American Literature; American Studies Journal; Amerikastudien; Anglia; Anglistik. Mitteilungen des Verbandes Deutscher Anglisten; a & e. Anglistik und Englischunterricht; AAA. Arbeiten aus Anglistik und Amerikanistik; Archiv für das Studium der Neueren Sprachen und Literaturen; Connotations. A Journal for Critical Debate; Contemporary Literature; DFU. Der Fremdsprachliche Unterricht; Eighteenth-Century Studies; EJES. European Journal of English Studies; Jahrbuch der Deutschen Shakespeare-Gesellschaft; Journal of American Studies; Kritikon Litterarum; LWU. Literatur in Wissenschaft und Unterricht; Literaturwissenschaftliches Jahrbuch; Modern Drama; MFS. Modern Fiction Studies; Narrative; Neusprachliche Mitteilungen aus Wissenschaft und Praxis; NLH. New Literary History; Nineteenth-

Century Studies; Orbis Litterarum; PMLA. Publications of the Modern Language Association of America; Poetica; Poetics; Poetics Today; Praxis Fremdsprachenunterricht (formerly Praxis des neusprachlichen Unterrrichts); Review of English Studies; Shakespeare Quarterly; Shakespeare Survey; Sprachkunst; Studies in English Literature 1500–1900; Style; Twentieth Century Literature; Victorian Studies; WLA. Wissenschaftlicher Literaturanzeiger; ZAA. Zeitschrift für Anglistik und Amerikanistik.

11. On Working Methods and the Composition of Academic Essays in Literary Studies

◆ ACZEL, Richard: How to Write an Essay. Repr., Stg.: Klett 2003 [1998].

GIBALDI, Joseph: MLA Handbook for Writers of Research Papers. 6th ed., New York: Modern Language Association of America 2003 [1977].

MEYER-KRENTLER, Eckhard & Burkhard MOENNIGHOFF: Arbeitstechniken Literaturwissenschaft. 10th, rev. ed., Munich: Fink 2003 [1990].

STANDOP, Ewald & Matthias L. G. MEYER: Die Form der wissenschaftlichen Arbeit. 16th, rev. ed., Wiesbaden: Quelle & Meyer 2002 [1959].

12. Useful Websites

A Guide to the Theory of Literary Genres: Poems, Plays, and Prose (http://www.uni-koeln.de/~ame02/ppp.htm)

Basics of English Studies: An introductory course for students of literary studies in English (http://www.anglistik.uni-freiburg.de/intranet/englishbasics/Home01.htm)

Bibliomania: Free Online Literature and Study Guides. (http://www.bibliomania.com)

Contemporary Writers in the UK and Commonwealth (http://contemporarywriters.com/)

Einladung zur Literaturwissenschaft: Ein Vertiefungsprogramm zum Selbststudium (http://www.uni-essen.de/literaturwissenschaft-aktiv/einladung.htm)

Literary Resources on the Net (http://andromeda.rutgers.edu/~jlynch/Lit/)

Projekt LesARTen (http://www.uni-regensburg.de/Fakultaeten/phil_Fak_IV/Germanistik/Braungart/mw1)

The English Browser (http://cobalt.lang.osaka-u.ac.jp/~krkvls/newsstand.html)

The Internet Movie Database (http://www.imdb.com)

Voice of the Shuttle (http://vos.ucsb.edu)

Information on further Internet addresses can be found in:

FELDMANN, Doris (ed.): Anglistik im Internet. Heidelberg: Winter 1997.

KRANZ, Dieter & Paul TIEDEMANN: Internet für Anglisten: Eine praxisorientierte Einführung. Darmstadt: Primus/WBG 2000.

Glossary

(with contributions by Gaby Allrath, Dorothee Birke, Klaudia Seibel, Annegret Stegmann and Carola Surkamp)

A

Absolute nature of dramatic texts *(Absolutheit dramatischer Texte):* in contrast to narrative texts, dramatic texts do not comprise a mediating communication system; intratextual communication is restricted to the → diegetic level of the → characters (for exceptions see → epic elements in drama).

Act *(Akt):* a discrete section of a drama, which is distinguished by a total change of → character configuration, a long pause, a change of scene or a major change in the → action (b).

Actant *(Aktant):* a literary → character regarded as an agent or function of the → plot (e. g. hero, helper, villain).

Action *(Handlung):* (a) term that refers in the broadest sense to → events enacted by → characters as a result of their abilities, needs, motivations and intentions; a corollary of → character perspective; (b) term used to describe the overall movement of → events, especially in drama. In the analysis of drama, the action is subdivided into individual units, for example → act and → scene.

Aesthetic illusion *(ästhetische Illusion):* the impression conveyed to the reader by means of the imitation of perceptual structures and information that he or she is personally experiencing the → fictional world of a dramatic or narrative text as though the → characters really existed and the → action really happened.

Aesthetic illusion, destruction of *(Illusionsdurchbrechung):* the reduction or shattering of the → aesthetic illusion in literary texts, for example, by means of the thematization of the → fictionality of a work, or by means of → epic elements in drama.

Anachrony *(Anachronie):* the disruption of the 'natural' chronology when giving an account of the sequence of → events (→ flashback and → flashforward); a category relating to the → order of events.

Analepsis *(Analepse):* → flashback

Analytical drama *(Analytisches Drama):* form of drama in which the → exposition extends throughout the entire text, and gradually discloses the past events that have led to the current situation.

Antagonist *(Antagonist):* the opponent of the → protagonist in narrative and dramatic texts.

Aside *(Beiseite-Sprechen):* in drama, form of monological speech in which the audience is acquainted with the thoughts and feelings of one (or more) → character(s), whilst other characters remain in ignorance (→ monologue, → soliloquy).

Assonance *(Assonanz):* phonological → rhetorical figure (see table 3.4.)

Authorial narrative situation *(auktoriale Erzählsituation):* one of the typical → narrative situations, of which the external perspective is the main constitutive element. The → story (b) is told by an → overt and individualised narrator, who is not part of the narrated world.

Autodiegetic narrator *(autodiegetische Erzählinstanz):* → homodiegetic narrator, who is also the main → character and narrates his or her own life story.

B

Blank verse *(Blankvers):* consists of unrhymed iambic pentameters (→ metre), and is used in drama (Shakespeare) and epic (Milton) as well as in poetry.

C

Caesura *(Zäsur):* syntactic division which separates a → line of a poem into units of meaning.

Canon *(Kanon):* corpus of texts that are considered by society to be particularly important, artistically superior or normative.

Character conception *(Figurenkonzeption):* the composition of a → character; we differentiate between a static character conception (the character's traits remain constant) and a dynamic character conception (the character's traits change as the action progresses); between a one-dimensional character conception (restricted, homogeneous selection of character traits) and a multidimensional character conception (large, complex selection of character traits), as well as the categories of → personification, → type and → individual.

Character configuration *(Konfiguration):* those members of the → *dramatis personae* in a drama who are present on stage at a particular moment in time.

Character constellation *(Figurenkonstellation):* term that refers to the relationships between → characters in dramatic and narrative texts and their attitudes towards one another; the character constellation is frequently represented graphically and serves to differentiate and structure the → *dramatis personae.*

Character perspective *(Figurenperspektive):* one → character's view of the → fictional world, which is generally limited to a greater or lesser degree, and is determined by the character's knowledge, psychological disposition, values and norms; a character's perspective generally correlates with his or her → actions (a).

Characterisation *(Figurencharakterisierung):* umbrella term used to refer to all the techniques used in literary texts to evoke mental images of → characters and their characteristics (see figure 4.4).

Characters *(Figuren):* the fictive agents of the → action (a) in narrative or dramatic texts, who appear on the level of the narrated or represented → story (b) and are differentiated from one another by means of relationships of → contrasts and correspondences.

Chinese-box structure: → hypo-narrative

Chronological narration *(chronologisches Erzählen):* the narrated → events occur in the same sequence as in their 'natural' temporal chronology (→ order).

Closed ending *(geschlossenes Ende):* form of conveying information at the end of narrative and dramatic texts, which, in contrast to the → open ending, generally comprises the resolution of all conflicts, conventional concluding → events such as marriage or death (see also → poetic justice) or glimpses into the → characters' future.

Consciousness, modes for presenting *(Bewusstseinsdarstellung):* the way in which → characters' thoughts, feelings, perceptions or memories are communicated to the reader or audience. Whereas narrative texts have a wide variety of possibilities at their disposal for the presentation of characters' consciousness and even unconscious (→ psycho-narration, → free indirect discourse, → interior monologue), the possibilities in drama are restricted to the → monologue, the → soliloquy and the → aside. The most important filmic mode for presenting consciousness is the → voice-over, although music and → word-image tropes can also be employed to imply or symbolise consciousness and internal processes.

Contrasts and correspondences *(Kontrast- und Korrespondenzrelationen):* term that is used in the study of narrative and dramatic texts as well as in film analysis to refer to all features that unite and differentiate between → characters; serves to differentiate and structure the → *dramatis personae.*

Covert narrator *(neutrales Erzählmedium):* → narrator who recounts the → action in a detached and factual manner, who is not presented as an individualised speaker, and whose role is restricted to the basic narrative functions (recounting the action and supplying deictic information concerning

→ place/space, time and → characters); common in the → figural narrative situation.

Cut *(Schnitt):* term that refers to the technical process of editing recorded material when making a film; the various types of cut, based on diverse types of → montage, range from 'invisible editing' to the 'jump cut', the latter of which deliberately draws attention to itself.

▰▰ D

Description *(Beschreibung):* → narrative mode of → telling; the → narrator attributes particular characteristics to → characters and objects within the narrated world, and describes conditions and → settings.

Deus ex machina *(der Gott aus der Maschine):* term used in drama to refer to the resolution of a conflict by means of sudden → events not motivated by the → action (b), or through the unexpected appearance of a → character or an external power (for example, a saint).

Diachrony/Synchrony *(Diachronie/Synchronie):* the term 'diachrony' refers to the temporal chronology of → events or circumstances; diachronic studies focus, for example, on changes in generic conventions (→ genre). 'Synchrony', by contrast, refers to the temporal coexistence of phenomena within a particular period of time; a synchronic study, therefore, could focus on the particular characteristics of a specific period.

Dialogue *(Dialog):* exchange between two or more → characters. In drama, the dialogue is the motor of the → action (b) (→ plot); in narrative texts it is situated on the → diegetic level and embedded in the → narrator's account of the action. Dialogue is also a constitutive element of the radio play and the film.

Diegetic level *(Ebene der Figuren/der fiktiven Handlung):* level of → action and communication within dramatic and narrative texts, which comprises all communication between the → characters.

Discourse: (in narrative texts) structure of the → narrative transmission. Complementary term to → story (b): 'story' refers to the 'what', 'discourse' to the 'how' of a text.

Discourse time *(Erzählzeit):* length of time needed in order to read or narrate a narrative text.

Dissolve *(Überblendung):* the connection of various visual and acoustic units in film by means of gradual transitions and slow fade-ins and fade-outs; can serve to blend the elements and harmonise perceptions of time and space.

Dramatic introduction *(dramatischer Auftakt):* (frequently non-verbal) form of introduction in drama which has the phatic function of establishing a channel of communication between the stage and the audience, of awakening the recipients' attention and of acclimatising them to the atmosphere of the → fictional world; can occur simultaneously with the → exposition, but also independently of it.

Dramatic irony *(dramatische Ironie):* results from discrepant awareness between the recipient and a → character; thanks to superior knowledge, the recipient has a privileged insight into the character's misjudgements, with the result that the character's words and → actions (a) take on additional, unintended meaning.

Dramatis personae *(Personal):* collective term for all the → characters who appear in a drama.

Duration *(Dauer):* the relationship between the → discourse time and the → story time; category relating to representation of time (→ time and representation of time; see also → ellipsis (b), → pause, → scene (b), → stretch, → summary).

▰▰ E

Ellipsis *(Ellipse):* (a) the omission of sentence elements that are necessary or important for the syntax; (b) the omission of → time and intervening occurrences between narrated → events; category of → duration.

End-rhyme *(Endreim):* → rhyme (see table 3.2.)

Ending: → closed ending, → open ending

Enjambment/run-on line *(Enjambement/ Zeilensprung):* term used in the analysis of poetry to refer to a sentence that extends beyond the end of the → line.

Epic elements in drama *(Episierungstendenzen im Drama):* suspension of the → absolute nature of dramatic texts by means of a mediating communication system, for example, the introduction of a → character from within or outside of the → action (b), who takes on the role of a → narrator; projections and banners or the exposure of the mechanisms of the theatre (for example, when a character steps out of his or her dramatic role momentarily) are also epic techniques.

Epilogue *(Epilog):* concluding part of a literary text; in drama, concluding speech which is addressed to the audience by one of the → characters. Counterpart to the → prologue.

Event *(Ereignis):* smallest unit of the → action (b).

Experiencing I *(Erlebendes Ich):* the former self of a → homodiegetic narrator (→ narrating I), presented as a → character in the narrated world.

Exposition *(Exposition):* information given in narrative and dramatic texts about preceding → events, the roots of future conflicts and the circumstances of the action (→ setting, → time, → characters); has a primarily informative and referential function. We differentiate between two different kinds of exposition, according to their location within the text as a whole: 'isolated exposition' (isolated text passage occurring at the beginning) and 'integrated exposition' (information is dispersed throughout the text and integrated into the → action [b]). The exposition can occur simultaneously with the → dramatic introduction, but also independently of it.

External focalization *(externe Fokalisierung):* perception of the → fictional world from an external perspective, in which the → heterodiegetic narrator is also the → focalizer (= external focalizer/*externe Fokalisierungsinstanz* or narrator-focalizer/*fokalisierende Erzählinstanz*).

Extradiegetic level *(Ebene der erzählerischen Vermittlung):* part of the communication structure of a text; level of → narrative transmission (→ narrator) or → discourse, which is external to the level of the → story (b) or → diegetic level.

Extradiegetic narrator *(extradiegetische Erzählinstanz):* → narrator or speaker on the → extradiegetic level.

F

Fictional world *(fiktive Welt):* the world represented in a dramatic or narrative text, which has been invented by the author, and is subject to its own rules and laws, which sometimes deviate from those governing extratextual reality.

Fictionality *(Fiktionalität):* term that refers to the invented or imaginative character of the world represented in a literary text.

Fictionality, signals for *(Fiktionssignale):* conventionalised signs, by means of which the → fictionality of a work is signalled; in addition to the communication situation and the external presentation of a book, these include the title, generic classification (→ genre), introductory and concluding formulae, as well as any information concerning → place/space (→ setting), → time and → characters which does not refer to extratextual reality, and also intertextual allusions (→ intertextuality) and polyvalence.

Fictive reader *(fiktiver Leser):* → narratee

Figural narrative situation *(personale Erzählsituation):* one of the typical → narrative situations; a → covert and → heterodiegetic narrator recounts the → events, restricting himself to a factual representation or using → internal focalization, thus creating the impression of immediacy.

First-person narrative situation *(Ich-Er-zählsituation):* one of the typical → narrative situations; → events are relayed by a → 'narrating I', who takes part in the action in the fictional world as a → character or → 'experiencing I' (→ homodiegetic narrator). There is frequently a temporal as well as a moral distance between the narrating I and the experiencing I.

Fixed focalization *(konstante Fokalisierung):* → focalization of the → fictional world through a single → focalizer, who remains constant throughout the text.

Flashback/analepsis *(Rückwendung):* category relating to the → order of events; communication of information about an → event that has already taken place earlier on in the 'natural' chronology of the → story (a); form of anachronic narration (→ anachrony).

Flashforward/prolepsis/foreshadowing *(Vorausdeutung):* communication of information about an → event that occurs later according to the 'natural' chronology of the → story; form of anachronic narration (→ anachrony); category relating to the → order of events.

Focalization *(Fokalisierung):* in contrast to categories relating to the → narrator, this term refers to the representation of the perception of the → fictional world; it includes internal processes such as thinking, feeling and remembering, in addition to sensory perception.

Focalizer *(Fokalisierungsinstanz):* subject of → focalization; centre of orientation, from whose perspective the narrated world is perceived; answer to the question *who sees?/who perceives?* (see also → external focalization, → internal focalization).

Foot *(Versfuß):* smallest rhythmical unit, consisting of one → stressed and up to two → unstressed syllables; based on the number of syllables and the position of the stress, we differentiate in English-language poetry between the iamb (˘/), trochee (/˘), dactyl (/˘˘), anapaest (˘˘/) as well as, occasionally, the spondee (//) and the amphibrach (˘/˘).

Free indirect discourse/narrated monologue *(erlebte Rede):* mode for presenting → consciousness in narrative texts, in which either the → narrator's or the → character's contributions can be dominant; linguistic features: third person singular, past tense.

Frequency *(Häufigkeit):* (here) quantitative relationship between the → events of the → story (b) and the narrative in which they are recounted; category relating to representation of time (→ time and representation of time).

▄▄ G

Genre/kind *(Gattung/Genre):* organisational category for literary texts, which involves sorting texts into groups based on common sets of characteristics; in addition to the three main genres/modes of writing (dramatic, lyric and narrative texts), we also differentiate between numerous subgenres (for example comedy, sonnet or detective novel).

▄▄ H

Heterodiegetic narrator *(heterodiegetische Erzählinstanz):* → narrator who is located outside the world he or she describes, and does not appear as a → character; conventionally accredited with → omniscience; the → speech situation is frequently deictically (i. e. temporally and spatially) undetermined.

Homodiegetic narrator *(homodiegetische Erzählinstanz):* → narrator who participates him- or herself as a → character in the fictional action of the narrated world; is by law of convention subject to the epistemological boundaries of real agents of the plot, and is therefore not 'omniscient' (→ omniscience).

Hybridization *(Hybridisierung):* the combination of two elements that are initially separate, for example, of different styles, → genres or media (for example, the historical detective novel is a hybrid genre).

Hypo-narrative *(eingebettete Erzählung):* a narrative that occurs on the → diegetic level (or on a hierarchically subordinate level) within one or more framing narratives, in which one of the → characters takes on the role of an → intradiegetic narrator; can theoretically recur *ad infinitum* (chinese-box structure).

▰ I

Imagery *(Bildlichkeit):* umbrella term embracing all types of linguistic images (for example, semantic → rhetorical figures).

Implied author *(impliziter Autor):* (confusing) term for the various phenomena relating to the structure and meaning of a narrative text, as well as to its underlying system of values and norms; not to be confused with the real, historical author.

Individual *(Charakter):* a literary → character which, in contrast to the → type, is a 'round' character, i.e. complex in structure and furnished with numerous characteristics, and therefore appears 'true-to-life'.

Interior monologue/quoted monologue *(innerer Monolog):* mode for presenting → consciousness in narrative texts, without apparent participation by the → narrator; high degree of authenticity in relaying internal, psychological processes; linguistic features: first person singular, present tense; often contains various features of oral language (elliptical constructions, colloquial expressions, etc.).

Intermediality *(Intermedialität):* umbrella term for the interaction between literature and other artistic forms such as music, painting, photography, film and television.

Internal focalization *(interne Fokalisierung):* perception of the → fictional world in which a → character functions as → focalizer (= internal focalizer/*interne Fokalisierungsinstanz*, reflector/*Reflektorfigur* or character-focalizer/*fokalisierende Figur*).

Intertextuality *(Intertextualität):* networks of thematic and formal references between

texts; many contemporary British and American works contain such references to earlier texts.

Intradiegetic narrator *(erzählende Figur):* speaker who narrates on the → diegetic level (or on a hierarchically lower level).

Isotopy *(Isotopie):* sequence of expressions linked by a common 'semantic denominator'.

▰ L

Line *(Vers/Zeile):* in poetry analysis: line of a poem which is offset typographically from the others. Often has a metrical structure (→ verse).

Literary adaptation *(Literaturadaption):* transferral of a literary work into another medium (for example, adaptation of a narrative text as a musical or radio play); → media change.

Lyric persona *(lyrisches Ich):* fictive speaker in a poem.

▰ M

Media change/change of media *(Medienwechsel):* transferral of a work from one medium to another (for example, film adaptation of literary text, the 'book of the film', radio play adaptations of novels, etc.)

Media genres, theory of *(Mediengattungstheorie):* area of study which focuses on research into generic designations (→ genre), on the expectations aroused by specific designations in media users, and on the effects and functions of generic designations.

Messenger's report *(Botenbericht):* a mode of conveying information in drama, whereby → events which for ethical or technical reasons cannot be represented on stage (violence, major battles) are relayed by a messenger (see also → teichoscopy).

Metaphor *(Metapher)* semantic → rhetorical figure (see table 3.7.); 'compressed simile', in which the denotations and connotations of a vehicle *(Bildspender)* are transferred onto a tenor *(Bildempfänger)*.

Method *(Methode):* systematic sequence of rules, principles or analytical steps, which proceed from particular angles of enquiry and points of departure towards a predetermined goal; different methods produce different results.

Metonymy *(Metonymie):* semantic → rhetorical figure (see table 3.7.)

Metre *(Metrum/Versmaß):* organisational principle according to which a → line of → verse is divided into feet (→ foot); we differentiate according to the number of → stressed syllables between trimeters, tetrameters, pentameters and hexameters (see table 3.1.).

Mimesis *(Mimesis):* aesthetic concept which defines the relationship between literary texts and extra-literary reality as one of imitation.

Model *(Modell):* abstract and simplified representation of a complex subject, which only takes into account those aspects and characteristics that are regarded as relevant.

Model of literary communication *(Kommunikationsmodell literarischer Texte):* idealised and generalised representation of the communicative interactions within literary texts, which differentiates between the various levels of communication, as well as between addresser and addressee (see figure 1.2.).

Monologue *(Monolog):* term that refers in dramatic texts to a speech addressed by a → character to him- or herself or the audience, and not to anyone else on stage; primarily a mode for presenting thoughts and feelings (→ consciousness, modes for presenting; → aside). If the figure is alone on stage when delivering the speech, it is known as a → soliloquy.

Monologue, interior *(innerer Monolog):* → interior monologue

Montage *(Montage):* term that is used to refer to the process of combining various parts to form a new unity in photography, radio plays, theatre and film. In cinematography and film theory, the term (which originates from the French word for 'cutting' or 'editing') refers to the process of combining or superimposing single → shots (and acoustic elements).

Multiperspectivity / multiperspectival narration *(Multiperspektivität/multiperspektivisches Erzählen):* form of → narrative transmission in which a subject, an → event or a → character is presented from one or more different perspectives.

N

Narratee *(fiktiver Leser):* more or less individualised fictive interlocutor of the → narrator on the → extradiegetic level, who is presupposed or even explicitly addressed in the text; not to be confused with the real reader.

Narrating I *(erzählendes Ich):* the present self of a → homodiegetic narrator in the → first-person narrative situation, who narrates on the → extradiegetic level.

Narration *(Narration):* superordinate account of → events on the → extradiegetic level, which is presented as an instance of communication between the → narrator and the → narratee.

Narrative embedding *(narrative Einbettung):* term that refers to the hierarchical and functional superordination or subordination of the → extradiegetic level and the → diegetic level.

Narrative modes *(Erzählweisen):* the way in which textual elements are represented on the → diegetic level or on the → extradiegetic level; we differentiate between → report, → description, commentary on the narrative and → scenic presentation.

Narrative perspective *(Erzählperspektive):* → narrative situation; → point of view

Narrative situation (Erzählsituation; also: narrative perspective): term that refers to the way in which → events, → actions (a) or thoughts are narrated. We differentiate between three 'typical narrative situations': the → authorial narrative situation, the → figural narrative situation and the → first-person narrative situation.

Narrative transmission (erzählerische Vermittlung): mode of constructing a fictional reality; comprises the functions of all → narrators and → focalizers.

Narrator (Erzähler/Erzählerin, Erzählinstanz): fictive textual speaker who functions as narrating subject on the → extradiegetic level, and who is the medium for the creation of the narrated world; answer to the question 'who speaks?' (see also → overt narrator, → covert narrator).

Narrator perspective (Erzählerperspektive): in contrast to the narrative perspective of a text (→ narrative situation), this term refers to the conception formed by the recipient of the → narrator's personality, psychological disposition, values and norms on the basis of the information supplied by the text.

████ O

Off stage: space outside the stage in theatre

Omniscience (Allwissenheit): a common but imprecise term for the privileged status of the → heterodiegetic narrator in psychological, cognitive, spatial and temporal matters; insight into the → consciousness of all → characters, simultaneous presence in all locations (omnipresence), and a commanding view over all past, present and future developments in the → plot.

Open ending (offenes Ende): form of conveying information at the end of narrative and dramatic texts, which, in contrast to the → closed ending, does not offer final solutions.

Order (Anordnung): term that (here) refers to the various possibilities of organising the temporal sequence of → events into a story; category relating to representation of time (→ time and representation of time; see also → anachrony, → chronological narration, → flashback, → flashforward).

Overt narrator (expliziter Erzähler): concrete, individualised speaker on the → extradiegetic level, who may analyse and evaluate the → character perspectives and → actions (a), as well as offering personal comments, interpretative judgements and generalising abstractions, as well as directly addressing the fictive reader (→ narratee).

████ P

Paradigmatic relations (paradigmatische Beziehungen): term that refers to the relationship between linguistic elements that can be substituted for one another in a particular position within a sentence. Paradigmatic relations are based on similarity (see also → syntagmatic relations).

Paratext (Paratext): a text which is supplementary to the actual literary text, for example, a text in a book jacket, title, subtitle, dedication, preface and concluding remarks.

Pause (Pause): category of → duration; the → story time freezes while the → discourse time continues.

Performance criticism: umbrella term for interpretative approaches that focus primarily on the performance of theatre plays (sometimes with reference to the implied performances within dramatic texts). 'Performance studies' are also concerned with multimedial representations in film, television and the new media.

Personification (Personifikation): term that refers to the representation of an abstract term as a → character (for example, vice or virtue).

Perspective (Perspektive): → narrator perspective, → character perspective.

Perspective structure (Perspektivenstruktur): in dramatic and narrative texts, the totality of all individual perspectives, including → character perspectives and → narrator perspective, and the relationships between them; results from the system of → contrasts and correspondences between the perspectives and, like all phenomena which derive from the structure of the entire text, concretizes only in the course of the interaction between the real reader and the text as a whole. We differentiate between a-perspectival, closed and open perspective structures.

Place/space *(Raum):* 'place' and 'space' are general expressions which encompass the conception, structure and presentation of such elements as locations and objects, scenery and the natural world within various genres (→ setting). 'Place' is used primarily but not exclusively for drama, 'space' primarily but not exclusively for the novel.

Plot: term that refers to the structure of the → action, i.e. the causal and logical sequence of the → events that occur in the narrated world; complementary term to 'story' (a).

Poetic justice *(poetische Gerechtigkeit):* in narrative and dramatic texts, conventional ending whereby the 'good' → characters are rewarded (for example, with marriage or riches), and the 'bad' characters are punished (for example, with death or financial or social ruin).

Point of attack: in a play, the beginning of the main → action (b), which is presented on stage.

Point of view: the perspective from which narrative information is regulated. Recent theories, however, distinguish between → focalization ('who sees?') and narration ('who speaks?'); → narrator.

Primary text *(Haupttext):* in tandem with the → secondary text, comprises a constitutive element of dramatic texts; consists of the → characters' utterances.

Prolepsis *(Prolepse):* → flashforward

Prologue *(Prolog):* introductory words addressed to the audience by one of the → characters, an additional character with no other role, or the author (for example, a greeting or information concerning the play); in classical drama, the most common form of → exposition. Counterpart to the → epilogue.

Protagonist *(Protagonist):* in a narrative or dramatic text, main → character, whose plans and intentions are often thwarted by an → antagonist.

Psycho-narration *(Gedankenbericht):* mode for presenting → consciousness in narrative texts, which includes a high degree of narrator participation and is relatively compressed; linguistic criteria: third-person singular, past tense.

▆▆ R

Reader address *(Leseranrede):* address by the → narrator, which has a predominantly conative function; the narrator may present the fictive reader (→ narratee) with hypotheses, ask questions or encourage him or her to adopt specific attitudes of reception.

Reader, fictive: → narratee

Reflector *(Reflektorfigur):* → internal focalization

Report *(Bericht):* → narrative mode concerned with → telling; a factual, frequently temporally compressed account of → events and → actions (a) in the narrated world given by a → narrator.

Rhetorical figures *(rhetorische Figuren):* conventionalised forms of deviation from everyday language, which have been in existence since Antiquity; we differentiate between phonological (see table 3.4.), morphological (see table 3.5.), syntactic (see table 3.6.), semantic (see table 3.7.) and pragmatic rhetorical figures.

Rhyme *(Reim):* consonance of words from the vowel of the last → stressed syllable in a → line; according to the degree of consonance, we differentiate between full rhyme and near rhyme (see table 3.2.).

Rhyme scheme *(Reimschema):* rhyme pattern over several → lines; we differentiate according to the way in which the → rhymes are grouped between rhyming couplets, alternate rhyme, embracing/envelope rhyme and tail rhyme (see table 3.3.).

S

Scene: (a) *(Szene)* used in drama to refer to the unit of → action (b) that is subordinate to the → act; generally consists of the appearance of one or more → character(s) and ends or begins with the entrance or exit of a further character; (b) *(Zeitdeckung)* category of analysis of time in narrative texts, occurs in the case of → dialogues as well as various modes for presenting → consciousness; → discourse time and → story time are coextensive; category of → duration.

Scenic presentation *(Szenische Darstellung):* a narrative mode that is a subcategory of → showing, whereby the reader is presented with the illusion of an unmediated view of the → events in the narrated world. The methods used range from a detailed account of events, → dialogue between the → characters or the use of modes for presenting → consciousness.

Secondary text *(Nebentext):* constitutive component of dramatic texts (together with the → primary text); consists of stage directions concerning the → setting, the temporal frame for the → action (b), the gestures and facial expressions of the → characters, divisions between → acts and → scenes, information identifying the character who is speaking, title, → *dramatis personae*, preface and dedication.

Semanticization of literary forms *(Semantisierung literarischer Formen):* expression which refers to the fact that literary structures and modes of representation not only serve representative and communicative functions, but are also themselves carriers of meaning.

Semiotics of theatre *(Theatersemiotik):* the study of the signs or codes of theatre communication (→ theatre codes).

Setting *(Schauplatz):* term that refers to the specific location of a → scene (a) or episode of a novel or drama in → space and/or time.

Shot *(Einstellung):* a single, uninterrupted camera take, which – along with the individual image – is the smallest unit of a film. The description of a shot includes information on size, frame rate and angle, as well as camera movements. Every shot is filmed and cut in such a way that it is related in form and content to preceding or following shots.

Showing: literary mode of representation that is closely related to dramatic performance; in contrast to → telling, it is usually recounted by a → covert narrator. Typical → narrative modes for showing include → scene (b) and various modes for presenting → consciousness such as → free indirect discourse and → interior monologue.

Sign systems of the theatre *(Zeichensysteme des Theaters):* → theatre codes

Soliloquy: form of monological speech in drama, in which the speaker is alone on the stage and talks to him- or herself or the audience. If other → characters are present, this form of speech is known as a → monologue.

Space: → place/space

Speech situation *(Sprechsituation):* in the narrow sense of the term, the speech situation of a literary text encompasses a speaker (for example, the → lyric persona in poems) and an addressee; in its broader sense, it also includes → place/space and → time.

Stanza *(Strophe):* in a poem, group of → lines that is typographically marked; the stanzaic structure of older poems in particular follows well-established rules.

Story *(Geschichte/story):* (a) sequence of → events in their 'natural' temporal chronology; complementary term to → 'plot'; (b)

totality of elements that constitute the → diegetic level of fictional action (as opposed to the level of mediation); complementary term to → discourse ('story' refers to the 'what', 'discourse' to the 'how' of a text).

Story time *(erzählte Zeit):* temporal → duration of the sequence of → events described in a narrative text.

Stream of consciousness *(Bewusstseinsstrom):* metaphorical term for an individual's often random, irrational and incoherent mental processes. The stream of consciousness can be relayed using various modes for presenting → consciousness.

Stressed syllable *(Hebung):* rhythmically accentuated syllable in a → line of → verse; indicated by ,/'.

Stretch/slow-down *(Zeitdehnung):* category relating to → duration; the → discourse time is longer than the → story time.

Structure *(Struktur):* the arrangement of and relationships between the individual parts of a whole.

Subjectivity *(Subjektivität):* relating to the perspective and use of language peculiar to an individual; particularly characteristic of poetry, where it can occur explicitly when the → lyric persona appears and speaks, or implicitly by means of a selection of words and images.

Summary/speed-up *(Zeitraffung):* category relating to → duration; the → discourse time is shorter than the → story time.

Sympathy, manipulation or direction of *(Sympathielenkung):* umbrella term referring to various strategies which engage the emotions of the reader or viewer; for instance, engaging or distancing comments by → overt narrators.

Synchrony *(Synchronie):* → diachrony/synchrony

Syntagmatic relations *(syntagmatische Beziehungen):* the links between and possible ways of combining elements within a sentence or text (see also → paradigmatic relations).

■■■ T

Teichoscopy *(Mauerschau/Teichoskopie):* a mode of conveying information in drama, whereby → events which for ethical or technical reasons cannot be represented on stage (violence, major battles) are reported by a → character located in a position of elevation (wall, tower, hill) to the other characters and thereby also the audience (see also → messenger's report).

Telling: literary mode of representation which, in contrast to the mode of → showing, features an → overt narrator who is clearly visible as a mediator. Narrative modes typical of the telling mode include the → report, → description, commentary and → psycho-narration.

Telling name *(sprechender Name):* → characterisation technique, in which a → character's name draws attention to a feature typical of him or her.

Theatre codes *(Theatercodes):* the verbal and nonverbal sign systems of the theatre (encompassing, for example, voices, sounds, music, facial expressions, gestures, hairstyles, costume, scenery, props, lighting); we differentiate between acoustic and optical signs, between signs relating to the actors and actresses and signs relating to representation of → place, and between durative and non-durative signs.

Time and representation of time *(Zeit und Zeitdarstellung):* terms that refer to the structure and presentation of temporal sequences and representations within the various → genres (→ order, → duration, → frequency).

Type *(Typ):* a one-dimensional → character (→ character conception), who has few individual characteristics, and is instead reduced to several general traits (for example, the grouch, the skinflint, the choleric person), or who represents a social class (for example, the courtier, the city-dweller, the peasant). There are also ethnic, regional and national stereotypes, as well as gender stereotypes.

U

Unreliable narrator *(unzuverlässiger Erzähler):* term used to refer to an → overt narrator whose account of → events, interpretation of the → story (b), or whose questionable norms and values give the reader cause to doubt his or her credibility.

Unstressed syllable *(Senkung):* element in a → line of → verse; indicated by a ‚–'.

V

Verse: poetic compositions written in metre.

Voice-over *(off-Kommentar):* the voice-over is added subsequently to audio- and visual material; it consists of remarks delivered by an invisible speaker, which comment on or supplement the central → events, or form them into a unit of meaning.

W

Word-image tropes *(Wort-Bild-Tropen):* rhetorical figures that are realised by images rather than linguistic expressions. The → metaphors, → metonymies and synecdoches expressed in filmic images are important considerations of film analysis (for example, when the image of a punk is used to represent the fringes of society or as an allegory for violence).

Word scenery *(Wortkulisse):* in drama, term that refers to the (mostly subjectively coloured) thematization of the spatial context within the → characters' dialogue or (in classical drama) the remarks of the chorus.

Pressestimmen zur Reihe UNI-Wissen

„Generell scheinen die Bücher der ›UNI-Wissen Reihe‹ eine neue Generation von ›Schulbüchern‹ einzuleiten, da sie endlich mal mit der Zeit gehen und nicht der Zeit hinterherhinken."
Amazon.de (1999)

„In den [...] Bänden dieser Reihe hat Professor Ansgar Nünning, einer der profiliertesten Vertreter dieser nun die Lehrstühle neu besetzenden Generation, als Herausgeber eine ungewöhnliche Homogenität in Form, Darstellung und Inhalt erreicht. [...]
Diese Reihe wird über Jahre hinweg der inhaltliche und finanzielle Maßstab von Konkurrenzbänden sein. [...] Die Bände sind rundweg zu empfehlen. Der erfreulich niedrige Preis [...] lässt das sonst leider gängige Kopieren zur unnötigen Zeitverschwendung werden."
Der fremdsprachliche Unterricht (1999)

„Die Bände der Reihe vermitteln auf wissenschaftlich solider und verständlicher Weise grundlegende Informationen und Überblickswissen zu ausgewählten Standardthemen der Literatur- und Sprachwissenschaft. Sie eignen sich sehr gut für die effiziente Einarbeitung in Teilgebiete der Anglistik/Amerikanistik, die Auffrischung bereits erworbener Kenntnisse ebenso wie die zielgerichtete Prüfungsvorbereitung. Besonders hervorzuheben ist die methodisch transparente Strukturierung der Bände und das übersichtliche layout."
Archiv für das Studium der Neueren Sprachen und Literaturen 237, 152 (2000)

Pressestimmen zu einzelnen Bänden

Uwe Baumann: *Shakespeare und seine Zeit*
„[...] Darüber hinaus vermitteln Baumanns Analysen einen informativen Einblick in eine Vielzahl thematischer [...] und formalästhetischer [...] Innovationen, die – trotz der erheblichen künstlerischen Unterschiede der vorgestellten Dramen – die Studierenden und auch Lehrenden auf ein leider noch immer marginalisiertes Gebiet der Ausbildung in unserer Anglistik aufmerksam machen." *Archiv für das Studium der neueren Sprachen und Literaturen, 237, 152 (2000)*

Vera und Ansgar Nünning: *Englische Literatur des 18. Jahrhunderts*
„Die in flüssigem Stil geschriebene Geschichte der englischen Literatur des 18. Jahrhunderts führt auf anschauliche Weise in die vielfältigen Formen, Gattungen und Entwicklungen der englischen Literatur des 18. Jahrhunderts ein. Dabei ist den Verfassern daran gelegen, nicht nur den Höhenkamm auszuleuchten, sondern sie steigen auch in die Niederungen der weniger bekannten Autoren und weniger populären Gattungen hinab. Alles in allem ergibt sich so ein sehr komplexes Bild der englischen Literatur des 18. Jahrhunderts, in dem sich nichtsdestotrotz noch klare Entwicklungslinien abzeichnen."
Sprachkunst 30,2 (1999)

Gottfried Krieger: *Das englische Drama des 20. Jahrhunderts*
„[…] Krieger gelingt es in seiner Einführung, die Entwicklungszusammenhänge einer Gattung in einem Jahrhundert sowie deren spezifische Ausprägungen interessant und fundiert zu vermitteln."
Arbeiten aus Anglistik und Amerikanistik 24,2 (1999)

Ansgar Nünning: *Der englische Roman des 20. Jahrhunderts*
„Die Leserin/der Leser gewinnt einen ausgezeichneten Überblick über inhaltliche wie formale Entwicklungsstränge des englischen Romans in diesem Jahrhundert. […] Das Buch ist eine wertvolle Bereicherung für jeden, der sich aus beruflichem oder privatem Interesse mit englischen Romanen dieses Jahrhunderts befassen möchte oder schlicht mit der Qual der Wahl konfrontiert ist, welchen Roman er mit seinem Oberstufenkurs lesen möchte."
Neusprachliche Mitteilungen aus Wissenschaft und Praxis 53,1 (2000)

Herbert Grabes: *Das amerikanische Drama des 20. Jahrhunderts*
„Mit dem Ziel, ›einen Überblick über die Grundformen und die Geschichte des amerikanischen Dramas im 20. Jahrhundert‹ (S. 5) zu geben, legt Herbert Grabes mit dem vorliegenden Band eine überzeugende Darstellung der Entwicklung dieser literarischen Gattung in den USA vor. […]
Dem vorliegenden Band ist zu bescheinigen, daß er eine bemerkenswerte und in ihrer Argumentation überzeugende Einführung in das amerikanische Drama des 20. Jahrhunderts darstellt."
Archiv für das Studium der Neueren Sprachen und Literaturen 237,152 (2000)

John F. Davis: *Phonetics and Phonology*
„… bei diesem Titel kann von einer überragenden Leistung, auch in didaktischer Hinsicht, gesprochen werden."
Anglistik 11,2 (2000)

Richard Aczel: *How to Write an Essay*
„Die zahlreichen Beispiele erleichtern später auch die Umsetzung in die Praxis und nehmen gerade den Schülern/Studenten, die zum ersten Mal ein essay schreiben, die Hemmschwelle zum ersten Schritt."
Amazon.de (1999)

Richard Humphrey: *Grundkurs Übersetzen Deutsch–Englisch*
„Der Autor behauptet zwar im Vorwort zu diesem Band sehr bescheiden, er würde ›nichts grundlegend Neues‹ (S. 6) bieten, doch einige Elemente des Übungsbuches sind durchaus als unkonventionell einzustufen."
Anglistik 11, 2 (2000)
„Das Buch ist [...] optimal fürs Selbsttraining. Es ist gerade für Erstsemester eine hilfreiche Anschaffung, die auch bestimmt ins studentische Budget paßt."
Amazon.de (1999)

Richard Humphrey: *English Idioms for University*
„[...] eine äußerst kurzweilige Lektüre [...] In der Breite der berücksichtigten Themen und der abwechslungsreichen Fülle des Materials wird dieses Übungsbuch seinem eigenen Anspruch mehr als gerecht. [...] Ein bescheidenes Büchlein, dabei aber mit offensichtlichem Spaß an der Sache zusammengestellt und von immensem sprachlichen Gebrauchswert – von den literarischen und landeskundlichen Nebeneffekten ganz abgesehen."
Mitteilungsblatt des fmf Westfalen-Lippe 19,1 (2001)